Contents

Th... ide to ... lom

Jonathan Reuvid

PA Consulting Group

Watson, Farley & Williams

Legend Business

Legend Business, The Old Fire Station,
140 Tabernacle Street, London EC2A 4SD
info@legend-paperbooks.co.uk
www.legendpress.co.uk

British Library Cataloguing in Publication Data available.

ISBN 978-1-9095938-1-7

Set in Times

Cover designed by EA Digital, Leicester
www.eadigital.com

PREFACE

This new edition of "*Investors' Guide to the United Kingdom*", like the five previous editions, focuses on the key information that inward investors need in order to develop their business plans for UK market entry.

At the corporate planning stage, company directors and senior managers need to have a detailed understanding of the business environment, how to structure their UK business, where it can be located to best advantage and what funding facilities are available. All these factors, of course, will be viewed against the background of UK commercial law and the taxation regime.

The essentials of the legal and regulatory environment are provided by Watson, Farley & Williams LLP, the London-based international law firm and a longstanding contributor to this book, which also provides chapters on key UK industries in infrastructure, the financial and other sectors of opportunity.

They are joined by Mazars LLP, the international accountancy and audit firm with global reach, who contribute the chapters on company formation, financial reporting and acounting, taxation and taxation planning. The UKTI Investment Services Team explains how locally-based grants and incentives can be accessed and has supplied chapters from the Automotive Investment Organisation and from the Life Sciences Investment Organisation on those sectors of the economy. Michael Boyd, Managing Director Investment of UKTI has written the Foreword to this edition our book.

Further chapters on key investment locations, industry sectors of opportunity, grants and incentives available in the UK and the AIM market of the London Stock Exchange are provided by longstanding regular contributors.

In the present conditions of a slowly recovering economy, the UK remains one of the easiest countries in which to do business safely and continues to be the leading European destination for inward investment. As previously, potential investors are invited to contact any of the contributors direct, who will be pleased to provide more detailed advice and hands-on assistance. Their contact details are listed in Appendix I.

Jonathan Reuvid
Editor

FOREWORD

Michael Boyd Managing Director, Investment UK Trade & Investment

It is my pleasure to introduce The Investor's Guide to the United Kingdom 2013/14.

Britain is a great place to do business. This has always been true, but the evidence shows that it is true even in times of significant economic uncertainty. Britain has created, and continues to create, a globally competitive, responsive and attractive economy which overseas investors of all sizes see as a sound investment environment.

That this is so is due to a combination of the right policies from Government, genuinely transformational opportunities for international investors, and a deep level of commitment from British companies, communities and people to make Great Britain a nation which is engaged, constructive, and rewarding for investment.

It does not automatically follow, of course, that simply because Britain is open for business, business will come to Britain. Competition in the global FDI market is increasing, both from our traditional competitors and from emerging markets.

The global pool of investment shrank significantly in 2012, and competitor economies felt the effects of that in sharp reductions in inward investment. The United Nations Conference on Trade and Development (UNCTAD) reported that global foreign direct investment (FDI) flows declined by 18 per cent in 2012 to

US$1.35 trillion, a level similar to the immediate aftermath of the financial crisis of 2008. Within that, the USA, for example, experienced a 26 per cent year-on-year decline in FDI inflows in 2012, while the European Union reported an even steeper decline of 42 per cent (with France falling by 35 per cent and Germany declining by 87 per cent).

It would be understandable if Britain had followed that trend. That we did not do so, and in fact bucked that trend by a huge margin, is clear evidence of the confidence that global business leaders have in Great Britain and the clearest possible commercial endorsement of the UK's business environment.

In 2012 the UK secured an annual increase of 22 per cent in FDI inflows in 2012, attracting US$62 billion, the highest level in Europe. The UK's share of global FDI flows rose to 4.6 per cent, up significantly from 3.1 per cent in 2011. The UK's stock of FDI increased in 2012 to an estimated £867 billion (US$1.3 trillion), an 11.5 per cent increase from 2011. Independently, Ernst & Young and the Financial Times confirm that the UK remained the number one FDI location in Europe in 2012.

These exceptional results, set against the backdrop of difficult times for FDI, are a genuine success for Britain. I am proud of the sheer hard work that national and local Government, investment partners and British companies put in to achieve this. I am very proud that my Investment team in UK Trade & Investment has played a leading part in this achievement too.

Every year, companies from around the world choose Britain to make new and expansion investments. These translate to real jobs for real people. Last year, 1559 investment decisions were made in Britain's favour. We estimate that these created or safeguarded 170,096 jobs in Britain – jobs which would not exist or would have been lost without inward investment. The great benefit to Britain from those people being in work, and the multipliers from it of reduced welfare costs, greater spending power in the high street, and the security that employment brings, are too often ignored – I think they should be celebrated.

Most companies understand that Britain is, at one and the same time, both a secure place to invest in the expectation of honest reward, and an exciting, dynamic global hub in which to deliver new and innovative products or services to market. These are not contradictions. We do both, and we do them well. And we build - investment opportunities in infrastructure are among our most important national assets and the highest value investments, and our National Infrastructure plan is valued at £330bn.

I think there are two reasons why Great Britain outstrips our competitors. Firstly, quite simply, Britain's offer stands among the best in the world. It improves every year. The UK is the easiest major economy in which to do business, and has the fewest barriers to entrepreneurship in the world. The British government is committed to a low tax, low regulation business environment. By 2015 our rate of corporation tax will be 20%, the lowest in the G7, with a special low rate of tax on patents and tax credits for research and development. This Government has cut the top rate of income tax to 45% from 50%.

We have a strong and flexible labour market and the second largest labour force in the EU. That labour force is highly skilled – we have the highest graduate output, and the highest number of leading MBA courses, in the European Union. We have four of the top ten universities in the world (three of the top five), acknowledged centres of excellence in research and internationally recognised expertise in a wide range of sectors, and hugely supportive business networks and associations. And we have a marketplace which is second to none in which to do business. Britain has 62m consumers within our borders and is a key gateway to 500m in the EU.

Secondly, and crucially to my mind, we listen to business and we act on what we hear. The Government understands that good business is the key to prosperity, and the whole resources of Government are employed to create an environment in which both domestic and international businesses can flourish. Government Ministers are wholly engaged in this and regularly meet with businesses of all sizes to build lasting relationships. My team in UK Trade & Investment exists to support international businesses in making their decision to invest in the UK, and help in making the experience simple, quick and effective. Whether you are a potential or existing investor looking to do business in Britain, UK Trade & Investment can provide a range of services tailored to suit your needs. We have dedicated officers who are available to help you – you can contact them by emailing enquiries@ukti-invest.com.

I hope you find this independent guide to investing in the UK as interesting and stimulating as I find working in this field. It focuses on what matters most to investors, and I hope the insight contained in its pages helps you make your investment decision.

Michael Boyd
Managing Director, Investment
UK Trade & Investment

List of Contributors

Watson, Farley & Williams LLP

Corporate

Christina Howard is a partner in the International Corporate Group of Watson, Farley & Williams LLP, dealing with a wide range of corporate and commercial work including corporate finance transactions, mergers and acquisitions, joint ventures and restructurings.

Tanvir Dhanoa is an associate in the International Corporate Group of Watson, Farley & Williams LLP. Tanvir's areas of practice include public and private mergers and acquisitions, equity capital markets and joint ventures, as well as general corporate and commercial work across a range of sectors.

Ravinder Sandhu is an associate in the International Corporate Group of Watson, Farley & Williams LLP, specialising in a broad range of domestic and international general corporate and corporate finance transactions including mergers and acquisitions, equity fundraisings, group reorganisations, joint ventures and regulatory matters.

Gareth Burge is an associate in the International Corporate Group at Watson, Farley & Williams LLP specialising in corporate and commercial transactions including corporate finance, strategic alliances (joint ventures and private equity fundraisings), mergers and acquisitions and group reorganisations.

Energy and Project

Heike Trischmann is a senior associate in the International Corporate Group of

Watson, Farley & Williams LLP. She specialises in all aspects of oil & gas law but has also been involved in electricity and water projects. Heike has advised governments, national oil companies as well as junior and major oil and gas companies, banks, energy trading companies, regulators and individual investors world-wide on a broad range of international and domestic corporate, commercial, regulatory and projects work. Through her work, she has developed an in-depth knowledge of various energy regulatory regimes in the UK, Continental Europe, Latin America and Africa including in relation to upstream E&P, LNG, gas storage and various energy infrastructure projects.

Sophie Yule is an associate at Watson, Farley & Williams LLP specialising in EU and UK energy regulation. She advises a global client base on renewable energy projects, including energy market reform implications for investment decisions. Sophie worked previously in-house at the UK Government's Department of Energy and Climate Change, where she advised on energy policy, the drafting of a number of energy bills, briefing Ministers and was also part of several major regulatory projects teams. Sophie also focuses on competition law and regulation.

Employment
Liz Buchan is a partner of Watson, Farley & Williams LLP, specialising in employment law and employee incentives. She heads WFW's Employment Group and is a former member of the Law Society's Employment Law Committee.

Asha Kumar is a partner of Watson, Farley & Williams LLP specialising in employment law and advises on a range of employment law issues affecting inward investors.

Rhodri Thomas is an associate at Watson, Farley & Williams LLP, specializing in employment law and a contributor to Discrimination in Employment – Law and Practice, 2006, Law Society Publishing.

Real Estate
Gary Ritter is a partner at Watson, Farley & Williams LLP. Gary specialises in advising on a broad range of residential and commercial property matters, including development, investment and landlord and tenant. He acts for substantial companies as well as for individual investors.

Felicity Jones is a partner in the International Corporate Group at Watson, Farley

& Williams LLP. Felicity is head of WFW's Hotel and Leisure Group and specialises in sales, purchases, funding, shareholders agreements and management structures in the hotel, leisure and technology sectors.

Charlotte Williams is an associate at Watson, Farley & Williams specialising In real estate. Charlotte advises on a range of commercial and residential property matters, including sales and purchases, landlord and tenant, investment and development. She is also experienced in the renewable energy sector, acting for developers in relation to onshore and offshore windfarms and solar energy installations.

Competition & Regulatory Law

Emanuela Lecchi is head of WFW's London Competition & Regulatory Group. She focuses in particular on competition law and regulation of communications and utilities. Emanuela has a Masters in International and Comparative Business Law, a Masters in Information Technology and Telecommunications Law, and a MSc in Economic Regulation and Competition.

Kristina Cavanna is an associate in the Competition, Regulatory & Networks group at Watson, Farley & Williams LLP. Kristina speacialises in competition law and regulation and has experience across several industry sector such as televoms, energy and the healthcare market.

Immigration

Angharad Harris is a partner at Watson, Farley & Williams LLP, specialising in all aspects of employment and immigration law. She is currently the Chair of the Law Society's Employment Law Committee.

Devan Khagram is an associate at Watson, Farley & Williams LLP specialising in employment and immigration law. His immigration practice includes advising on all aspects of the Points Based Immigration System including investors, entrepreneurs and application for settlement and naturalisation.

Intellectual Property

Mark Tooke is a partner in the International Corporate Group at Watson, Farley & Williams LLP. Mark is head of WFW's London intellectual property department, and has a particular focus on the corporate and commercial aspects of IP, including assisting clients in the communications, media and technology sectors.

Mazars LLP

Mazars is an international, Integrated and independent organisation, specialising In audit, accountancy, tax and advisory services. Mazars can rely on the skills of 13,000 professionals in Europe, Africa, the Middle East, Asaia Pacific, North America, Latin America and the Caribbean. The organisation also has correspondents and joint ventures in 15 additional countries.

Financial Report & Accounting
Stephen Brown is a Partner at Mazars LLP specialising in Audit and Assurance services. His client base ranges from owner-managed businesses, charities and not for profit organisations to international groups, either based in the UK or reporting to overseas parenbt comnpanies.

Business Tax and Business Tax Planning
A ndrew Ross is a Tax Director at Mazars LLP with extensive experience of both UK and non-UK/cross-border tax Issues, including tax efficient corporate restructuring and transaction planning (for both acquisitions and disposals/exists). He advises a range of clients, ranging from multi-national corporate groups to owner-managed businesses.

Company Formation
Mark Jackson is a Director in the Company Secretarial Department of Mazars LLP and a Fellow of the Institute Chartered Secretaries and Administrators. Mark has over 25 years' experience of advising all types of UK companies in all areas of concern to the Company Secretary. He is also currently the company secretary of a listed asset management business.

UK Taxation for Foreign Nationals
Janet Pilborough-Skinner is a Private Client Director at Mazars LLP specialising in all aspects of Individual international tax planning, including tax residency issues and offshore trust tax planning. She is the firm's national expert on the rules surrounding non-domiciled individuals and regularly advises clients on a range of remittance planning from small remittances to transfers in excess of £1 million.

Money Laundering
Donald Plane is the Compliance Director within the Standards and Risk

Management team at Mazars LLP. He us also the firm's Money Laundering Reporting Officer.

Immigration

Kay Bains is Mazar's Head of UK Immigration. Qualified as a solicitor with vast experience across the whole spectrum of UK immigration matters, her client base covers most industry sectors and a diverse range of individual applications. Kay also heads the Mazars India desk in LOndon and is fluent in Punjabi and Hindi.

Simon Kenny is an Immigration Manager at Mazars LLP. He spent time at the Home Office as an Immigration Officer before qualifying as a solicitor and applying his knowledge to immigration for the private client and corporate sectors.

UK Trade & Investment and the Investment Services Team

Michael Boyd is Managing Director Investment, having joined UKTI in 2011. His previous career was at Ernst & Young (now EY) where he was a member of the Global Executive Board and International Council. His executive responsibilities at EY included Global Managing Partner, Quality and Risk Management, Chairman and Area Managing Partner in the Far East and Vice Chairman, Global Accounts.

Anna Francis is Director for Relationship Management within the Investment Services Team, and has worked with Local Enterprise Partnerships since the beginning of the contract with UKTI to build and develop effective relationships around the delivery of inward investment. Anna has worked in the Government Practice within PA Consulting Group for over five years, working with a range of government departments specializing in stakeholder management and communications. Anna has an MPhil in European Studies from the University of Cambridge and a BA Honours Degree in History and French from the University of Bristol. She is based in London.

Mark Treherne is Chief Executive of the Life Sciences Investment Organisation

Will Harman and **Tim Padgett** are managers at the Automotive Investment Organisation

Other Contributors

Nick Hood is a Partner within Carter Jonas, a Director of St. John's Innovation Centre Ltd, The City of Cambridge Education Foundation, and is a Chartered Surveyor. Nick leads the the Carter Jonas Technology Team which specializes in the development and marketing of Science Parks and Innovation Centres. Carter Jonas is one of the leading property consultants in the Science Park sector. The Technology Team offers a broad spectrum of services to both public and private sector clients including feasibility studies, demands and needs studies, development agreements, marketing strategy reports, lettings and acquisitions of incubators, laboratory and/or R&D buildings.

Mark Norcliffe has been closely involved, for over 15 years, in promoting business partnerships between British and overseas automotive companies – formerly as Head of International Services at the Society of Motor Manufacturers and Traders and latterly as a specialist adviser to UK Trade & Investment. He is now Managing Director at TheSourcingSolutions Ltd.

Tony Rawlinson is a Chartered Accountant who has around 25 years experience advising quoted companies on a broad range of transactions. Tony was a founder of Dowgate Capital plc, a specialist AIM Market Nominated Adviser and Broker. He was appointed Chief Executive on 2004 and led the successful development of the Group until its sale in Summer 2009. Since then, Tony and his team from Dowgate have successfully established Cairn Financial Advisers LLP, an AIM Nominated Adviser, Plus Adviser and Takeover Code specialist. Tony is a member of the AIM Advisory Group of the London Stock Exchange.

Jonathan Reuvid is an editor and author of business books and a partner in Legend Business. He has edited all six editions of *The Investors' Guide to the United Kingdom* and has more than 80 editions of over 30 titles to his name as editor and part-author including *The Handbook of International Trade*,*The Handbook of World Trade*, *Managing Business Risk* and business guides to China, the 10 countries that joined the EU in 2004, South Africa and, more recently, Morocco. Before taking up a second career in business publishing Jonathan was Director of European Operations of the manufacturing subsidiaries of a Fortune 500 multinational. From 1984 to 2005 he engaged in joint venture development and start-ups in China. He is also a founder director of IPR Connections, the quality conference organiser.

Olaf Swanzy is the PNO Group UK sector specialist for innovation with close working relationships with all principal funding bodies in this sector. He joined the PNO Group in 2004 to help establish the UK operation with an initial focus on technology development within the Environmental Sector. Over the past 7 years Olaf has worked with an extensive range of SMEs and large companies across all industry sectors and academia to advance research and innovation activities through the procurement of government funding from national and EU sources. Since 2008, he has been involved in the delivery of training to SMEs in the areas of government funding for innovation investment activities. In 2009 alone he secured in excess of £15 million of grant support for clients.

Part One:

Investment in the United Kingom – The Current Climate

1.1 THE UK ECONOMY AND INVESTMENT ENVIRONMENT

Jonathan Reuvid, Legend Business

On 9th September 2013 the Chancellor of the Exchequer was able to declare with a degree of confidence that the UK economy "has turned a corner" although "the upswing is still in its early stages". His statement was supported by the reported 0.6% growth in GDP and the upward revision of the National Institute of Economic and Social Research forecasts in August for full year GDP growth in both 2013 and 2014 to reach 1.2%. The forecasts contrasted encouragingly with doomsayers' predictions twelve months ago of a UK double-dip recession this year.

MACRO-ECONOMIC INDICATORS

Forecasts for 2013/2014

Table 1.1.1 highlights more recent 2013 and 2014 composite forecasts for the basics of the UK economy published by HM Treasury on 18th October.

Table 1.1.1 Macro-economic indicators October 2013

	Independent 2013		2013	2014
	Lowest	Highest	Average of new forecasts	
GDP growth (%)	1.2	2.1	1.4	2.2
Inflation (Q4 %)				
- CPI	2.1	2.9	2.5	2.3
- RPI	2.5	3.4	3.1	3.1
Claiman Unemployment (Q4: mn)	1.30	1.60	1.41	1.32
Current account (£bn)	-61.0	-33.4	-52.1	-40.0
PSNB (2013-14: £bn)	93.0	120.0	103.4	92.2

Source: Macroeconomic Prospects Team, HM Treasury, No. 318

The independent averages are based on the forecasts made during the previous 3 months by 22 city banks and investment firms, and 16 non-City research institutions and forecasters including the OECD, IMF, EC and Confederation of British Industry (CBI).

Comparing prospects for the UK with those for other major developed economies the OECD summarised their relative growth performances in Table 1.1.2, implying a brighter short-term outlook for the UK than for its EU neighbours.

Table 1.1.2 2013 implied GDP growth vs 2012

	2012 %	2013 %
UK	0.2	1.5
US	0.2	1.7
Japan	2.0	1.6
Germany	0.9	0.7
France	0.0	0.3
Italy	-2.4	-1.8
3 largest euro economies	-0.2	-0.1

OECD forecasts at 03.09.2013

THE UK POPULATION

For readers unfamiliar with the ethnic diversity of the UK, the population stands at an estimated 63.7 million (Source:ONS, 2013), with 29.28 million in work, comprising 21.23 million in full-time work and 7.97 million in part-time work. The employment level (the proportion of working age people in work) in the UK is high at 70.6% compared with the European Union (EU) average of 64.3% Applying the international "standardised" measurement, the UK's rate of unemployment was 8.2% which also compares favourably with the EU average of 10.3% (source: Eurostat, 2012). 83.9% of the population are English, 8.3% Scottish, 4.9% Welsh and 2.8 % Northern Irish. According to the 2001 census, 1.9% of the population were black, 1.7% Indian and 1.6% Pakistani with a further 2.5% of mixed and other nationalities. Immigration rose sharply in the first decade of the millennium, but is now capped for non-EU entrants.

UK INWARD INVESTMENT

In the World Investment Report 2013 by the UN Conference on Trade and Development (UNCTAD), the UK stock of inward foreign investment is quantified at US$1,321 billion (£867 billion), an increase of 11.5% over the previous year. As Michael Boyd, Managing Director,Investment, at UK Trade & Investment (UKTI) notes in his Foreword, UNCTAD also reports a 22% growth in the UK's FDI inflows in 2012 to US$62 billion, ranking the UK as the largest recipient of FDI stock in Europe where FDI flows declined year-on-year by 18 per cent. The UK performance contrasts strongly with the experience of other leading developed economies still suffering from slow economic recovery or recession (declines of: US 26%; France 35%; and Germany 87%). These statistics provide evidence-based confirmation of the Ernst & Young and Financial Times assessments of the UK's continuing status as the preferred European FDI location.

The total number of inward investment projects in the year to March 2013 at 1,559 was the highest for three years and an advance of 10.8% over the previous year. However, the number of new jobs generated by overseas investors was 59,153, an increase of 12% on 2011/2012, and FDI activity also safeguarded a further 110,943 jobs, a quantum leap of 85% year-on-year over the 20111/2012 recorded total of 59,918 recorded. Together, the total of new and safeguarded jobs at 170,096 was nearly 51% above the 2011/12 total. In the prevalent recessionary climate, this was a more than satisfactory outcome.

The top 10 sources of investment over the past four years are detailed in Table 1.1.3.

Table 1.1.3 Top ten sources of investment

Country	Projects 2009/10	2010/11	2011/12	2012/13	New and Safeguarded Jobs 2009/10	2010/11	2011/12	2012/13
USA	484	388	336	396	15,443	36,424	37,525	48,802
Japan	90	71	88	114	1,434	4,360	7,818	7,442
France	74	59	65	93	760	1,471	12,038	16,001
Italy	107	105	98	93	2,293	5,508	1,763	6,892
China	92	97	92	70	3,271	6,096	2,116	3,409
India	99	69	81	89	3,729	5,902	5,454	7,255
Germany	62	68	66	78	2,033	1,947	4,994	14,589
Canada	38	56	59	63	1,193	3,542	1,342	21,208
Australia	55	53	51	61	762	2,940	1,500	1,297
Switzerland	67	53	54	52	549	4,344	2,970	2,056

Source: UK Inward Investment Reports: 2009/10, 2010/11 and 2012/13, UKTI

As in the three previous years, the US remains by far the biggest source of investment projects, accounting for 25% and 29% of created or safeguarded jobs (one-third in 2010/11). Project numbers recovered for Germany and France, although not yet to their 2009/10 levels, and both countries contributed significantly to the new and safeguarded jobs total (9.4% in the case of French and 8.5% for German projects). Japan ranked second in 2012/2013 after the USA as the source of 114 new investment projects, a significant increase of more than 29%, but generated only 7,442 new and safeguarded jobs against 7,818 in 2010/2011. Ranking third with France, Italy provided 93 new investment projects in 2012/2013 against 98 in 2011/2012 but generated 6.892 new and safeguarded compared with 1,763 in the previous year. India, Canada, Australia and Switzerland were also sources of more projects year-over-year in 2012/13 and the 63 Canadian investments generated 21,208 new and safeguarded jobs, representing 12.5% of the total, and second only to employment from US investments. Only 70 projects this year originated from China compared to 92 in 2011/2012 but the 3,409 jobs generated were more than 50% up on the previous year.

Composition of investment projects
Inward investment by category
The 2012/2013 proportions of completely new investments, expansions of previous investments and mergers and acquisition (M&As) including joint ventures (JVs) are compared with the 2010/2011 and 2011/2012 proportions in Table 1.1.4.

Table 1.1.4 UK inward investment by category

	2010/2011	2011/2012	2012/2013
New investments	724	752	777
Expansions	544	506	577
M & A (inc. JVs)	166	148	205
TOTAL	**1,434**	**1,406**	**1.559**

Source: UK Inward Investment Reports 2010/2011, 2011/2012 and 2012/2013, UKTI

While there were satisfactory improvements in all three categories of FDI, perhaps the most significant was the year-on-year increase of 14% in the expansion category, the highest ever, which reflects the commercial value placed by existing investors on the UK skills base and advanced research, and the open economic investment environment, particularly in infrastructure.

Inward investment by sector
The dispersion of FDI by primary business sector in 2012/2013 and jobs created or safeguarded is detailed in Table 1.1.5.

Table 1.1.5 UK inward investment projects 2012/2013 by primary sector

Sector	Projects	Total jobs
Advanced Manufacturing	380	51,568
Life Sciences	142	11,238
Creative industries and ICT	369	20,837
Electronics and Telecom	109	5,671
Finance and Professional	309	35,636
Energy and Infrastructure	250	45,149
TOTAL	**1,559**	**170.096**

Source: UK Inward Investment reports 2012/2013, UKTI

Within the manufacturing sector, the 85 automotive and 58 aerospace projects registered the highest average of total jobs.

Inward investment by type of operation
Table 1.1.6 completes the analysis of 2012/2013 FDI projects by type of operation. Within the period, there were overall increases in each sector of operation other than HQs and manufacturing. The outstanding year-on-year increase of 84% in R&D projects emphasises the attractiveness of the UK as a global centre for innovation. Chapter 3.5, provides an overview of science parks and business incubators in the UK where much of the private sector R&D is located.

Table 1.1.6 UK Inward Investment by operation type

	2009/10	**2010/11**	**2011/12**	**2012/13**	
				Projects	**Jobs**
Services	711	587	629	666	69,261
HQ	277	274	286	283	4,726
Manufacturing	248	210	256	235	44,438
R & D	278	218	162	298	34,800
Distribution	56	66	38	40	4,866
Contact centres	49	69	35	37	13,005
TOTAL	**1,619**	**1,434**	**1.406**	**1,559**	**170,096**

Source: UK Inward Investment Reports 2009/2010, 2010/2011and 2011/2012, UKTI

KEY AREAS OF INVESTMENT OPPORTUNITY

Looking forward to 2014 and beyond among the many areas of business opportunity for inward investors the UK industry sectors which continue to attract high levels of interest are:

- Advanced engineering
- Creative and media
- Electronics and communications
- Energy
- Financial and business services
- Food and drink
- IT and software

However, there are four individual areas where prospects are particularly exciting and which merit specific attention:

Infrastructure

UKTI's Global Entrepreneur Programme has yielded 60 business ventures from international entrepreneurs generating more than 4000 jobs. Over the programme's eight year life entrepreneurs will have raised approximately £1 billion of venture capital.

Key elements of the programme include:

- implementation of a ground-breaking commercial-scale carbon capture and storage project;
- improvements to selected road and local transport schemes across the UK;
- Crossrail and the new HS2 high-speed rail network;
- launch of the Green Investment Bank to stimulate growth in the green economy;
- support for major regeneration projects around the UK, including Elephant and Castle, Nine Elms and the Atlantic Gateway;
- increase in the UK's nuclear power capability;
- construction of the Thames Tideway Tunnel;
- development of electricity generation capacity through offshore wind.

London Olympic Games Legacy

The London Legacy Corporation continues to build on the highly successful London 2012 Olympic and Paralympic Games by transforming the Olympic Park into a new metropolitan centre that will provide significant development opportunities for business enterprises and investors, such as:

- the International Quarter, a £1.3 billion project that will provide four million square feet of Grade A commercial office space; and
- Landprop, a 30 acre mixed development with 1.3 million square feet of housing and half a million square feet of office space.

The official 12-month report on the initial impact of the 2012 Games to be published shortly confirm that the UK is on course to achieve its economic legacy targets from this historic event.

Tech City

The Tech City Investment Organisation (TCIO), was established in 2010 to support the growth of the technology cluster in East London around Shoreditch and Old Street and extending into the Olympic Park at Stratford.

Life Sciences
The significant investment opportunities in this key sector of the UK economy are explored in detail in Chapter 5.3.

THE ROLE OF UK TRADE AND INVESTMENT (UKTI)

In 2012/2013 UKTI played an active role in attracting 1,322 (85%) of the national total of projects secured. UKTI works with new and existing investors to ensure that clients are fully integrated into UK networks and UK market opportunities with access to information and people to ensure that their inward investment decisions are made on a sound economic basis. Following the investment decision, UKTI provides a comprehensive "after sales" programme to help every new investor to connect with local partners, relevant UK business communities and to make use of UKTI's Trade Services.

Note: Much of the content for this chapter is derived from the Great Britain and Northern Ireland Inward Investment 2012/2013 published July 2012 by UK Trade & Investment.

1.2 OVERVIEW FOR INWARD INVESTORS

Christina Howard
Watson, Farley & Williams LLP

INTRODUCTION

The UK is one of Europe's most favoured jurisdictions for inward investment[1], that is, the investment of money from an external source into a region. Despite continuing global economic uncertainty, inflows of foreign direct investment (FDI) into the UK have increased year on year for the second time since 2008, reaching nearly US$62 billion in 2012[2]. Once established in the UK, foreign-owned companies are treated no differently from UK firms. London is seen to be a particularly attractive place to invest and has been voted the number one destination in Europe for FDI[3], attracting 45% of the UK's FDI[4].

There are many reasons for investors and businesses to choose to invest or establish a presence in the UK, including:

- its sophisticated infrastructure and telecommunications;
- its position as a leading financial centre;
- its recognized and respected legal system;
- its financial incentives and tax environment;
- its stable political environment; and
- its skilled workforce.

1 Ernst & Young's UK Attractiveness Survey 2013.
2 United Nations Conference on Trade and Development - World Investment Report 2013 - Country Fact Sheet - UK.
3 FDI European Cities & Regions 2012/2013.
4 Ernst & Young's UK Attractiveness Survey 2013.

Once a business has chosen to establish a presence in the UK, there are a number of factors, in addition to other, broader commercial issues, that need to be considered, including the following:

1. What type of entity should I choose?
2. What will the tax treatment be on my investment?
3. How do I go about employing people in the UK?
4. Which type of premises do I need for my investment?
5. Is the UK a good place to raise finance?
6. What if my business becomes involved in a dispute?

TYPE OF ENTITY TO BE CHOSEN

There are a number of entities or arrangements that may be chosen when establishing a business presence in the UK, including trading partnerships, limited liability partnerships, agency arrangements and European Economic Interest Groupings. However, the most common arrangements chosen by those investing or establishing a presence in the UK are the incorporation of a UK company (which may be a subsidiary of the overseas parent company) or the opening of a UK establishment (a branch or place of business in the UK).

UK companies and establishments are all regulated by UK companies' legislation. Companies House, operated by the Registrar of Companies, is the key government organisation that coordinates the registration and administration of businesses in the UK.

Where a business establishes a presence in the UK through a company or UK establishment, a number of consequences will follow, which will to some extent vary with the form or presence chosen, but will include obligations to file certain documents at Companies House and to submit tax returns to HM Revenue & Customs.

Establishing a UK company

The most common method of establishing a business presence in the UK is through the incorporation of a limited liability company. The company may be incorporated as a wholly owned-subsidiary of a non-UK parent entity, or by one or more individuals. The company will have its own legal personality as an entity separate from its parent undertaking or individual shareholders, and will be able, therefore, to enter into contracts and operate in its own name.

In certain cases, the best way to develop a presence in the UK may be to partner experienced and established local representatives or undertakings through cooperation or joint venture arrangements, which will often be structured through a UK company as the joint venture vehicle. For further discussion on joint ventures, reference should be made to Chapter 6.4 of this book entitled "Mergers and Acquisitions and Joint Ventures".

In order to establish a UK company, certain documents must be filed with Companies House, including the company's constitutional documents (namely, the Memorandum and Articles of Association). Depending on the nature of the company's business going forward, standard documents may be adopted, or these can be tailored to specific requirements (for which a solicitor's advice should be sought). Once the constitutional documents have been finalised, these and other incorporation documents are filed at Companies House, and a certificate of incorporation and company number are issued. It can take as little as a day to register a company at Companies House.

Opening a UK establishment

As an alternative to incorporating a UK company, a non-UK business may simply register a UK establishment in the UK. An overseas company will be required to register its UK establishment at Companies House and will also be subject to certain on-going accounting requirements and requirements to deliver returns. In simple terms, if an overseas company has a presence in the UK from which it regularly conducts business or premises in the UK where it may be contacted, this will constitute a UK establishment requiring registration. A single registration regime applies for all overseas companies that carry on business in the UK through a UK establishment, irrespective of whether it is a place of business or a branch.

THE TAX TREATMENT ON INVESTMENT

The format chosen for establishing a business presence in the UK will vary as a result of the taxation implications as well as the commercial considerations and objectives of the investors involved. The basic principles of UK corporation tax and the taxation consequences of each format are briefly set out below.

When deciding which entity would be most suitable for an inward investor, it should be noted that the tax implications of establishing a company, branch or a place of business/representative office in the UK may vary significantly from entity to entity depending on, for example, the size of the business or the nature of the trade that is being undertaken.

Since the taxation implications of any investment will vary from case to case and may be complex, it is advisable to seek more detailed tax advice from a solicitor specialising in UK tax before establishing any sort of UK presence.

Companies resident in the UK

A company incorporated in the UK will generally be regarded as resident in the UK for tax purposes and will consequently be liable to pay UK corporation tax on its worldwide profits (subject to double taxation relief for foreign taxes).

In the UK, local and foreign-owned UK resident companies are taxed alike. Inward investors may have access to certain regional grants and incentives that are designed to attract industry to particular areas of the UK, but no tax concessions are granted.

The main corporation tax rate is currently 23%, with a small profits rate (previously the small companies' rate) of 20%. The coalition government continues to reduce the headline rate of corporation tax. The main rate will be reduced to 20% by April 2015, down from 28% in 2010, with a view to increasing the UK's competitiveness from a tax perspective.

The UK has a fairly simple system of personal income tax, with a basic rate of 20% for income up to £32,010 (excluding personal allowances), a higher rate of 40% for income between £32,011 and £150,000 and a rate of 45% for income over £150,000. There is also a National Insurance system into which taxpayers and their employers make mandatory payments.

Companies that are not resident in the UK:

Companies that are not resident in the UK are subject to corporation tax only if the company trades through permanent establishment in the UK. Profits that are attributable to the activities of a UK permanent establishment are subject to UK corporation tax as if the permanent establishment were a separate entity.

A non-UK resident company that does not have a permanent establishment in the UK, although not liable to corporation tax, may be liable to income tax on its UK source profits (e.g. rents from a UK property) at the basic rate of 20%, subject to certain limitations.

Where a company is resident in a country with which the UK has a double taxation treaty, the impact of that treaty must be considered.

EMPLOYING PEOPLE IN THE UK

Businesses wishing to establish a presence in the UK have various options in relation to their staff. These, along with connected immigration issues, are discussed in more detail in Chapters 2.5 and 4.5 of this book entitled "UK Immigration" and "UK Employment Law".

Due to the challenging economic conditions, there has been some downturn in the UK's employment data over the last few years; however, between February and

April 2013, the number of people in work in the UK was still 29.76 million and the unemployment rate was at 7.8% (down 0.4% compared to the same period last year).[5]

Much of the employment legislation currently affecting the UK workforce originates from the European Commission in Brussels. EU regulations affect working patterns, wage structures and employee protection rights in the UK; for example, the European Working Time Directive creates an entitlement to minimum daily and weekly rest periods, an average working week limit of 48 hours, and restrictions on night work. As it has implemented the EU directives, the UK government has been proactive in trying to maintain its flexibility and competitiveness; for example, it has currently negotiated a special provision under the Working Time Directive that allows employees to opt out of the 48-hour working week limitations.

Whilst citizens of EEA Member States can usually enter the UK to live and work without restriction, migrants from other countries will usually require a visa. Individuals from certain countries can enter as business visitors for up to six months without applying for a visa in advance but their activities whilst in the UK are restricted. The UK immigration regime is dealt with in more detail in the chapter of this book entitled "UK Immigration".

RAISING FINANCE

The City of London is widely regarded as one of the leading financial centres in the world. London offers a huge variety of financial services, including:

- commercial and investment banking;
- insurance;
- venture capital;
- stock and currency brokering;
- fund management;
- commodity dealing;
- accounting and legal services;
- electronic clearing and settlement systems; and
- bank payments systems.

Notwithstanding the continuing difficult global economic conditions, London remains attractive to inward investors because of its solid regulatory, legal and tax environment, a supportive market infrastructure and a dynamic and highly skilled workforce.

5 Office for National Statistics - Labour Market Statistics (June 2013).

UK government policies are intended to facilitate the free flow of capital and to support the flow of resources in the product and services markets. The principles involved in legal, regulatory and accounting systems in the UK are transparent, and they are consistent with international standards. In all cases, regulations have been published and are applied on a non-discriminatory basis by a single regulatory body: the Financial Conduct Authority.

The London Stock Exchange (LSE) is one of the most active equity markets in the world, combining its robust and liquid nature with a high degree of integrity. An increasingly popular forum for inward investment into the UK, particularly for smaller companies, is the LSE's AIM market, which is examined in Chapter 6.2 of this book entitled "The AIM Market of the London Stock Exchange".

REAL ESTATE

The UK has one of the most dynamic and transparent property markets in the world, with a wide range of property options and flexible short term lease arrangements. For inward investors in the UK, one of the first decisions to make regarding real estate is whether to rent premises (known as a "leasehold" interest) or to buy premises (known as a "freehold" interest). There are no restrictions on overseas companies either buying or renting property in the UK.

Renting or leasing

Companies can either rent premises that are already available or enter into what is known as a "pre-let". A "pre-let" is an agreement with a developer to lease premises before construction is completed, enabling prospective tenants to specify the design, layout and fittings of the building. Commercial leases in the UK typically run for a term of 5-10 years with the tenant paying a full-market rent, normally quarterly, with rent review provisions and usually with no premium. It may be possible to negotiate "break rights" at set times throughout the lease (enabling the tenant to "break" the lease before the end of the term).

The majority of leases of commercial premises in the UK are let on "full repairing and insuring terms", which places the responsibility and costs for all upkeep, decoration and repairs on the tenant. In addition, most leases over 5 years in length will have a provision to increase the rent in line with market conditions at pre-determined points throughout the lease. The standard clause allows for "upwards-only" rent reviews at 3-5 yearly intervals. This means that if the market rent rises, so too will the rent payable under the lease, but the rent payable will not come down if the market falls.

Businesses choosing to rent property must also pay stamp duty land tax

("SDLT"), which is calculated using the lease premium (if any) and the net present value of the rent payable, which is based on the value of the total rent over the life of the lease.

Buying

Buying property in the UK is usually a relatively straightforward process and, importantly, there are no restrictions on overseas companies buying real estate. In addition to the price of the property, purchasers must pay SDLT, which is currently chargeable at a rate of up to 15% of the purchase price or lease premium of residential property (depending on the statutory value bands) and up to 4% for commercial property, as well as Land Registry fees payable on purchases and, in some circumstances, on a letting.

Companies purchasing or leasing property should appoint an agent to represent them and are expected to pay legal fees, which incorporate conveyancing fees, as well as the costs for local authority and other conveyancing searches and bank transfer fees. An experienced property solicitor is necessary to assist in the preparation of all the required legal documentation.

Location

London may be the obvious choice for most investors establishing their business in the UK, due to its position as an internationally accessible city, its international time zone, its proximity to the EU and its excellent telecommunications infrastructure.

However, running an office in London can be expensive, and some businesses may prefer to locate elsewhere in the UK. As the legal and tax regulations do not tend to vary between locations in the UK, the considerations when choosing a location are primarily practical and will include, for example, cost, physical geography, labour and transport.

DISPUTE RESOLUTION

Disputes in the UK are generally resolved through litigation in UK courts or by arbitration/mediation. Numerous disputes a year take place in London, many with an international dimension, reflecting London's strong position as an international centre for legal services.[6]

The London Court of International Arbitration and the International Chamber of Commerce's International Court of Arbitration are leading international arbitration institutions. As a signatory to the 1958 Convention on the Recognition and Enforcement of Foreign Arbitral Awards (the New York Convention), the UK

6 Doing Business in the United Kingdom, 2012 Country Commercial Guide for US Companies - US Commercial Service

permits local enforcement on arbitration judgements decided in other signatory countries. The UK is also a member of the International Centre for Settlement of Investment Disputes and as such accepts binding international arbitration between foreign investors and the state.

Bilateral investment treaties (BITs) have been used as a means of protecting international investment and ensuring a more predictable and fair treatment of investors. The UK is party to 94 BITs that are currently in force[7]. A key feature of most of these BITs is investor-state dispute settlement arrangements that provide rights to those investing in the UK to seek redress for damages arising out of alleged breaches by the UK government of investment-related obligations. Key elements include provisions for equal and non-discriminatory treatment of investors and their investments, compensation for expropriation, transfer of capital and returns and access to independent settlement of disputes.

CONCLUSION

For the reasons discussed throughout this chapter, the UK continues to be attractive to overseas businesses and inward investors.

7 Ibid.

1.3 GRANTS AND INCENTIVES WITHIN THE UK

Olaf Swanzy, PNO Consultants Ltd

INTRODUCTION

Thousands of different grant schemes, worth well in excess of £5 billion each year, are available for UK companies in an attempt to encourage, amongst others, innovation and economic development.

In general there are four types of public funding incentives available in the UK:

- Grants - where funding is secured ahead of the launch of a project.
- Soft loans – where loans are secured for projects that fall outside the parameter of normal business banking.
- Tax incentives – recognising advanced financial incentives for those with leading edge Research and Development (R&D) or capital programmes that are aligned with government strategy.
- Awards – that retrospectively recognise industry excellence in many functional areas of business – usually a financial prize, which has the advantage of significant PR.

Outside of the obvious fiscal benefits, for successful applicants the receipt of public funding can be also be used to achieve the following:

- Increased project leverage and project development
- Improved company image (being awarded a grant is the equivalent of being awarded a quality stamp from a grantor body)
- Offers a competitive advantage over others in your sector
- Help raise additional 'harder finance'
- Increased knowledge transfer and collaborative relationships with external parties.

In all cases, funding is used by a Governmental Body or Policy Maker to address key policy issues and to stimulate first movers by reducing financial risk in that area. Such incentives are therefore always in line with Government policies and key drivers. It is important that this is kept clearly in mind for any potential applicant when positioning their applications.

MAIN GRANTS AND INCENTIVES IN THE UK

One of the key funding bodies to support UK businesses is the Technology Strategy Board (TSB), a fully public funded executive body established in July 2007. The TSB is the UK's national innovation agency, dedicated to driving innovation for wealth creation in the UK, so that technology-enabled businesses sustain or attain global significance. It provides support for R&D to build partnerships between business, research and Government to address major societal challenges; and to run a wide range of knowledge exchange programmes to help innovation flourish. Funding is available for business and in some cases the academic base. The vision for the TSB is to make the UK a global leader in innovation and a magnet for innovative businesses, where technology is applied rapidly, effectively and sustainably to create wealth and enhance quality of life. Further information can be found at www.innovateuk.org

Other sources of guidance and support for UK investment include: www.ukti.gov.uk, www.scottish-enterprise.com, www.wales.gov.uk, www.investni.com.

In general, the range of funding programmes available for UK businesses can be broken down into the following three principle areas:

1. Research and Development
2. Training and Education
3. Capital Investment

1. Research & Development

Innovation remains the key focus area for the majority of UK funding bodies. A range of schemes are available for businesses irrespective of sector, company size and Technology Readiness Level (TRL). The key national funding programmes, designed to support businesses in their R&D activities, have been summarised below.

The Smart Programme

Smart is a UK small and medium-sized enterprise (SME) single company scheme, managed by the Technology Strategy Board. It is available on a rolling basis and is open to all sectors.

Three types of grant are available:

- *Proof-of-market grant:* assess the commercial viability of a project. Projects will last up to 9 months, have a maximum grant of £25k, and up to 60% of total project costs may be funded.
- *Proof-of-concept grant:* explore the technical feasibility and commercial potential of a new technology, product or process. Projects will last up to 18 months, have a maximum grant of £100k, and up to 60% of total project costs may be funded.
- *Development of prototype grant:* develop a technologically innovative product, service or industrial process. Projects will last up to 2 years and have a maximum grant of £250k; up to 35% of total project costs for medium enterprises, or up to 45% for small and micro enterprises, may be funded.

Collaborative Research & Development (CR&D) Programme

CR&D is designed to assist the industrial and research communities to work together on R&D projects in strategically important areas of science, engineering and technology - from which successful new products, processes and services can emerge. Regular calls are announced throughout the year and topics vary with each call. Example calls have featured in ICT/Digital, Low Carbon Vehicles, Biotechnology, and Healthcare sectors. Projects must comprise industry led activity which is collaborative, either science-to-business or business-to-business interactions involving a minimum of two partners. Grant levels can be between 25% (for experimental development) and 50% (for applied research executed by Universities). Funding is typically £100K - £800K.

Biomedical Catalyst

There are also a range of sector specific funding programmes such as the

Biomedical Catalyst programme. This scheme supports SMEs and academics, from any sector or discipline, looking to develop innovative solutions to healthcare challenges e.g. stratified healthcare, diagnostics and regenerative medicine.

There are three types of grant available:

- Feasibility award (enables the exploration and evaluation of the commercial potential of an early-stage scientific idea
- Early stage award to evaluate the technical feasibility of an idea and establish proof of concept in a model system,
- Late stage award takes a well-developed concept and demonstrates its effectiveness in a relevant environment eg Phase I&II Clinical trial

Under this scheme, funding proportions vary from up to 60% (for a late or early stage award) and 75% (for a feasibility award). The maximum grant available ranges from £150k - £2.4 million.

Small Business Research Initiative (SBRI)

The SBRI supports the engagement of the public sector with industry during the early stages of development, supporting projects across a range of industry sectors through the stages of feasibility and prototyping. The initiative is particularly suitable for SMEs and early stage businesses, as it provides them with vital funding for the critical stages of product development, and gives them a fast track and simplified process for working with the public sector. Typically, funding available is £100k for a feasibility stage project and £1 million for a development stage project.

Energy Entrepreneurs Fund

Entrepreneurs with innovative ideas and products in energy efficiency, storage and low carbon generation can apply for a share of £19million of funding managed by the Department of Energy & Climate Change (DECC). Projects will be assessed in terms of their the potential impact of the innovation on 2020 and/or 2050 low carbon targets or security of supply; the technical viability of their innovation and coherent development plan that will commercially progress the innovation; value for money; and the size and nature of the business opportunity. Calls open every three months. The maximum amount of funding that a company may receive shall not exceed 1 million euros. SMEs need to demonstrate a minimum 10% cash match.

Horizon 2020 (H2020) – European Funding

At a European Level, H2020 is the latest European funding programme for research and innovation, which will be launched on the 1st January 2014. H2020 combines three separate funding programmes, including Research Framework Programme 8 (FP8), to create a budget of 70.2 billion euros for research and innovation across Europe over the next seven years. Unlike Framework Programme 7 (FP7) H2020 will not be limited to research, it will also support the conversion from research to real-life demonstration and commercialisation of products and services. This round of European funding will increase the UK's innovation capacity, boost its ability to commercialise knowledge and enable the Government to tackle major societal challenges; resulting in sustainable growth, job creation and social progress for the UK.

2. Training

Training or re-training of employees is of eminent importance to keep the workforce up to speed in rapidly changing environments. In some areas within the UK, these types of training courses may be eligible for public funding. Focus is on training for personnel below NVQ level 2 or minority groups such as asylum seekers.

3. Capital Investment

Few CAPEX support programmes remain in the UK, with a greater number of smaller schemes available at a Regional/local level, depending on location. For larger scale investments, the main National funding programme is the Regional Growth Fund (RGF). RGF is a £3.2 billion fund, helping companies throughout England to create jobs between now and the mid-2020s. The payment of RGF money is spread between 2011 and 2017. RGF supports projects and programmes that are using private sector investment to create economic growth and sustainable employment. Its principle aims include:

- To support in particular those areas and communities that are currently dependent on the public sector make the transition to sustainable private sector led growth and prosperity.
- The fund is competitive and there will be several bidding rounds – and is open to Private sector and Public/Private partnerships based in England
- All areas of UK are eligible. Projects can be: CAPEX, R&D, Training or productivity boosting technology.
- Support will only be given to projects that will not be pursued without RGF funding – the least amount required to deliver the project

- All projects should lever private sector investment for long term growth and private sector employment.
- The bid threshold (a minimum amount of funding that can be applied for) is £1 million
- An award could take the form of a grant, loan and/or loan guarantees
- RGF support will phased in line with expenditure and/or job creation/safeguarding.

THE GRANT APPLICATION PROCESS

Thorough preparation is the key to success in applying for grants. Having a credible business plan, a clear commercial/marketing strategy as well as a quality management team, before an application is submitted is a very important part of the application process. Application processing times differ significantly from scheme to scheme, with timescales ranging from four weeks to 9 months. For any potential applicants it is important that project costs are not incurred before the grant application process is completed and grant agreements signed with the appropriate funding body.

Careful preparation of applications will naturally increase the chances of success; however there are no guarantees that an application will succeed, regardless of its merits, as the majority of UK grants are discretionary, meaning that they are awarded on a case-by-case basis and, more commonly, on a competitive basis. It is therefore of vital importance to ensure that the application is of the highest quality so that it stands out against the competition. It is also prudent to maximise the chances of success by developing a total grants strategy, rather than pinning everything on just one application. Sectors that currently attract the most funding include agriculture, food services, manufacturing, chemicals, waste management, bioscience, aerospace and ICT, while pet projects the government bodies are currently seeking to encourage are those involving energy, transport, the environment, education, research and development activities and training.

SUPPORT IN THE GRANT ACQUISITION PROCESS

Finding the most appropriate grant and applying for funds can often be prohibitive. Successful grant procurement requires dedicated time and resources which companies often do not possess internally. As a result some businesses choose to maximise the funding opportunities available, appointing external expertise. Support advice and providers can be found through bodies such the UK Government Business Link network and the Enterprise Europe Network as well as specialist funding consultants.

One such public funding advisory is the PNO Group. Employing just under 250 staff across the EU, PNO's core business is advising organisations, across a range of sectors, in the context of the UK and EU grant funding landscape, helping them to identify and secure funds through available schemes. Their client base include SME's, Universities and Multinationals which include companies such as HP, Microsoft, Philips, P&G and Solvay. (www.pnoconsultants.com)

PNO Consultants adopt an 'end to end' approach to funding, with a range of services that can be broken down into three main areas:

- Identify (the identification and building of fundable projects, partner/partner linking and consortium development)
- Apply (proposal writing and submission)
- Comply (support in financial project management)

CONCLUSION

Grants can assist enterprises to achieve their aims, and with the correct approach and some thorough planning, companies can minimise the inconvenience and maximise the possible returns. With many businesses struggling to raise private and bank finance to advance their activities, it has never been more important to review all forms of funding available including public funds. If you are serious about being a market leader in your field, grant funding is the ideal mechanism to help you achieve this.

Note: Further information on grants and incentives currently available in the UK may be found in UKTI factsheets on wwww.ukti.gov.uk.

1.4 SUPPORTING THE FOREIGN INVESTOR: THE ROLE OF LOCAL ENTERPRISE PARTNERSHIPS

Anna Francis, Director for Relationship Management, Investment Services Team, UKTI

Depending on where you locate in the UK, you will be able to access grants and financial incentives which are bespoke to that local area....
Following the closure of the Regional Development Agencies in the UK, 39 Local Enterprise Partnerships were established to promote economic growth locally and support the delivery of foreign inward investment into their areas. UKTI, through the Investment Services Team, works closely with these Local Enterprise Partnerships to understand their local assets, for example talent pool, research excellence at local universities or access to markets. A key part of this local offer is, however, the multitude of grants and financial incentives that exist. These vary considerably locally depending on local funding and delivery arrangements and will of course also vary by sector. This article provides a first step to you understanding the kinds of grants and financial incentives available and how to access them through UKTI.

Direct financial support to help set up your business....

Many UK localities will be able to provide some kind of direct financial support to potential investors landing in the UK. This direct financial support can be used to help set up the company and provide training to staff. The amount of money available typically depends on the amount of jobs created by the company and the average staff salary costs. Again, this will vary across the UK and will depend on the size or profile of the company investing. Often this direct financial support will include money to support the training and development of staff (in some cases up to 50%) or incentives to recruit unemployed people within the area.

Access to Regional Growth Fund money once you have located in the UK.....

The Department for Business and Skills in the UK runs the Regional Growth Fund, a £3.2 billion fund that businesses across England can apply for and will run until 2017. The Fund supports projects and programmes that are using private sector investment to create economic growth and sustainable employment. It aims to help areas and communities currently dependent on the public sector to make the transition to sustainable private sector led growth and prosperity. Local Enterprise Partnerships play an important role in bidding for RGF money through supporting and endorsing private sector bids and can also bid direct for Regional Growth Fund money which they can then use to distribute to local companies or to run programmes, for example, to support small businesses. Once you have located in the UK, it may be possible for you to apply for Regional Growth Fund money to support further research or technological innovation within your company. Companies that benefited from Round 4 RGF funding include Jaguar Land Rover, Tata Steel UK and Augusta Westland UK. The funds are discretionary and each has specific qualifying criteria but UKTI, supported by the relevant Local Enterprise Partnership, can support you in the process for applying for these funds and submitting the application.

Business rate relief and Enhanced Capital Allowances if you locate in an Enterprise Zone...

There are 24 Enterprise Zones in the UK, ranging from city centre locations to globally competitive science parks. Many of these Enterprise Zones have a particular sector focus based on the cluster of companies already located there, and will often have a particular R&D or technological focus. Enterprise Zones in the UK do vary from those with world-class capability in a particular sector, such as Sci-Tech's Daresbury's High Performance Computing proposition and MIRA's focus on Advanced Enigneering and R&D in the Automotive sector, to those with a more property focused offer, such as city centre Enterprise Zones in, for example, Manchester.

Whatever the Enterprise Zone focus, there are significant financial incentives across all. Companies locating in an Enterprise Zone are able to claim up to 100% Business Rate Relief, worth up to £275,000 over a 5 year period and some offer Enhanced Capital Allowances for investment in plant and machinery for your business. Others offer lease payment holidays, low-rent incubator units, development funding and 'soft landing' packages with local service providers including pre-agreed deals with developers, accountants, or estate agents to make it easier for your business to establish a base there. They will also make it easier for you to apply for planning through the use of simplified planning procedures. Some examples of the Enterprise Zone offer are provided below:

Leeds Aire Valley Enterprise Zone

Situated at the heart of the Leeds City Region – a £53 billion economy with a 3 million population and a workforce of 1.5 million – the Aire Valley Leeds Enterprise Zone represents an unrivalled opportunity for business expansion and relocation. Strategically located just minutes from the centre of Leeds and the national motorway network, the Enterprise Zone offers access to a thriving regional economy, well-established supply chains and markets across the UK. The combination of strategic location and transport connectivity make the Aire Valley Leeds Enterprise Zone the ideal location for modern manufacturing, healthcare and renewable technologies, logistics and distribution businesses.

Lancashire Advanced Engineering & Manufacturing Enterprise Zone

The Lancashire Advanced Engineering and Manufacturing Enterprise Zone (EZ) lies across BAE Systems' Samlesbury and Warton sites with 74 hectares available for development. It can provide you with business rate relief of 100% up to 55K per annum for 5 years for businesses locating to the Enterprise Zone before April 2015, planning permission available for typical advanced manufacturing uses without a detailed application and local investor support packages available depending on the scale and economic value of the proposed investment by new occupiers. Other selling points of this Enterprise Zone are they are planning to establish a world-class skills development and supply chain excellent facility for the advanced enigneering and manufacturing scetor.

Depending on where you locate in the UK, some local areas have developed innovative ways of pooling resources and funds which are then available to businesses locating there...

One example of an innovative way in which resources and funds have been pooled to better support companies locally is the Greater Manchester Fund. The combined authority of Greater Manchester has created a revolutionary new way of investing in its future that will see the public sector act as a £100 million lender to business projects in exchange for an equity stake to kick start the regions economic recovery. Pooled from both government and European funding, this agreement is the first of its kind whereby all 10 local authorities in Greater Manchester are working to deliver a single investment strategy, underpinned by a new Regional Investment Team. Funds will be provided as short-term loans to companies in return for an equity stake in the hope that it will encourage them to invest in projects which create jobs and provide economic growth. Once repaid, the money will be "recycled" into further schemes, to support the development of a strong regional economy.

For companies looking to apply for such loans, a number of criteria will be taken into conideration, such as the sustainable economic growth of the operation, job creation, value for money (amount spent versus econonic outputs), private sector funding leverage, GVA contribution to the Greater Manchester region. Applications must be compliant with state aid regulations. Some examples of funding that comply with state aid regulations include; in Tier 2 Assisted Areas, up to 15% project for capital investment (Manchester benefits from a number of these areas to the north of the conurbation). For training aid to companies, up to 25% for specific training (non transferable skills) and up to 60% for general training may be available. For Research and Development Aid, funding for fundamental research is available up to 100%, for industrial research around 50% and experimental development around 25%.

In Liverpool City Region, for example, the Local Enterprise Partnership won £10million from Regional Growth Fund Round 3 to provide expansion grants to businesses. Miniumum grants available are £50k and maximum is £175k under de minimis regs. The funds are to fund capital equipment costs for businesses with expansion plans that will create jobs and bids need to demonstrate leverage of the money, so £5 million of additional investment for every £1 of the grant. The fund is currently administered by the LEP.

And there are a range of sector specific funding opportunities locally....

UKTI can also support you to understand what sector specific funding opportunities exist across the UK, both nationally and locally. For example, if you are a company in the Life Sciences sector investing in the UK, there are a range of local or regionally based funds available.

The North West Fund for Biomedical, for example, provides a flexible equity package for growth orientated businsses operating within the Biomedical Sector ranging from £50k to £1.5M to support a broad range of needs from start-up and early development through to expansion plans for trading businesses. The types of companies that it can support include those involved in pharmaceuticals (research, development and manufacture of drugs and biopharmaceuticals); biotechnology; diagnostics; clinical research organisations; contract manufacturing organisations; analytical services and sciences; and healthcare technologies and medical devices. In return for the equity loan, the Fund Manager will require an equity share in the business. Capital structures can include a combination of equity, quasi-equity or mezzanine capital and loan support as best suits the needs of the company.

BioCity in Nottingham, for example, has a range of specific funding available to businesses in the Life Sciences sector. They work with venture capital providers and government based agencies to secure funding for companies in the life sciences sector. http://www.biocity.co.uk/finance. The Mobius Life Sciences Fund, the first investment fund in the Midlands region dedicated to the life sciences sector, is operated by a subsidiary of and receives its investment funds directly from BioCity - http://www.mobiuslifesciences.com/. BioCity is based within the Nottingham Enterprise Zone which also contains the Boots Alliance based on life sciences sector. The Alliance Boots Campus is also within easy reach of Nottingham's two universities, University of Nottingham and Nottingham Trent University, which have some of the UK's leading research centres in Pharmaceuticals, Oncology and Clinical Technologies. The wider Enterprise Zone site also offers a wide range of property solutions from incubator facilities, location for SMEs, to sizeable business to major business accommodation.

You can access detailed information about these grants and financial incentives via UKTI's Investment Services Team…

UKTI's Investment Services Team supports foreign investors to land in the UK and works with you to understand your requirements and what the UK has to offer. We will work with you to understand whether your location drivers are cash driven, access to talent pool or access to markets. The Investment Services Team works very closely with Local Enterprise Partnerships and Enterprise Zones to understand the most up to date picture of the specific grants and financial incentives available for potential investors. Depending on your requirements, we will work with Local

Enterprise Partnerships on a package of benefits in that local area depending on your sector as well as information about skills availability, regulatory and policy issues affecting your area of business, property options, and access to markets. To access this package of support from UKTI, please contact enquiries@ukti-invest.com

Part Two:

The Regulatory Environment

2.1 COMPETITION LAW AND POLICY IN THE UK

Emanuela Lecchi and Kristina Cavanna, Watson, Farley & Williams LLP

INTRODUCTION – SUBSTANCE & ENFORCEMENT

Competition law has two levels of complexity. First, it is *substantively* complex. Second, it is complex when it comes to *enforcement* due to the interplay between the workings of various regulators and courts both at the national level (in each member State of the European Union) and at the European level.

In this short chapter we aim to bring some clarity to the main concepts of competition law as it applies in the UK, and give a brief overview of recent reforms to the existing regime. Readers with an interest in competition law should consider a specialised text for an in-depth analysis.

COMPETITION LAW – THE SUBSTANTIVE RULES

Competition law at the European level and in most member States of the European Union (including the UK) is designed to deal with three main substantive situations, namely:

(a) anticompetitive agreements (Art. 101, Treaty on the functioning of the

1 This chapter is condensed from a longer chapter on competition law published in 2009 in the Law Society Commercial Law Handbook, edited and co-authored by David Berry.

European Union ("TfEU"); Chapter I Prohibition, UK Competition Act 1998 ("UKCA 1998"));

(b) merger control (EU Merger Regulation; UK Enterprise Act 2002 (EA 2002); and

(c) abuse of a dominant position (Art. 102, TfEU; Chapter II Prohibition, UKCA1998).

In addition, both at the European level and in some member States (including in the UK) the competition authorities (and, in the UK, the sector regulators) can investigate sectors which may show features (often structural features) which impede competition in some way (so-called "market investigations").

There are then two sets of rules often dealt with by lawyers specialising in competition law. These are, on the one hand, rules designed to deal with **State Aids** and rules designed to ensure a level playing field amongst companies **bidding for public works and services**; and, on the other hand, rules to ensure that **parallel imports** (usually of pharmaceuticals, or cars) are not impaired throughout Europe. State Aids, public procurement and parallel import have a "common market" *raison d'être* and are assessed, amongst others, with reference to underlying concepts of distortion of competition. Space dictates that they cannot be considered further here.

RECENT COMPETITION LAW REFORM IN THE UK – THE COMPETITION AND MARKETS AUTHORITY

Over the last year there have been several important changes to competition law in an attempt by the UK Government to make the existing regime more effective in terms of enforcement and quality of decision making. The Enterprise and Regulatory Reform Act 2013 (ERRA) received Royal Assent on 25 April 2013 and contains important competition law reforms which are discussed as they arise under the relevant sections below. Some of the ERRA's provisions came into force at Royal Assent, others will be coming into force later via commencement order.

The most notable change is to the institutional architecture. A new body, the Competition and Markets Authority (CMA) will replace the OFT and the CC both of which will be abolished, in April 2014. The rationale behind this institutional reform is that the CMA, a single authority, will be able to deploy resources more effectively and will have new powers, for example in relation to information gathering and the use of interim measures in merger situations. One obvious concern is the degree of separation between investigation and decision-making in Competition Act cases, and whether the safeguards in place will be sufficient to maintain this.

The Government also intends to increase the application of general competition policy and law in the areas covered by sector regulation, which will necessitate greater cooperation between the CMA and sector regulators than has previously been the case. The reforms allow for joint action, cases being transferred to the CMA, or for powers being removed in certain cases. The rationale behind this is to increase the use of competition law powers in regulated sectors, since to date there have been very few cases brought by sector regulators using competition powers, and consequently even fewer infringement decisions.

THE THREE MAIN SUBSTANTIVE SITUATIONS

In the experience of the authors, the following Figure 2.1.1 helps to understand the three main situations with which competition law is mostly concerned, by visualising each situation by reference to a bar designed to represent market concentration.

Figure 2.1.1 The three main situations addressed by competition law.

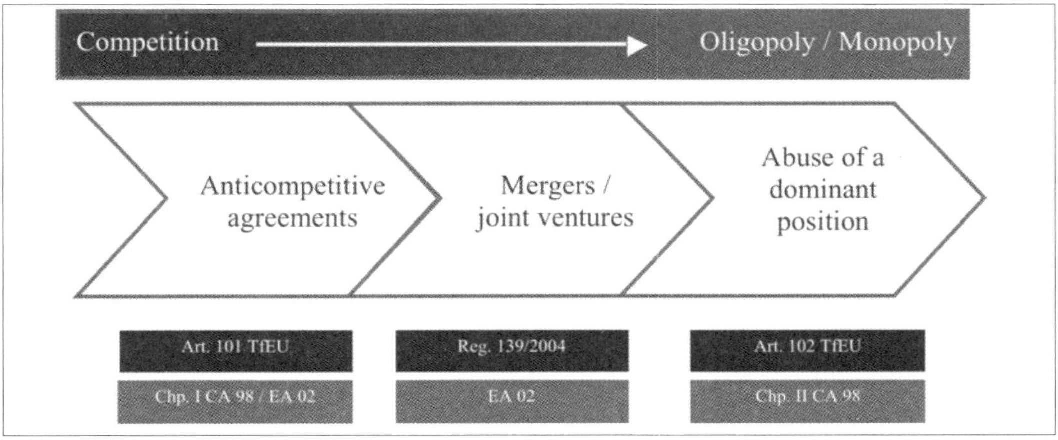

The left-hand side reflects a situation where the marketplace is close to a situation of perfect competition, progressively moving towards a situation of "dominance" and, on the extreme right, monopoly.

Anticompetitive agreements

The first situation, *"anticompetitive agreements"*, occurs in a relatively unconcentrated marketplace, where there would remain a sufficient number of "undertakings" to compete, provided that the market remained competitive. If these undertakings enter into anti-competitive agreements, and, for example, agree to fix prices, or partition marketplaces, then the fact that there may continue to exist a number of undertakings is irrelevant as those undertakings will effectively agree to act as one single independent undertaking (a monopolist), rather than as an individual profit maximising firm might.

The most pernicious form of anticompetitive agreements is, of course, the "cartel". In Europe, the focus is on tackling cartels: leniency and immunity applications are accepted by "whistleblowers" and the amount of fines has increased considerably. A number of jurisdictions in the European Union have introduced criminal sanctions for executives involved in cartels (cfr. Ireland, the UK, Hungary and Romania amongst others). One of the more controversial reforms resulting from the ERRA is the removal of the requirement of "dishonesty" as an element to the offence. Some have argued that this effectively removes the "mens rea" of the offence. There is an exclusion where customers were given the "relevant information" which includes the names of undertakings involved and nature of the agreement. One issue with this is that it may not be commercial, or practical in some cases to publish information of a commercial nature and whether this will have a chilling effect on deals remains to be seen.

Defences to the cartel offence exist where the individual did not intend to conceal the nature of the arrangements from customers (or the CMA) and where reasonable steps were taken to ensure the nature of the arrangements would be disclosed to professional legal advisers for the purposes of obtaining legal advice.

When practitioners talk about "block exemptions", they refer to a set of guidelines and rules that can offer a "safe harbour" for agreements which may otherwise, on first consideration, be caught by the prohibition against anticompetitive agreements (the first situation, (a) above). Under no circumstances (at least under the law as it currently stands) can the block exemptions offer a "safe harbour" for conduct amounting to an abuse of a dominant position. The role of the block exemptions is often misunderstood: it is not the case that undertakings must ensure that their agreements fall within a block exemption to be permitted; agreements outside of the block exemption are not automatically void, but they do not benefit from a presumption of compliance with the competition rules. More information on the block exemptions is provided in Appendix 1.

There are limited exclusions from the prohibition on anticompetitive agreements in the UK. These are typically for public policy and national security reasons. Until 6 April 2011, there was a more general exclusion for land agreements. This exclusion has now been revoked and as of 6 April 2011, land agreements (whether entered into before or after that date) are subject to the Competition Act 1998.

Abuse of a dominant position

The third situation, *"abuse of a dominant position"* occurs in a relatively concentrated marketplace, where one undertaking (or a small number of undertakings together) can act in a manner that impedes competition, usually because of their market shares and the existence of reasons why these market shares cannot be eroded over time (for example, barriers to entry). The assessment of market dominance and of abuse is complex. There is no exhaustive list of conduct that constitutes abuse of a dominant position but competition lawyers distinguish between *Exploitative Abuses*, those which affect companies and entities dependent on the dominant undertaking (customers and suppliers) and *Exclusionary Abuses*, which relate to actions which have as their object the elimination of competitors and/or competition. There are two principal types of exploitative abuse: excessive pricing and price discrimination. Exclusionary conduct can be categorised as either price related or non-price related. Exclusionary price abuses include predatory pricing, margin squeezes and discounts. Exclusionary non-price abuses include refusal to supply and tying and bundling.

Under the ERRA the CMA will have powers to compel individuals to provide information for the purposes of an investigation, and increased powers of intervention to impose interim measures where it considers that "significant damage" is likely. Previously this was set at the lower threshold of "serious irreparable harm", so interventions by the CMA pending investigative outcomes are likely to be more frequent.

Merger control

In the middle between anticompetitive agreements and abuses of a dominant position is *"merger control"*: markets become more concentrated as undertakings merge. Pre-screening of mergers is considered to be essential for the proper workings of the system. The European Commission has exclusive jurisdiction under the *EU Merger Regulation* ("EUMR") (Council Regulation (EC) No. 139/2004) to investigate mergers with a community dimension. Mergers must be notified to the European Commission if they meet each element of either of the tests set out in Appendix 2.

If a merger falls outside the scope of the EUMR, it is still necessary to determine whether clearance is required from any national merger authorities. (If the merger is notified to three or more countries within the EEA, the notifying party may request that the merger is referred to the European Commission (Art. 4(5) EUMR)).

When a merger taking place in the UK does not have a community dimension,

2 The Department of Business Innovation and Skills is currently consulting on possible changes to the UK merger control regime, which may result in the introduction of a mandatory notification regime.

the UK system of merger control needs to be considered. The UK currently has a voluntary merger notification regime. Parties are not required to notify mergers to the regulatory body, currently the Office of Fair Trading (OFT) and as of April 2014, the CMA). Although the system is voluntary, and will remain so under the ERRA, parties should be mindful of the OFT's ability to open own-initiative investigations into mergers after they have been completed. The OFT has, (and the CMA will have) jurisdiction to investigate mergers where either:

- the target has an annual UK turnover that exceeds £70 million; or
- the merging parties will together supply or acquire at least 25% of a particular description of goods or services in the UK, or in a substantial part of the UK, and the merger leads to an increment in share.

The thresholds will remain the same under the ERRA, and the regime will remain voluntary, however there are a number of reforms in order to strengthen the existing rules. These include penalties for parties for failing to respond to information requests from the CMA; suspension powers for proposed and completed mergers (previously these only existed for completed mergers); financial penalties of up to 5% of worldwide group turnover for breach of CMA orders and increased fees for filing merger notification forms.

MARKET INVESTIGATIONS

Currently, where the OFT considers that particular features of a market may give rise to anti-competitive effects which may not be caught by the Art. 101 and 102 TfEU or UKCA 1998 provisions, it may investigate these markets where it considers that consumer harm may result. Generally speaking, these market investigations focus on industry practices rather than the actions of specific firms. Following a market study, the OFT may (under the EA 2002) make a market investigation reference to the CC where it has reasonable grounds for suspecting that any feature, or combination of features, of a market in the UK for goods or services prevents, restricts, or distorts competition in connection with the supply or acquisition of any goods or services in the UK, or a part of the UK. A reference may also be made by a sector regulator.

Under the ERRA all market investigation powers will be transferred to the CMA. A shorter statutory timetable will be introduced for the first phase (market study) and there will be a reduction in the timetable for the second phase (market investigation reference) from 24 months to 18 months. This can be extended up to 24 months where there are "special reasons" for doing so, with a six month time limit (extendable to ten months) for the implementation of remedies. In addition the ERRA introduces formal information-gathering powers in the market study phase, impose interim measures to reverse pre-emptive action by parties.

CORE CONCEPTS IN COMPETITION LAW

In each of the three situations outlined in the diagram (Figure 2.1.1) above, there are two main concepts to be considered at the outset. First, that the rules apply to "undertakings". Second, that "market definition" is the foundation of competition analysis.

The Concept of an "Undertaking"

"Undertaking" is not defined in either the TfEU or the Competition Act 1998, which applies in the UK. The ECJ (now the Court of Justice of the European Union) has stated that the term "undertaking" "*encompasses every entity engaged in an* ***economic activity****, regardless of the legal status of the entity and the way in which it is financed*" (see *Höfner & Elser v. Macrotron* [1991] ECR I-1979).

Generally speaking, all companies, individuals and other entities (including charities) that engage in a commercial or economic activity will be undertakings for the purpose of competition law. There are two key difficulties with the definition of an "undertaking":

(a) what activities are "economic activities"; and
(b) whether two legally separate bodies (such as two companies) can be considered a single undertaking.

A group of companies can be a 'single economic entity' if they have unity of conduct on the market. For example, a subsidiary company and a parent company may be one undertaking if they act as a single unit on the market, e.g. if the parent company is the directing mind of the subsidiary. Therefore, coordinated conduct between a parent and subsidiary company that distorts competition is unlikely to be prohibited as there is only one undertaking (the test under Art. 101 TfEU is that there are "two or more undertakings"). Similarly, commercial agents, such as those falling under the Commercial Agents Directive, and their principals will usually be considered to be the same undertaking for the purposes of competition law as the agent typically provides goods or services on behalf of the principal.

The Concept of a "Market"

An agreement can only be anticompetitive when it has as its "object or effect" the "prevention, restriction or distortion of competition" in a "market". Every one of the block exemptions will only confer a "safe harbour" provided that the parties to an agreement have a market share in a "relevant market" below prescribed thresholds (parties whose market shares are above the thresholds do not necessarily fall foul of the competition rules). Merger control is designed to prevent those (and only those) mergers that lead to a significant impediment to effective competition in a market. Equally, an abuse can only occur when an undertaking is "dominant" (can exercise market power) in a market.

An undertaking is said to have market power if it can raise prices without suffering a significant decline in demand.

The definition of a product market involves consideration of demand-side substitutability and supply-side substitutability. Demand and supply-side substitutability are used to delineate the products concerned by and the geographic scope of relevant markets, which in some (limited) scenarios will also have a temporal dimension; for example, in the case of markets where it is not possible for customers to substitute between time periods, as in the case of, e.g. the supply of train tickets at certain times of day (see OFT Notice on Market Definition, Guidance Notice OFT 403, section 5).

The exercise of market definition consists in identifying the effective alternative sources of supply for customers of the merging undertakings, both in terms of products or services and the geographic location of suppliers. Detailed rules on market definition apply.

ENFORCEMENT ISSUES

The CMA will be the body responsible for enforcement following the abolition of the OFT and CC, and where an undertaking is found to be in breach of the UK or EU competition rules, that undertaking can be fined up to 10% of its annual turnover. An "undertaking" means a single economic entity: a parent company can be fined up to 10% of the group's turnover if its subsidiary is in breach of competition law. Therefore, parent companies should take an active role in ensuring that all of their group companies are compliant with the competition rules.

Additionally, individuals that breach competition rules could be imprisoned, face personal fines and could be disqualified from being a director for fifteen years. In the UK, individuals may be extradited under the EA 2002 s.191, if they breach competition rules in the USA or in any other country that has a criminal offence that corresponds to the cartel offence in the EA 2002.

SECTOR REGULATORS

Utilities and communications services were historically provided by State-owned companies. With liberalisation, the sectors were opened up to competition. The UK regulators in the key sectors are listed below in Table 2.1.1.

Table 2.1.1 UK key regulators

Regulator	Responsibilities
Ofcom	Communications and post
Ofgem	Gas and electricity
ORR	Rail regulation
OFWAT	Water services
Utility Regulator NI	Northern Ireland energy, water and sewerage regulation
CAA	Aviation

COMPETITION ENFORCEMENT INSTITUTIONS

The key European and UK competition enforcement institutions, together with some of their responsibilities are set out in Table 2.1.2 below.

Table 2.1.2 Competition enforcement institutions

UK Institutions	
Office of Fair Trading (OFT)	The OFT has dual roles – as competition authority and consumer authority
Competition Commission (CC)	The CC follows on from the OFT and other sector regulators in conducting in-depth investigations. Following Government consultation in 2011 the CC and OFT are to be merged to form the Competition and Markets Authority. Please see the section on the CMA below.

Competition Appeal Tribunal (CAT)	• hears appeals on the merits of decisions made under Competition Act 1998 – appeals against decisions of the OFT or other sector regulators; • hears actions for damages under Competition Act 1998; • reviews mergers and market references; appeals against regulatory decisions of Ofcom.
CMA	• The Competition and Markets Authority (CMA) will bring together the CC and the competition functions of the OFT. • The CMA should be in place by April 2014 and will have a primary duty to promote effective competition.
High court	Claimants can bring private actions for damages to the High Court. Claims can follow on from an adverse finding by the OFT, CC or CAT or can be brought directly to the High Court.
EU Institutions	
European Commission (DG Competition)	• enforces competition rules of the TfEU; • reviews mergers (phase I and phase II); • publishes guidelines on the application of competition rules for consumers, industry and national competition authorities.
General Court (was Court of First Instance (CFI))	Hears appeals against decisions of Community institutions, including DG Competition.

Court of Justice of the EU (was European Court of Justice (ECJ))	• hears references for preliminary rulings – the Court of Justice provides decisions or reasoned orders on specific points of law referred from national courts; • hears appeals against decisions of the General Court.

SUMMARY CHECKLIST
Activities in the contexts of:

- A. Negotiating with customers
- B. Cooperation with competitors
- C. Mergers/joint ventures
- D. Information gathering
- E. Unilateral action by "dominant" companies which are likely to be permitted and those which are likely to be prohibited under EU Law are listed in Table 2.1.3 below.

The main block exemptions at the time of writing are identified in Appendix I and threshold for European notification under merger control are listed in Appendix II.

Table 2.1.3 Activities likely to be permitted and prohibited

LIKELY TO BE PERMITTED	LIKELY TO BE PROHIBITED
A. NEGOTIATING WITH CUSTOMERS OR SUPPLIERS	
• Checking aggregated industry-wide statistical data. • Offering discounts to customers based on the suppliers' costs. • Setting recommended retail prices ("RRPs") for distributors, provided that there is no explicit	• Agreeing minimum or fixed resale prices with a distributor or a supplier. • Preventing a distributor from exporting a product to another EU member State. • Charging a distributor prices that vary according to whether the goods are to be resold in a specific country or exported to another EU member State.

LIKELY TO BE PERMITTED	LIKELY TO BE PROHIBITED
or implicit pressure on the distributor to follow the RRPs and that you are not dominant.	• Preventing a distributor from selling a product to a customer because they intend to export the product to another EU member State. • Preventing manufacturers of components from selling these components as spare parts.
B. CO-OPERATION WITH COMPETITORS	
• Attending meetings of trade association. • Discussing health and safety. • Discussing proposed regulatory changes.	• Bid-rigging, i.e. allocating tenders between competitors. • Agreeing production quotas with competitors. • Agreements or arrangements with the effect of dividing product or geographic markets with competitors. • Warning a competitor to stay away from "our territory" or specialist field. • Discussing prices, profit margins, rebates or discounts with competitors. • Discussing the cost of key raw materials with competitors that also source similar materials. • Agreeing to boycott particular suppliers or distributors. • Discussing prices or profit margins with competitors. • Agreeing current or future prices with competitors. • Discussing terms of sale or supplier/ customer business relationships. • Discussing strategic plans, such as pricing strategy or product/territorial expansion.

LIKELY TO BE PERMITTED	LIKELY TO BE PROHIBITED
	• Agreeing with a competitor to fix the timing for the introduction of a new technology that has been developed independently. • Delaying quoting a price until you know a competitor's price.
C. MERGERS / JOINT VENTURES	
• Entering into a research & development co-operation agreement with a competitor, where both parties are free to exploit the results independently.	• Agreeing with a competitor to fix the timing for the introduction of a new technology that has been developed independently.
D. INFORMATION GATHERING	
• Obtaining information on competitors' sales and prices from publicly available sources or from customers in the ordinary course of business. • Giving historical sales data to a third party which distributes aggregated, industry-wide sales figures to participants.	• Contacting customers specifically to gather competitors' pricing information ("fishing trip").
E. UNILATERAL ACTION BY "DOMINANT" COMPANIES	
	• Excessively high pricing, i.e. where the price has no reasonable relation to the economic value of the product. • Selling goods below cost in order to foreclose competitors from the market.

LIKELY TO BE PERMITTED	LIKELY TO BE PROHIBITED
	• Offering discounts to customers in a discriminatory manner, e.g. offering discounts to customers if they source all or most of their supplies from you. • Suggesting recommended retail prices to a distributor. • Refusing to sell a product to a purchaser with an existing business relationship. This will be permitted only if there are sound commercial reasons for refusing to sell, such as poor credit history. • Refusing to sell a particular product unless it is purchased with another non-essential product from your dominant market. • Insisting that a distributor must stock the whole range of your products.

APPENDIX 1
BLOCK EXEMPTIONS

The main EU block exemptions in force at the time of writing are listed below:

Block exemption	Council Regulation
Vertical agreements – agreements between non-competitors – new block exemption	Regulation 330/2010 Expires 31 May 2022
Specialisation/production agreements – unilateral specialisation; outsourcing; reciprocal specialisation; joint production agreements	Regulation 1218/2010 Expires 31 December 2022
Research and development – joint R&D and joint exploitation of findings	Regulation 1217/2010 Expires 31 December 2022
Motor vehicle distribution – purchase, sale and resale of motor vehicles or spare parts; repair and maintenance services	Regulation 461/2010 Expires 31 May 2023
Technology transfer agreements – certain patents, know how and software copyright licensing agreements	Regulation 772/2004 Expires 30 April 2014
Insurance – joint establishment of calculations and tables; establishment of non-binding standard policy conditions for direct insurance	Regulation 267/2010 Expires 31 March 2017
Road and inland waterways groupings	Regulation 169/2009 Indefinite duration
Liner consortia – joint operation of liner shipping transport services	Regulation 906/2009 25 April 2015

The *Commissions Notice on Agreements of minor importance (de minimis notice) 2001/C368/07* applies to agreements where the combined market share of competing/potentially competing undertakings ("horizontal agreements") is less that 10% and less than 15% for non-competitors ("vertical agreements"), provided they do not contain any hardcore restrictions.

APPENDIX 2
MERGER CONTROL :
THRESHOLDS FOR EUROPEAN NOTIFICATION

Issue	Primary test	Alternative test
Combined worldwide turnover	> €5,000 million	> €2,500 million
Individual EU-wide turnover	At least two parties > €250 million	At least two parties > €100 million
Presence in three member States		Combined turnover of all parties in at least three member States > €100 million AND Individual turnover of two or more of the parties in three of the member States referred to above > €25 million
Exception	A merger will not have a Community dimension if each of the parties achieves more than two-thirds of its EU-wide turnover in one and the same member State.	

The European Commission can refer the merger analysis to a national authority where the concentration would affect competition in a distinct market of a specific member State (Art. 4(4) or Art. 9 EUMR)..

2.2 REGULATION OF FINANCIAL SERVICES

Ravinder Sandhu,
Watson, Farley & Williams LLP

INTRODUCTION

The existence of a legal and regulatory framework that provides investors and others with confidence in the market as a place to do business has never been more important than now.

The financial crisis that started in 2007 led to significant reforms to the system of financial services regulation in the UK, resulting in a new regulatory regime provided for in the Financial Services Act 2012 (FS Act) which came into force on 1 April 2013.

Until 1 April 2013, the structure of the regulatory system in the UK comprised a single central regulator, the Financial Services Authority (FSA), responsible for both the prudential and conduct regulation of all types of financial firms, and an overriding framework statute, the Financial Services and Markets Act 2000 (FSMA), governing businesses in the UK undertaking financial services – a term that encompasses a broad and diverse range of activities from banking and insurance to fund management, securities trading and even funeral contracts.

On 1 April 2013, the FSA was abolished and replaced with a "twin peaks" structure where the prudential and conduct of business regulation is to be carried out by two separate entities, the Prudential Regulation Authority (PRA), which is aimed at ensuring the stability of financial services firms, and the Financial Conduct Authority (FCA), referred to as the City's behavioural watchdog.

The Bank of England is responsible for the direct supervision of the stability of the whole of the UK banking system through its Financial Policy Committee (FPC), which can instruct the two new regulators.

The FS Act implemented significant changes to the UK financial regulatory framework. Its main role was to make extensive changes to the FSMA to establish the new regulators and to set out their additional powers.

THE FCA

The FCA is the financial services regulator responsible for both the conduct of all firms authorised under the FSMA (including those regulated for prudential matters by the PRA) and for the prudential regulation of firms not regulated by the PRA.

The FCA has taken on a majority of the FSA's roles and functions, including its function as the United Kingdom's Listing Authority (UKLA). In addition the market abuse regime is within the FCA's remit.

In carrying out its role, the FCA needs to comply with both its strategic objective of "ensuring that the relevant markets function well" and advance the following three operational objectives:

- the consumer protection objective – securing an appropriate degree of protection for consumers (which covers a broad spectrum of persons);
- the integrity objective - protecting and enhancing the integrity of the UK financial system; and
- the competition objective - promoting effective competition in the interests of consumers.

So far as is compatible with advancing the consumer protection objective or the integrity objective, the FCA is to discharge its general functions in a way which promotes effective competition in the interests of consumers.

THE PRA

The PRA is a subsidiary of the BoE and is responsible for the prudential regulation and supervision of banks, building societies, credit unions, insurers and major investment firms.

The PRA has a general objective to promote the safety and soundness of PRA-authorised persons. In promoting safety and soundness, the PRA focuses primarily on the harm that firms can cause to the stability of the UK financial system.

When dealing with insurers, the PRA must have regard to the insurance objective of contributing to the securing of an appropriate degree of protection for those who are or may become policyholders.

The Board of the PRA includes the Governor of the BoE (as Chairman) and the Chief Executive of the FCA.

THE FPC

The FPC is a committee of the Court of Directors of the BoE. It is chaired by the Governor of the BoE and other members include the PRA chief executive (who is also the BoE Deputy for prudential regulation) and the FCA chief executive.

Unlike the FCA and PRA, it does not have direct regulatory responsibility for firms. Instead, it is responsible for macro-prudential regulation – regulation aimed to mitigate risks of the financial system as a whole.

The FPC has a primary objective of identifying, monitoring and taking action to remove or reduce systemic risks with a view to protecting and enhancing the resilience of the UK financial system. The secondary objective of the FPC is to support the economic policy of the Government which includes growth and employment objectives. It is required to produce financial stability reports detailing how each action it takes is consistent with its objectives.

The FPC also has the power to give directions and make recommendations. In particular, it may give directions to the FCA or the PRA requiring it to exercise its functions so as to ensure the implementation, by or in relation to a specified class of regulated persons, of a macro-prudential measure described in the direction. The FPC's "macro-prudential toolkit" currently consists of the sectoral capital requirements tool, which allows the FPC to adjust financial institutions' capital requirements against exposures to specific sectors over time.

The FPC may also make recommendations to the FCA and the PRA about the exercise of their respective functions. The recommendations may relate to all regulated persons or to regulated persons of a specified description, but may not relate to the exercise of the functions of the FCA or the PRA in relation to a specified regulated person. Should the FCA and PRA decide not to implement recommendations made on a "comply or explain" basis, they are required by the FS Act to explain publicly their reasons for not doing so.

THE FSMA

The FSMA is a framework statute. Its principal provisions form the basis of the

UK's regulatory system, with secondary legislation, rules and regulations being made under and pursuant to those primary provisions. The two main provisions setting the overall parameters within which financial services businesses are required to operate are the general prohibition on the carrying on of regulated activities (section 19, FSMA) and the restriction on the making of financial promotions (section 21, FSMA). These two sections provide that persons are prohibited from carrying on or promoting regulated business activities unless licensed, authorised or exempt by the FCA or PRA. These provisions are at the centre of the structure of the FSMA and form the basis for the regulatory system established beneath it.

General prohibition

As noted above, the FCA's and PRA's regulation of financial services within the UK is based on a system of approval and licensing of market participants, whether they are commercial or investment banks, insurance companies, securities dealers, financial advisers or others. The system provides for minimum standards and criteria for persons to qualify for approval and licensing where the legislators consider that the end-consumers may require regulatory protection.

The activities requiring licensing are termed "regulated activities". The FSMA prohibits the carrying on of a regulated activity in the UK other than by authorised or exempted persons. This prohibition is referred to as the "general prohibition" and is the central building block around which the FSMA and secondary legislation is structured. A person who undertakes a regulated activity without authorisation will be subject to criminal and civil sanctions. Furthermore, an agreement that results from a breach of the general prohibition will be unenforceable against the other contracting party.

Although the FSMA provides examples of regulated activities, this term is not exhaustively defined in the FSMA itself. Instead, it is defined in secondary legislation - the Financial Services and Markets Act 2000 (Regulated Activities) Order 2001 (RAO) - and includes the following activities:

(a) accepting deposits (i.e. banking business);
(b) dealing in investments as principal or agent;
(c) arranging deals in investments;
(d) managing investments;
(e) safeguarding and administering investments;
(f) establishing or operating collective investment schemes;
(g) advising on investments; and

(h) insurance related activities, including (i) effecting and carrying out contracts of insurance and (ii) assisting in the administration and performance of contracts of insurance.

Investments are defined by the RAO and include deposits, contracts of insurance, shares, debt instruments, units in collective investment schemes and various derivative instruments.

As stated above, only authorised or exempt persons may carry out regulated activities. Such persons may include securities traders and advisers, firms of accountants or UK corporate finance firms that act as sponsors or brokers on a market listing. Exempt persons include recognised investment exchanges, such as the London Stock Exchange.

The regulated activities a person carries on determines whether it will be regulated by the FCA for conduct and prudential purposes (a FCA-Authorised Firm) or whether it will be regulated by the FCA for conduct purposes and by the PRA for prudential purposes (a PRA-Authorised / Dual-Regulated Firm). The FSMA (PRA-regulated Activities) Order 2013 (SI 2013/556), which came into force on 1 April 2013, identifies which of the RAO activities are PRA-regulated activities. Activities which are designated as PRA-regulated activities include accepting deposits and effecting and carrying out contracts of insurance.

Financial promotion

In addition to regulating the activities described above, the FSMA also regulates communications made to third parties in relation to those activities. In particular, the FSMA prohibits a person from communicating, in the course of business, an invitation or inducement to engage in investment activity. This is more commonly known as "financial promotion". The FCA is responsible for the regulation and supervision of financial promotions.

The financial promotion regime is based on similar foundations to the general prohibition and does not apply if the person making the communication is an authorised person under the FSMA, or if an authorised person approves the contents of the communication.

Breach of the financial promotion restriction may give rise to civil liability or constitute a criminal offence. Resulting agreements may also be unenforceable and recipients of the unlawful communication may be entitled to recover their investment and to claim compensation for any loss suffered.

Details of the financial promotion regime are set out in secondary legislation: the Financial Services and Markets Act 2000 (Financial Promotion) Order 2005

(FPO). The term financial promotion is itself cast in extremely broad terms to encompass any communication on whatever medium. It includes face-to-face oral representations and representations made during telephone conversations (referred to as 'real time communications') as well as communications made in letters, emails or on a websites (referred to as 'non-real time communications'). Hence, communications with potential investors, inviting them to purchase shares or other investment products, will be caught, as will communications concerning insurance and banking products and the provision of investment management and investment advisory services.

Although the financial promotion restriction is wide, the FPO contains a large number of exemptions from the restriction. Examples of exemptions include intra-group communications and communications made by a company to its members, creditors or employees. The application of certain exemptions depends on the type of communication being made and whether or not it is solicited by the recipient. Exemptions may also apply by virtue of the nature of the recipients, for example, communications made to investment professionals, certified high net worth individuals or companies will be exempt from the financial promotion prohibition, as such investors are not regarded as requiring higher levels of investor protection.

The financial promotion regime will generally apply to all communications with a UK link, irrespective of whether the recipients are located inside or outside the UK and whether the communication is an incoming or outgoing communication. Communications originating outside the UK will, however, only be caught if they are capable of having an effect in the UK, otherwise they are exempt. It is important to note that, if relevant, the general position may be altered by European Union (EU) legislation.

The intention is to regulate the provision of business advice or the making of statements upon which a customer or client (other than sophisticated investors) may seek to rely in making a financial or investment decision. The aim is to ensure that individuals and businesses establish the necessary credentials, legitimacy and expertise through a system of approvals and licensing before they engage with third parties and take a pecuniary reward as a result. This is supported by the requirement to treat customers fairly by recommending that, when preparing and approving financial promotions, authorised persons consider whether the material:

- is clear, fair and not misleading;
- provides a balanced picture of the product or service;
- matches what the product or service delivers; and
- will be easily understood by their customers.

SECONDARY LEGISLATION AND THE FCA HANDBOOK

Secondary legislation is issued, modified, replaced and supplemented as the marketplace develops, and is tailored to particular kinds of businesses, such as the carrying on of deposit-taking businesses by banks, dealing in securities and derivatives and the operation and promotion of investment funds and other collective investment schemes.

Secondary legislation is further supplemented with rules and guidance issued by the FCA and the PRA and contained in the FCA Handbook (which applies to both FCA-Authorised Firms and PRA-Authorised Firms, containing conduct of business requirements) and the PRA Handbook (which applies to PRA-Authorised Firms only, and contains the relevant PRA prudential requirements).

Both the FCA and the PRA Handbooks include overriding standards for all market participants, as well as detailed conduct of business rules and a code of market conduct. The FCA Handbook is also responsible for implementing the requirements of the Markets in Financial Instruments Directive (MiFID), which aims to harmonise financial services regulation within the European Economic Area and increasing competition and consumer protection in investment services. There are proposals to replace MiFID, by implementing the MiFID II Directive. This is currently being considered by the European Parliament, and is expected to be implemented by 2015 at the earliest.

Conduct of Business Rules

The FCA's Conduct of Business rules apply to all firms with investment business customers in the UK. The extent to which the rules apply depends upon the nature of the products and services provided, and the type of client to which they are offered. The rules are set out in the Conduct of Business Sourcebook (COBS).

The COBS is designed to provide guidance on the regulatory requirements across the range of activities that may be carried on by regulated persons and covers, amongst other things:

- financial promotions;
- the provision of information and advice to clients;
- dealings in investments; and
- the management of investments.

The previous COBS was widely criticised by the financial services industry for imposing unnecessary burdens on the businesses being regulated. The new COBS is intended to free companies from the prescriptive nature of the previous sourcebook and enable them to design their business processes and promotional material to suit their particular circumstances and those of their customers. To this end, the COBS has been simplified and is based on general principles rather than detailed rules and processes. The COBS also implements the conduct of business requirements of the MiFID.

Market abuse

Although the FSMA primarily regulates financial services through a system of authorisation and licensing, it also sets out a framework for tackling wrongful behaviour in the financial markets (better known as market abuse), which complements the criminal offence of insider dealing. These rules are designed to enhance market integrity and confidence for the benefit of market participants.

The FCA has taken over the FSA's responsibilities for regulating the market abuse regime and targeting market abuse is a regulatory priority, particularly in an uncertain economic climate where market instability can increase the scope for market abuse.

The current market abuse provisions implement the Market Abuse Directive, and harmonise the requirements relating to insider dealing and market manipulation across the EU.

Market abuse arises in circumstances where market participants have been unreasonably disadvantaged (whether directly or indirectly) by others in the market who, amongst other things, have:

- used to their own advantage information that is not generally available;
- created a false or misleading impression; or
- distorted the market.

Under the FSMA, the FCA has the power to impose financial penalties for market abuse. The FCA has a published Code of Market Conduct, which forms the first chapter of the FSA's Market Conduct sourcebook (MAR) to supplement the provisions that deal with market abuse and provide guidance as to whether or not behaviour constitutes market abuse.

Other provisions

In addition to the above, the FSMA also establishes the FSA's powers of intervention, which include broad powers of investigation and powers to penalise persons contravening the FSA's rules or the provisions of the FSMA, including the ability to fine contraveners or withdraw a person's authorisation.

The FSMA is a comprehensive statute. This chapter provides a summary of the principal provisions upon which financial services regulation in the UK is based, but the FSMA also makes provisions in relation to other relevant matters, including provisions for:

- the official listing of securities, derived from EU legislation;
- an investors' compensation scheme;
- the establishment and operation of an independent financial ombudsman to whom investors and market participants can complain;
- the establishment and operation of regulated and unregulated collective investment schemes; and
- changes of control over authorised persons.

In addition, under the FS Act, there is a prohibition on certain kinds of market behaviour, including making false or misleading statements or creating false or misleading impressions, which are in addition to the provisions relating to "market abuse" referred to above.

FUTURE

In April 2014, the FCA will take over the OFT's responsibilities for consumer credit (which will also include amendments to the FSMA).

In order to comply with EU reforms to the capital requirements regime, it is envisaged that the FPC will have a countercyclical capital buffer (CCB) tool and a leverage ratio tool. A CCB will increase firms' capital requirements at the discretion of the BoE and responsibility for taking policy decisions will be delegated to the FPC. The leverage ratio tool will allow the FPC to set a maximum ratio of total unweighted liabilities to capital and to vary it over time.

2.3 INTELLECTUAL PROPERTY

Mark Tooke, Watson, Farley & Williams LLP

INTRODUCTION

Intellectual property rights ("IPRs") play an important and often essential role across business activities. There are many different types of IPRs that include the protection of intangible business assets, such as know-how, reputation and goodwill, and the products of creative effort. Most IPRs have a commercial value and can be bought, sold and licensed.

It makes good business sense to identify the IPRs you have (particularly where your business is investing in innovation and research, or sells goods or services on the basis of its reputation) and to ensure that they are properly protected. It is also important, where possible, to identify as early as possible areas of potential conflict with IPRs owned by third parties, so that infringements of their IPRs can be avoided.

Some IPRs attract protection automatically on their creation or commercialization; others require registration with an official body (usually the UK Intellectual Property Office; IPO) before they are recognized and afforded protection by the courts. This chapter gives a description of the main commercially significant IPRs that may be protected and exploited in the UK.

COPYRIGHT AND RELATED RIGHTS

Copyright is the collective name for the body of law that grants to makers of written, dramatic, musical and artistic works the ability to control how their creations are used. Both economic and moral rights are provided under the copyright law of the UK:

- Economic rights allow the creator to control the commercial exploitation of their work and to prevent it from being copied without permission.
- Moral rights protect works from being manipulated or distorted in a way that is detrimental to the interests or reputation of the creator.

In the most basic terms, copyright is a right to prevent unauthorized copying. Rights related to copyright include the ability for the owner of a work to prevent others from doing things that, although not strictly copying, are essential to the commercial exploitation of a work; for example, the public performance of music, the adaptation of a play or the broadcasting or public showing of a film or television programme.

Automatic protection

Copyright protection covers original literary, dramatic, musical and artistic works, published editions, sound recordings, films and broadcasts, where the creator has expended a sufficient level of "skill, judgement and labour" in creating the work.

Protection is automatic as soon as the work is recorded, in any form or medium. There is no official registration system in the UK and, therefore, there are no fees to pay or formal action required in order to obtain copyright protection. However, it is good practice to keep a detailed record of how and when the work was produced in case a creator is ever obliged to prove (eg. in court) that they created the work and that it was not copied. Although not a legal requirement in the UK, owners can mark their work with the international copyright symbol ©, together with their name and the year of publication.

The UK is a member of several international copyright conventions, and works created by UK nationals or residents are automatically protected by the copyright law of other signatory countries; nationals or residents of these countries are automatically afforded reciprocal protection in the UK.

Ownership and duration

Copyright can be bought, sold, inherited, transferred or licensed (wholly or in part). As a result, the economic rights to a copyright work can belong to someone other than the creator. Moral rights can be waived, but cannot be transferred. The length of protection offered by copyright depends on the type of work and there are specific rules for each work, but in general, the length of protection is as follows:

- literary, dramatic, musical or artistic works and film: the life of the author, plus 70 years;
- sound recordings and broadcasts: 50 years; and
- published editions: 25 years.

Infringement

Copyright infringement occurs when a work is copied or used without permission. Matters of infringement are ultimately decided in court. Infringement will not occur if the work is used with the permission of the owner or in relation to certain very limited purposes, which include non-commercial research, private study, criticism, review and teaching in schools.

DATABASE RIGHT

A database, for the purposes of protection, can be defined as a collection of independent works, dates or other materials that are, firstly, arranged in a systematic and methodical way and, secondly, are individually accessible by electronic or other means. Copyright protection will apply to a database if there is originality in the selection or arrangement of the contents. If there has been substantial investment in the creation of a database then, in addition to copyright protection, a separate, stand-alone database right may also apply. Copyright and the database right can both apply to the same database.

Database right gives automatic protection as soon as a database exists in recorded form and applies to both electronic and paper databases. It provides protection against the unauthorized appropriation and distribution to the public of the whole or a part of the contents of a database, and lasts for 15 years.

TRADEMARKS AND PASSING OFF

A trademark is a distinctive sign that identifies certain goods and/or services as those produced or provided by a particular person or enterprise. The owner of a registered trademark has the exclusive right to use or identify goods and/or services using that trademark. If a sign is being used by a business as a trademark but is not registered, it may be capable of protection using the law of passing off.

Trademarks can greatly assist the customers of a business by serving as a badge of origin for the business's goods and services. Registered trademarks also offer businesses the ability to protect the investment it makes in its brand identity and in the reputation of its goods and services. Additionally, without trademark protection the competitors of a business may try to take unfair advantage by using confusingly similar, distinctive signs to market their products and services.

Types of trademarks

Trademarks may be words, letters, numerals, symbols, drawings, fragrances, colours used as a distinguishing feature and/or three-dimensional signs (eg. the shape and packaging of goods and sounds, as long as the trademark is capable of being represented graphically). Although the possibilities are many, and may seem almost limitless, a trademark must be distinctive and capable of distinguishing the goods or services of one undertaking from that of another.

Registration process

To be registered, a trademark must be distinctive, not similar to any earlier marks and not be deceptive, or contrary to law or morality. Both British trademarks and European Community (EC) trademarks have effect in the UK. There are two main ways to acquire such a trademark:

1. apply to the IPO for a British trademark; or
2. apply to the Office for Harmonization in the Internal Market for an EC trademark.

Official fees must be paid to obtain both types of registered trademarks. A British trademark offers protection in the UK only. An EC trademark has effect in every member State of the EC, as well as the UK, but the application process is generally more expensive and slower than for a British trademark.

A trademark application must specify the types of goods and services in respect of which protection is sought (the more types, the more expensive the application). Prior to registration, the application can be rejected by the relevant office on a number of grounds, or challenged and blocked by third parties. Once granted, registration lasts for 10 years but can be renewed indefinitely on payment of a renewal fee for successive ten year periods as long as the trademark is being used.

Benefits of registration

Registering a trademark confers on the owner the exclusive right to use the mark for the goods and services it covers in the UK. Once a trademark has been registered, the symbol ® can be put next to the trademark to warn others from using it.

Care must be taken, however, as use of the symbol ® for unregistered trademarks is a criminal offence.

Other benefits conferred to the owners by registered trademarks include the following:

- the ability to sell or license the trademark;
- the ability to commence legal action against anyone who uses it without permission;
- the generation of value in an asset that may be used as collateral for financing; and
- the ability to involve the UK Trading Standards, the police and the other law enforcement agencies, who can bring criminal charges against counterfeiters and pirates.

Passing off

If an unregistered mark is used without the owner's permission, it may be possible to claim protection from the courts under the law of passing off. To be successful in a claim for passing off, a claimant must prove that:

- he/she is the owner of the unregistered trademark and has built goodwill or reputation attached to the goods and services he/she supplies to the public;
- the defendant has made a misrepresentation to the public (intention is irrelevant), leading or likely to lead the public to believe that goods or services offered by the defendant are the goods and services of the claimant; and
- he/she has suffered or is likely to suffer damage from the illegitimate use of the mark.

A legal action claiming passing off can be expensive, as proving the sufficient reputation or goodwill in an unregistered trademark is often difficult for the claimant, and usually involves showing an extensive and lengthy prior use of the trademark in the UK (five years or more).

PATENTS

If you have invented a product that is new or a new way of doing something, a patent may be granted. A patent having effect in the UK can be acquired in two ways:

1. by application to the IPO for a British patent; or

2. by application to the European Patent Office for a European patent (which is in fact a single-application process, leading to the grant of a "bundle" of separate national patents, including a UK patent).

Irrespective of which application process is used, a UK patent (once granted) has effect only in the UK, and lasts for 20 years from the date of filing of the application provided the prescribed annual renewal fees are paid following the expiry of the fifth year. A patent may not be the best or only way to protect an invention. It may be possible to protect aspects of the invention as registered or unregistered designs, registered trademarks or using the law of copyright.

Scope

In basic terms, a patent is designed to protect how things work, what they are made of or how they are made. To be granted a patent, the invention in question must be new, must involve an inventive step, must not be obvious to someone with knowledge and experience in the subject and must be capable of being applied on an industrial scale.

A patent will not be granted for certain types of innovations, including:

- scientific or mathematical discoveries;
- literary, dramatic, musical or artistic works;
- most computer programs;
- animal or plant varieties;
- methods of medical treatment or diagnosis; and
- inventions that are deemed against public policy or morality.

Application process

The process of applying for a patent can be complicated, and the assistance of a qualified patent attorney is recommended. It is also recommended that a search of published patents and existing public know-how (so-called "prior art") be conducted before an application is made to confirm that the invention is new and has not already been patented.

The registration process requires full disclosure to the IPO of information explaining how the invention works, and this information is made available to the public whether the application is successful or not. Once a patent is granted, yearly renewal fees must be paid for the rights to continue.

Protection
The owner of a patent can prevent anyone from using, distributing, selling or commercially making the invention without permission. If a patent is infringed, it is up to the owner to take appropriate action.

DESIGNS

In the UK, a design may be legally protected in one of the three ways.

- Registered designs: the look of a product (including its surface decoration, colour and ornamentation) may be protected by seeking registered design protection, provided certain requirements are met, the main ones being that the design is new and has individual character (ie. it is distinctively different from existing designs). To obtain a registered design, an application must be made to the IPO, with the required fee. Registration lasts for a maximum of 25 years.
- Design right: the shape or configuration of a product may be protected from illegal copying by use of the law of unregistered design right. Design right is free and, subject to certain qualifications, arises automatically where the shape of a new product is original. Design right lasts for the shorter of the 10-year period after the first marketing of products that use the design or the 15-year period after the creation of the design. Licences of right (meaning that anyone is entitled to a licence to make and sell products copying the design) may be available toward the end of the protection period. Design right does not protect two-dimensional designs (in respect of which registered designs or copyright may be relevant).
- Copyright: if an original design is artistic and is not intended to be mass-produced, it will be protected against illegal copying by the law of copyright.

PLANT VARIETY RIGHTS AND GEOGRAPHICAL INDICATIONS

There are a number of IPRs that, although less well known than those mentioned previously, can be valuable to those engaged in certain specialist areas of business. These include the following:

- plant variety rights (which offer protection to plant breeders); and
- geographical indications (which offer protection to producers of foodstuffs with a strong connection to a particular area, eg. Stilton cheese).

CONFIDENTIAL INFORMATION AND TRADE SECRETS

Information that is not covered by one of the IPRs may nonetheless be protected by its owner if it is not public knowledge and the owner keeps it a secret. The law imposes or implies certain duties of confidentiality in particular situations, but these can be strengthened or widened by contract; for example, a new and distinctive business proposition may not meet the requirements for patent protection, but before disclosing it to potential new business partners the owner may require them to sign a confidentiality agreement that will prevent them from using the idea themselves or disclosing it to third parties.

REMEDIES FOR INFRINGEMENT

A range of remedies is available to the owner of an IPR depending on the IPR in question. These include the following:

- Account of profits: if the defendant has made profit out of infringing another's IPRs, the IPR holder can elect to have this awarded instead of damages.
- Damages: damages are usually calculated on a loss of profits or on a royalty basis. Generally, they are compensatory in nature and are to put the holder back in the position that they would have been in if the infringement had not occurred.
- Criminal penalties: serious infringement of certain IPRs, such as copyright, trademarks and patents, may amount to a criminal offence (eg. piracy on a commercial scale), leading to criminal sanctions including imprisonment and fines.

Other remedies include delivery up and destruction of articles infringing IPRs.

Injunctions ordering a defendant not to carry on certain activities may be granted by the court; however, injunctions are discretionary remedies and may not always be awarded, and interim injunctions (awarded before the final decision of the court in an action for infringement) are granted only if it is a matter of urgency or in the interests of justice.

EMPLOYEES AND IPRS

In many cases, the IPRs created by an employee in the course of their employment will, according to UK law, belong automatically to their employer. However, the type and nature of the IPRs created and the scope of the employee's duties can sometimes result in the employee being considered the first owner of the IPRs; for example, a junior employee who invents something that is not directly connected with the main business of the employer may claim that they are the first owner of the invention, on the basis that it was not created in the course of their employment or as part of their normal duties.

To avoid such problems, it is strongly recommended that every UK employment contract contains clauses that expressly set out who will be the first owner of the IPR created while the employee is employed by the employer.

Where the creator of an IPR is not an employee of the business but is a contractor engaged by the business, the usual rule (that the business is the first owner of any IPRs created at its request) does not apply in the absence of an express agreement between the parties to the contrary. In this situation, the IPRs will usually belong to the consultant who created it, with an express or implied licence being granted to the business to use the IPRs. Although in some circumstances it may be inferred that a contractor is under an obligation to assign the IPRs to the business, a clear written agreement between all parties engaged in the work is highly recommended.

THE PATENT BOX

There are a range of incentives for R&D administered by HM Revenue & Customs, particularly for small and medium enterprises (SMEs). A new addition to these incentives is the Patent Box, which came into effect in April 2013 and seeks to reward those innovations that result in a qualifying patent. In simple terms, profits that arise from certain patents will be taxed at 10%. The regime will also apply to other qualifying intellectual property rights such as regulatory data, supplementary protection certificates and plant variety rights.

2.4 COMPANY FORMATION – METHODS AND LEGAL IMPLICATIONS

Mark Jackson, Mazars

INTRODUCTION

The UK has an open and transparent system for setting up companies. No permission is required to set up a business, although some industries, such as financial services, may require specific authorisation before they can commence trading. This chapter looks at the options available to investors wishing to set up a new enterprise in the UK or expand an existing one.

COMPANY TYPES

In the UK, there are four main types of company that can be separated into two categories:

Unlimited liability

The owners of organisations having unlimited liability are personally liable for all the debts that the business may incur. Should the enterprise fail, the owners may have to liquidate some (or all) of their personal assets in order to pay the enterprise's outstanding debts. Examples of such businesses are sole traders, unlimited companies and partnerships.

Limited liability

The owners of these types of business are only liable for the amount that they originally invested in the company. Should the business fail, investors in the failed company will only lose the original value of their investment or the amount they agreed to contribute, as set out below.

In the UK there are three main types of Limited Liability Company:

1. A private company limited by shares – the liability of members is limited to the amount unpaid on shares they hold.
2. A private company limited by guarantee – members are only liable for the amount they agreed to contribute to the company's assets should the company be wound up.
3. A public limited company – these companies are permitted to sell shares to the general public, and their liability is limited to the amount unpaid on shares they hold.

FORMING A COMPANY

The majority of businesses setting up in the UK register as limited companies and are therefore subject to the Companies Act 2006. This Act sets out the rules governing the setting up and day-to-day running of companies.

To set up a company in the UK, you can use a company formation agent, arrange for your professional adviser (solicitor or accountant) to form the company, or you can incorporate a company yourself by using the web incorporation services operated by Companies House.

Companies House is the government agency responsible for incorporating, dissolving and registering companies, and making company information available to the public.

Eligibility for company directorship

Any company setting up in the UK must have formally appointed officers. The number of officers depends on the type of company that is being set up:

- A private company must have at least one director and may have a company secretary. The company's sole director cannot also be the company secretary.
- A public company must have at least two directors and the company secretary must hold a formal qualification.

Procedure to incorporate a company

To register a private or public limited company, the following documents must be sent to Companies House:

- A Memorandum of Association
- Articles of Association
- Form IN01

The Memorandum of Association is a document that sets out the company's name and the address of its registered office (which must be a valid UK address).

The Articles of Association set out the standard rules and procedures that state how the company runs its internal affairs. A company can adopt the model articles in their entirety as prescribed by the Companies Act 2006.

Form IN01 provides details of the first director(s) and company secretary (if appointed), the address of the company's registered office, a statement of the issued share capital on incorporation and the names and addresses of the subscribers (first shareholders). The directors must also include personal details such as their address, date of birth, occupation, nationality and country of residence.

CAPITAL FOR PRIVATE AND PUBLIC LIMITED COMPANIES

When first registering, the first members of the company must each agree to take at least one share and their names must also be included on the memorandum. Shares have a par value, which can be of any amount. The value of the shares held by the shareholders (number of shares multiplied by their par value) is the company's 'Issued Share Capital'.

The amount of share capital required differs depending on the type of company you are setting up and the requirements of the business. A private limited company has no maximum or minimum authorised or issued share capital required in order to commence trading, save that it must have at least one share in issue unless the regularity requirements of its particular industry require a specific minimum. The rules for public limited companies are more complex.

Capital for public limited companies

For a public limited company to trade, the requirement is that it must have at least £50,000 or Euro equivalent of issued share capital, of which 25% must have been paid up and the whole of any premiums (that is the amount investors are asked to pay for the shares less the par value) on these shares. As with private companies a company operating in a particular industry may be required to have a significantly higher issued share capital.

Once the share capital has been paid the company will need to send the relevant information to the Registrar of Companies, who will then issue a 'Certificate to commence business and borrow'. Without this certificate the company cannot trade or carry on business.

MANAGEMENT OF COMPANY

A private limited company must have at least one director, and a public limited company must have at least two directors. In both types of company, the directors are responsible for the day-to-day running of the business, and are personally responsible for any decisions made. The main responsibilities include:

- Producing the annual accounts and making sure that a copy of these is sent to Companies House (a legal requirement for both public and private limited companies);
- Making sure any other information required by Companies House is sent there (for instance, notification of a change in address of the company's registered office or a change in the identity of the directors of the company).

Some of these responsibilities are required by law and, as such, any breach by the directors is a criminal offence for which the penalties can be severe (prosecution, fines, and/or imprisonment).

OTHER FORMS OF COMPANY

Sole Traders

Sole traders are businesses set up by individuals. They are typically small and usually financed by the individual. They are unlimited liability businesses, so the owner is responsible for meeting all the debts of the business. Sole traders are not required to publish annual accounts, although they must keep financial records for tax purposes.

Partnership

Regarded as a step up from a sole trader, this is where a group of two or more individuals set up a business together. Partnerships are regulated by the Partnership Act 1890 (as amended). Normally, a partnership agreement is drawn up before trading commences and this agreement usually contains information on the names of the partners of the business, how profits and/or liabilities will be shared, how the partnership will be run, and the procedures for dissolving the partnership.

As with a sole trader, partnerships have unlimited liability, with the partners jointly and severally liable for all debts, that is, if one or more of the partners is unable to meet these debts, then the remaining partners will become liable for them. A partnership in England and Wales does not have a separate identity from its partners, as a company has from its members. Partnerships are not required to publish their annual accounts, although they must keep financial records for tax purposes.

Limited Partnership

It is still possible to register a limited partnership under the Limited Partnership Act 1907, although they have been superseded in the main by the Limited Liability Partnership (see below). Limited partnerships are very similar to partnerships with these exceptions:

- There are two types of partner: general partners, who are liable for all the businesses debts, and limited partners, who have limited liability up to the amount of money they have invested as capital in the business. Limited partners cannot take back any money invested in the business during the partnership's lifetime, nor can they have a management role in the business.
- By law, limited partnerships must be registered at Companies House by sending a form signed by all partners giving the name of the business, what the business does, and details of all the money invested by the limited partners.

Limited Liability Partnership (LLP)

The Limited Liability Partnerships Act 2000 created a new business vehicle, the Limited Liability Partnership (LLP) which combines the organisational flexibility and tax status of a partnership with limited liability for its members.

Members of limited liability partnerships benefit from limited liability because the partnership, rather than its members, is liable to third parties. However where the members of an LLP are professional people, a negligent member's own personal assets may still be at risk because under general law, a professional person owes a duty of care to his or her client. While the government originally intended to restrict the use of LLPs to members of regulated professions, the LLP Act makes LLPs available to two or more persons carrying on any trade or profession. In view of this, as the LLP combines the tax/NIC (National Insurance Contributions) advantages of partnerships with incorporation and limited liability, it may well become a popular vehicle for small businesses.

LLP profits are taxed as if the business were carried on by partners in partnership, rather than by a body corporate. There are no special tax treatments, or reliefs, available to LLPs or members of LLPs beyond the treatments or reliefs available to partners and partnerships.

The European Public Limited-Liability Company

The European Public Limited-Liability Company or 'Societas Europaea' (SE) is available to businesses operating in more than one member state. It has been possible to set up this type of legal entity in the UK since October 2004.

The purpose of the SE is to make it easier for businesses to structure and carry out cross-border activities within the EU. In practice, however, they are probably of more value for presentational purposes, although the ability to change the domicile of an SE by an administrative procedure can prove to be useful in certain circumstances.

The SE European Public Limited – Liability Company.

An SE may be created on registration in any one of the Member States of the European Economic Area (EEA). Member States are required to treat an SE as if it is a public limited company formed in accordance with the law of the Member State in which it has its registered office. UK national laws that apply to public limited companies also apply, in many respects, to SEs registered in the UK.

Overseas companies carrying on business in the UK

Some companies might still want to do business in the UK without registering a company in the United Kingdom. This can be done by setting up a branch.

A branch is part of an overseas limited company that employs local representatives in the UK to carry out its trading activities. To register a branch with Companies House, the company must complete a OSIN01 Form (this lists details such as the company's name and directors, and details of the branch being set up), the most recent set of audited company accounts, and a certified copy of their constitutional documents (both these must be in the home language of the company). If these are not in English, then a certified translation made in the country where the company was incorporated must also be submitted. A non-UK company can establish one or more branches and must register each one separately, but it is only necessary to file the constitutional documents once.

Overseas companies may also wish to set up a joint venture with a UK firm, usually through a partnership or a limited company.

2.5 UK IMMIGRATION

Angharad Harris and Devan Khagram,
Watson, Farley & Williams LLP

INTRODUCTION

The UK government is keen to promote economic opportunities by encouraging overseas investment and the immigration of skilled individuals. The government implemented a points-based system (PBS) in 2008 to replace the various immigration options that were previously available to individuals wishing to enter the UK to seek employment or to explore business and investment opportunities. The aim of the PBS is to enable the UK to:

- control migration more effectively;
- tackle abuse; and
- attract the most talented workers into the economy.

This chapter sets out an outline of the main business immigration options and key requirements under each category.

CAN I VISIT THE UK ON BUSINESS?

It is possible to enter the UK as a business visitor, although there are restrictions on the type of activities that can be undertaken. Permitted activities include:

- board-level directors attending board meetings in the UK, provided they are not employed by a UK company (however, they may be paid a director's fee for attending the meeting);
- attending meetings, including interviews that have been arranged before coming to the UK, or conferences;
- arranging deals or negotiating or signing trade agreements or contracts;
- acting as an adviser or consultant to a UK firm;
- speaking at a conference where this is not run as a commercial concern and the conference is a "one off";
- undertaking fact-finding missions; and
- undertaking specific, one-off training in techniques and work practices used in the UK, provided this is not on-the-job training.

Advisers, consultants, trainers or troubleshooters entering the UK as business visitors must be employed abroad, either directly or under contract, by the same company (or group of companies) to which the UK company belongs. In addition, they must not get involved in actual project management or provide direct consultancy services to clients of the UK company. A business visitor must:

- only intend to transact business directly linked to his/her employment abroad;
- normally live and work abroad and have no intention of transferring his/her base to the UK (even on a temporary basis); and
- receive a salary from abroad (although reasonable expenses may be paid for travel and subsistence during the visit).

Recent changes also mean that in restricted circumstances, secondees from overseas companies that are not linked to the UK company may also qualify as business visitors.

HOW DO I KNOW IF I NEED TO OBTAIN A VISA BEFORE TRAVELLING TO THE UK?

Not all individuals travelling to the UK require a visa if they are visiting the UK. The UK Border Agency website[1] has a list of all countries from which nationals will require a visa before travelling to the UK to visit.

Entry clearance

For longer term categories, if an individual is already legally in the UK but is

1 http://www.ukba.homeoffice.gov.uk/

changing their immigration status from one category to another, they can sometimes "switch" their immigration status without leaving the UK. This requires the applicant to make an application to the UK Border Agency before their current leave to remain ends, although they will need to check whether they are eligible to "switch" in-country.

Most visa applications under the PBS will require an application for prior entry clearance before the individual can travel to the UK. If an application for entry clearance is required, the applicant must make their application to a British Diplomatic Post in their country of nationality or legal residence before travelling to the UK.

IF I HAVE A SCHENGEN VISA, DOES THIS ALLOW ME TO TRAVEL TO THE UK?

A Schengen visa allows an individual to travel freely among certain European member countries. The UK is not part of the Schengen Treaty and therefore having a Schengen visa will not permit someone who would otherwise need a visa and/or other immigration permission to enter the UK. As of July 2013, the Schengen Treaty countries are:

Austria	Greece	The Netherlands
Belgium	Hungary	Norway
Czech Republic	Iceland	Poland
Denmark	Italy	Portugal
Estonia	Latvia	Slovakia
Finland	Lithuania	Slovenia
France	Luxembourg	Spain
Germany	Malta	Sweden
Switzerland		

Schengen visas are issued for varying amounts of time, but an individual will be allowed a maximum stay of 90 days within any six-month period. The scheme is intended for individuals who wish to move around Schengen member states for the purposes of business and tourism. A Schengen visa does not provide a right to work in a Schengen participating country, and in order to do so, an individual will generally need to obtain permission to work from the relevant country.

WHAT RIGHTS DO I HAVE AS A EUROPEAN UNION NATIONAL?

Nationals of certain countries have the right to live and work in the UK. This is known as a right of residence. Nationals with a right of residence include:

- nationals of the European Union (EU);
- nationals of Iceland, Liechtenstein and Norway; and
- Swiss nationals.

Iceland, Liechtenstein and Norway are not EU countries but are part of the European Economic Area (EEA) Agreement, which provides nationals of these countries with the same rights to enter, live and work in the UK as EU citizens. Swiss nationals are also included in the definition of "EEA nationals". Although not essential, people from the EEA can apply for a UK residence permit. Nationals of Bulgaria and Romania, from 1 January 2014, will have the same rights as other EU citizens.

Croatia has now joined the EU. However, Croatian nationals will still need to obtain authorization to work before starting any employment. Once they have been working legally in the UK for 12 months without a break, they will acquire full rights of free movement; they can then apply for a residence permit confirming their right to live and work in the UK.

Where an individual has a right of residence, their spouse/partner, children under 21 and other dependant relatives may generally join them in the UK. However, if their family members are non-EEA nationals, they should get an EEA family permit, which is a form of entry clearance (like a visa) prior to travelling to the UK, followed by a Residence Card once here. The spouse/partner of an EEA national is permitted to work in the UK without requiring his/her own permission to do so.

If an individual is not an EEA national or the family member of an EEA national, they will generally require permission to undertake employment in the UK. Permission will be required even if they are going to undertake work-based training for a professional or specialist qualification, or a period of work experience.

TIER 1 OF THE PBS

The Tier 1 (General) visa which was designed to allow highly skilled workers to come to the UK has now closed to new applicants; however those who already have a visa under this category can extend their visas from within the UK.

Until April 2012, applicants who obtained their Bachelor's or Master's degree and certain other post-graduate qualifications in the UK could apply for a Tier 1 (Post-Study Work) visa within 12 months of obtaining the relevant qualification. This route has now closed; however migrants with existing valid leave to remain as a post-study worker can continue to live and work in the UK until their visa expires. It should be noted that, as with student visas, time in the UK under Tier 1 (Post-Study Work) cannot be taken into account when calculating the length of UK residence required for Indefinite Leave to Remain in the UK (ILR) (see below).

CAN I ESTABLISH A BUSINESS IN THE UK?

Under Tier 1 (Entrepreneur) of the PBS, an individual may apply for entry into the UK in order to set up, take over and be actively involved in the running of one or more businesses. To apply under the PBS and be accepted into the Tier 1 (Entrepreneur) category, an applicant must pass a points-based assessment, and must score a minimum of 75 points for attributes, 10 points for English language and 10 points for available maintenance (funds). They will need to have access to £200,000 (see exceptions below), which must be in a regulated financial institution and disposable in the UK. They must also provide the UK Border Agency with a letter from each financial institution holding the money, confirming the amount of money available, as well as additional evidence if they are receiving third-party funding.

This £200,000 fund should be invested into a new or existing UK business within three months of the visa being granted. The amount of money invested must not include residential accommodation, property development or management, nor can it be in the form of a director's loan (unless it is subject to certain conditions).

Recent changes to this category have made it more attractive for those setting up business in the UK. It is now possible for an entrepreneur to team up with another entrepreneur as part of an entrepreneurial team to rely on the same £200,000 to qualify under this visa category whereas previously they would have needed to show £200,000 each. Furthermore, those applicants who have access to £50,000 from a venture capitalist firm regulated and listed with the FSA, from a UK entrepreneurial seed funding competition endorsed by UK Trade and Investment or from a UK government department can now also apply for a visa under this category. Applicants switching into this Tier 1 (Entrepreneur) category from certain other UK visa categories, such as student visas on the graduate entrepreneur visa (this is separate from the Tier 1 (Entrepreneur) category), may also benefit from these and other similar provisions.

The UK Border Agency has also recently introduced a "genuine entrepreneur" test to allow them to assess whether the applicant genuinely intends to set up a business in the UK.

One of the requirements for an extension under this visa is to create the equivalent of 2 full time jobs for persons settled in the UK, for a period of 12 months. Employers can rely on combinations of employment to create the equivalent of 2 full time jobs, by the UK Border Agency. Where an Entrepreneurial team has been granted a visa, both team members can rely on the jobs created by the team at the point their visas are extended. In addition, the applicant must also have registered as the director of a new or existing business, or registered as self-employment with HMRC, no more than 6 months after the grant of their visa.

Those who are very successful in their business in the UK and create the equivalent of 10 full time jobs for a period of 12 months have an accelerated route to settlement and can obtain ILR in 3 years (usually it takes 5 years). Entrepreneurs who have generated business income of at least £5 million during a 3 year period also have an accelerated route to settlement.

Tier 1 (Entrepreneurs) can now spend as much as 180 days per year outside the UK and still qualify for ILR. However, please note that the permitted absences for nationality are more restricted (see below). Therefore, if the applicants aim is to obtain British citizenship they will have to spend a greater amount of time in the UK.

ARE THERE SPECIAL RULES FOR INVESTORS IN THE UK?

An application under Tier 1 (Investor) is suitable for individuals who have substantial capital assets available to invest in the UK. In order to be granted leave to enter the UK under this category, an applicant needs to show that they have at least £1 million to bring to the UK (this can either be their own money over which they have full control, i.e. not held in a trust or similar restriction, or be money borrowed from a Financial Services Authority regulated institution if they have a personal net worth of at least £2 million).

Where the loan method is chosen, the calculation of net worth may include not only financial assets, but also property. Assets held through an offshore company or trust, where the applicant is the beneficiary, can be taken into account when assessing personal net worth.

These funds need to be held by the applicant for the three months prior to the application or they need to show the source of the funds in a manner specified by the UK Border Agency. Within three months of the visa being granted or the date they first enter the UK under this visa, the applicant must bring £1 million into the

UK (if it is not here already) and invest at least £750,000 of their capital in UK government bonds, or in share capital or loan capital in active and trading UK registered companies (other than property investment companies), subject to certain restrictions. There is more flexibility regarding the remaining £250,000, however it must be held or invested in the UK. Any shortfall in the investments during the validity of the visa must be made up by the next reporting period.

Applicants are permitted to seek employment or can be self-employed or non-executive directors/consultants.

In addition, it is possible for a potential investor currently in the UK under certain other immigration categories to "switch" into the Tier 1 (Investor) category. Furthermore, once established in the UK, the investor can extend their stay in the UK, provided that they can show sufficient evidence that they have invested the £1 million as permitted by the UKBA within three months of arriving in the UK and still have permitted investments of over £1 million in the UK.

To provide an incentive for applicants as Investors in the UK, the government have provided for an accelerated route to settlement for those who invest £5 million or £10 million in the UK. Whilst a Tier 1 (Investor) is usually eligible for ILR after 5 years in the UK, if the applicant invests £5 million in the UK they can obtain ILR after 3 years and if they invest £10 million in the UK they can obtain ILR after 2 years. The investments need to have the same 75% and 25% split as when investing £1 million. It should be noted that the fast track is for ILR only. Those who invest £5 million or £10 million still have to be in the UK for 5 years before they are eligible to apply for British citizenship. Whereas investors who invest £1 million will have to be in the UK for 6 years.

Like Tier 1 (Entrepreneurs), Tier 1 (Investors) can now spend as much as 180 days per year outside the UK and still qualify for ILR. However, the permitted absences for nationality are more restricted (see below). Therefore, if the applicant's aim is to obtain British citizenship they will have to spend a greater amount of time in the UK.

Unlike most of the other categories, there is no English language or maintenance requirement to qualify for this visa.

TIER 2 OF THE PBS

Tier 2 of the PBS incorporates and adapts the old work permit regime. The main change to the system is that employers require a sponsorship licence and are required to issue certificates of sponsorship to employees they wish to employ. The employee will then apply to their local entry clearance officer (embassy/visa application centre) for entry into the UK to work, at which stage the UK Border Agency will assess the application to ensure the applicant scores sufficient points to qualify. Points will be awarded based on prospective salaries and the circumstances around their recruitment as well as the level of need in any given sector. Tier 2 (Skilled Migrant) is available in two categories:

1. Tier 2 (General); and
2. Tier 2 (Intra-Company Transfer).

Tier 2 (Intra-Company Transfer) applications involve a simplified procedure where the employee of a global company is transferring to a skilled post in a UK-based branch of the same company. Since April 2010 this category has been split into 4 subcategories:

1. Long-term Staff - for those who have worked for the company outside the UK for 12 months or more and who's annual salary will be £40,600 or more. They are permitted to come to the UK for up to 5 years;
2. Short-term Staff - for those who have worked for the company outside the UK for 12 months or more and who's annual salary will be less than £40,600 but more than £24,300. They are permitted to come to the UK for up to 12 months;
3. Graduate Trainees - to allow multi-national organisations to transfer recent graduate recruits to the UK business for up to 12 months of training; or
4. Skills Transfer - for migrants to transfer to an organisation or UK business to learn or transfer skills and knowledge to/from the UK offices for a period of 6 months.

Before an application is made under this category, the applicant must have:

- a valid sponsor; and
- certificate of sponsorship.

When an application is made, the applicant is awarded points based on their:

- future expected earnings;
- sponsorship;
- English language skills; and
- available maintenance (funds).

When applying for permission to come to the UK under this category, or extending their permission to stay, the applicant does not have to meet the English language requirement.

Other applications, usually where the individual does not already work for the organisation abroad, may fall within the Tier 2 (General) category and this usually requires the employer to show that it cannot fill the post with a "resident worker" (including EEA nationals). This usually involves advertising the post in Jobcentre Plus (if the migrant's prospective salary is less than £71,000 per annum) and other methods, which depend on the relevant industry sector that the job is in. Those earning more than £152,100, those in shortage occupations or exempt categories, Tier 1 (Post-Study Work) migrants or certain students are exempt from the advertising requirements. By contrast to Tier 2 (Intra Company Transfer) all applicants under Tier 2 (General) need to meet the full English language requirement.

Those migrants applying under Tier 2 (General) from outside the UK and whose prospective earnings are less than £152,100 will be subject to the monthly limit on migrants. Their employer will have to apply for a certificate of sponsorship and this will be granted if the applicant scores sufficient points to come within that particular month's limit.

Those already in the UK in certain other specified categories, those extending their stay or those who's prospective earnings will be more that £152,100 are not subject to the annual limit on economic migrants.

CAN I COME TO THE UK AS A SOLE REPRESENTATIVE OF AN OVERSEAS FIRM?

A sole representative application is only suitable where an overseas company that does not have a presence in the UK wishes to send one of its existing employees to set up a wholly owned subsidiary or register a branch. The overseas parent company must be in genuine operation; where it has been established for less than one year, it is unlikely to be deemed an eligible sponsor for these purposes.

In order for an application to be considered, the individual must:

- be authorised to take operational decisions on behalf of the overseas parent company without reference to the overseas parent company;
- have been recruited to the overseas parent company from outside of the UK;
- be directly employed by the overseas parent company; and
- have been employed by the overseas parent company for some time and hold a senior post.

The employee must not, however, be a major shareholder in the overseas parent company and should not intend to carry out any other work while in the UK. In addition, the individual must be able to support themselves (and any dependants) in the UK, without recourse to public funds.

A sole representative application is normally made by the individual employee at a British Diplomatic Post in their country of nationality or legal residence. Applicants are expected to spend a minimum of nine months a year in the UK; those who spend less time than this are not considered to be making genuine efforts to establish a commercial presence.

Once an application has been successful, the sponsor company must continue to conduct the majority of its business overseas. It will not be permitted to gradually move its operation to the UK by exploitation of this category.

INDEFINITE LEAVE TO REMAIN (SETTLEMENT)

Generally speaking, an individual will become eligible to apply for ILR after they have spent a requisite period of time in the UK; for most people, this is five years of continuous lawful residence in a qualifying category (although see the accelerated route for Tier 1 (Entrepreneurs) and Tier 1 (Investors)). This category has been restricted and those entering under the Tier 2 (Intra-Company Transfer) category can no longer apply for settlement (unless they were in the UK before 6 April 2010). Those in the UK under Tier 2 (General) can currently apply for ILR. From 6 April 2016, Tier 2 (General) migrants applying for ILR must be paid at least £35,000 per annum in order to qualify for settlement.

Adult applicants (aged 18-65) are required to demonstrate knowledge of language and life in the UK, in addition to meeting the usual requirements for settlement. Most applicants now will need to pass a "Life in the UK" test and many applicants will also need to demonstrate that they have sufficient English language skills, either by way of a degree taught in English, or having passed an approved English language test.

Once settlement is granted, there will no longer be any immigration related restrictions on the work or business the individual may do in the UK, and no time limits on their stay here, provided that in general they do not spend longer than two years outside of the UK, maintain ties here and consider the UK to be their home.

BRITISH NATIONALITY

An individual can normally apply for naturalization as a British citizen one year after being granted ILR and as long as they meet the residence requirements and they have been in the UK for 5 years in total. There are two ways to naturalize as a British citizen:

1. naturalization based on five years' residence in the UK; and
2. naturalization based on marriage/civil partnership and residence in the UK.

There are various requirements that will need to be satisfied, such as age, capacity, residence requirements, good character, language skills and intention. The applicant will also need to meet an English Language requirement and pass the "Life in the UK" test (if they did not do so at the ILR stage). If the application is approved, the applicant will be required to attend a citizenship ceremony after which a certificate of naturalization is issued. Once naturalized, they are eligible to apply for a British passport.

When applying for British citizenship an applicant is only permitted absences from the UK of up to 450 days over 5 years with no more than 90 days in the final year.

The information contained in this chapter is correct at the time of writing, but the authors would recommend that readers check the current position.

2.6 IMMIGRATION OPTIONS FOR START-UP COMPANIES IN THE UK

Kay Bains and Simon Kenny, Mazars

Immigration controls in the United Kingdom require that citizens of countries outside the European Economic Area must apply for permission to live and work in the UK if they intend to move here to establish and develop a business.

There are a number of options open to such applicants, depending on a range of criteria including their net worth, the amount they intend to invest in their business enterprise, their role in the enterprise (whether they are active or passive investors, or employees to be moved to the UK to develop the business) and the scale of the enterprise. This chapter therefore introduces the different routes for these applications and summarises the benefits and restrictions of each.

THE LEGAL FRAMEWORK

The law regarding permission to live and work in the UK is determined by the Immigration Rules as published by the UK Border Agency. The Immigration Rules determine the requirements of each of the immigration categories concerned and specify their requirements. The four principal immigration applications being considered within this chapter are:

- Tier 1 Investor applications

- Tier 1 Entrepreneur applications
- Applications based on registration of the business entity as a Sponsor, then applications for individual employees within Tier 2 of the Points Based System
- Sole Representative visa applications
- Visitor visas (limited use in these circumstances)

(NB: For several years, many individuals starting new businesses in the UK tended to use the Tier 1 General immigration category; this allowed well educated and remunerated applicants to live and work in the UK, initially with very few restrictions. The category was closed to new applicants in 2011 though those already in the UK within this immigration category are able to extend their immigration status further under certain conditions.)

There are further requirements in respect of the extension of stay (or leave to remain) in the UK after arrival in each of these categories. Most, but not all, can lead to permanent residence, also known as settlement, in the UK after meeting the immigration requirements for five consecutive years. They can also lead to naturalisation as a British Citizen, under certain circumstances.

The requirements of each category are different and should be carefully considered.

Tier 1 Investors

There have been provisions within the Immigration Rules for investors to come to the UK for many years and the current government is keen to encourage and promote new investment into the UK via this immigration category. Damien Green, the UK's former Immigration Minister, has previously stated:

"Entrepreneurs and investors can play a major part in our economic recovery, and I want to do everything I can to ensure that Britain remains an attractive destination for them. Last year we issued far too few visas to those who wish to set up a business or invest in the UK -- I intend to change that."[1]

Tier 1 Investor visas are granted to applicants who plan to make investments in the UK economy of at least £1 million for 5 years or more. The investments must be made in UK government bonds or share or loan capital in UK registered entities. Proof of the maintenance of the investment is required in the form of a quarterly statement from a Financial Services Authority approved investment manager.

The main advantages of this route are that applicants are not required to show English language ability to qualify and that the route leads to the right to live permanently in the UK. Qualification for settlement does not depend on success

1 Home Office Press Release, 16 March 2011

in business, a wider contribution to society (as required in other countries) or any element of judgment by Home Office immigration caseworkers. If an applicant is awarded a Tier 1 Investor visa and maintains an investment of £1 million, as specified by the UK government, during the requisite period, they will be able to stay permanently after five years, subject to passing a test to confirm knowledge of life in the UK and meeting certain residency requirements.

On application for a Tier One Investor Visa, evidence is required to demonstrate that sufficient funds in order to make this investment are held within a regulated financial institution and are disposable in the UK. On issue of the visa, the funds must be transferred to the UK within one month and the qualifying investment in the UK must then be made within three months in order to qualify for extension of stay and/or settlement.

At the £1 million level, permission to stay is initially granted for three years (plus the four months for transfer of funds to UK and the actual investment). Provided the investment is maintained at the required level during that three year period, an application is then required to extend the visa for another two years to the five year point, following which an application for permanent residence can be made.

Settlement

To make the category more attractive, residency requirements applicable to settlement applications have been relaxed. Those seeking entry as an Investor are able to meet the residency requirement by restricting their absences from the UK to 180 days (or six months) in each consecutive 12 month period during the relevant five years. It is also important to note that there are no restrictions on absences from the UK in respect of dependants, allowing dependants greater freedom to travel.

Eligibility for settlement can be accelerated for applicants who make a larger investment in the UK economy. Applicants who invest at least £5,000,000 are able to qualify for settlement after three years' residence in the UK. Those who invest £10,000,000 qualify after two years.

Figure 2.6.1: Comparative data on the number of entry clearance applications approved in each of the assessed immigration categories, April 2011 to March 2013

	Investor	Entrepreneur	Tier 2	Sole Representative	Visitor
Approved 2011-12	387	455	38,413	653	2,275,000
Approved 2012-13	475	878	40,264	666	2,230,000

Source: Home Office Quarterly Statistical Bulletin

Tier 1 Entrepreneur

This immigration category is designed for those with limited capital but a solid business proposition in the UK and a determination to be active in the development of the enterprise.

Qualification requires the intention to invest in the UK by setting up (or taking over) and being actively involved in the running of a business registered in the UK or, alternatively, buying into a partnership. Applicants must show that they have access to £200,000 of disposable funds for the purpose of investing in the business. Third parties can undertake to provide these funds by way of legal declaration. Up to two business partners can qualify for this visa by relying on the same £200,000 funds, provided they have equal control over the funds and the business. English language ability is required to qualify for this visa.

The initial visa grant is for three years with an option to extend by a further two years so long as certain conditions are met, such as that reasonable business activity has been undertaken to establish the business; that the funds have been invested and that at least two full time roles have been created for resident workers which have lasted for at least 12 months within those three years.

A hybrid version of this immigration category for Graduate Entrepreneurs already in the UK with a valid study visa also exists, whereby only £50,000 of capital is required for those who have graduated from UK universities and are now seeking to switch immigration status. Alternatively, applicants can qualify with access to £50,000 should that come from one or more venture capital firms regulated by the Financial Conduct Authority; UK entrepreneurial seed funding competitions which have been endorsed by the UK Trade & Investment website or; from UK government departments (or those of the devolved government authorities in Scotland, Wales or Northern Ireland) provided to the applicant in order to start or grow a UK business.

This immigration category was amended in early 2013 by the introduction of a "genuineness" test to the process. Immigration officials are now able to make an assessment of the likelihood of the proposed business succeeding in the UK.

Settlement

Those in the UK under this category can also apply for permanent residency after five years if they have made the necessary investment in the business, are actively engaged in it and have created the roles referred to above. As with the Investor route, an option of accelerated settlement is available, after the initial three year grant, if either 10 full time equivalent posts for resident workers have been created for at least 12 months or if the company has generated a total turnover of £5m over the three year period.

Tier 2 Sponsor Licence

All UK trading companies wishing to sponsor the employment of workers from outside the EEA (including those companies who want to transfer employees from an overseas office to the UK office) must hold a government licence in order to do so.

The process of securing the licence includes a requirement that the company has established a genuine trading presence in the UK, maintains UK regulation compliant HR practices, and has at least one UK based employee, although not necessarily a British citizen, able to hold a key position with regards to the licence (this is known as the "Authorising Officer"). This individual would be responsible for the proper management of the licence requirements and should have a reasonable knowledge of the requirements together with the necessary authority within the organisation to enforce them.

The licence application also requires certain company documents to be submitted in support. Such evidence varies based on the type of entity being registered but can include registration with the relevant tax department to pay UK tax, documentation to show the UK trading premises, employee liability insurance and evidence of appropriate professional registration in the UK. Such applications can, at the time of writing (August 2013), be processed within a matter of weeks.

Companies applying for such a licence have numerous duties with which they must comply. Careful assessment is made as to whether companies are able to adhere to these duties. Failure to do so and to maintain certain documentation can result in a loss or suspension of the licence and fines of up to £10,000 in respect of each employee not legally employed within the UK.

Tier 2 sponsorship

Once the necessary licence has been obtained, the process of transferring employees to the UK can commence. The process involves two stages - securing the initial work permit (known as a Certificate of Sponsorship) and subsequent visa for the employee by way of an application to the British Embassy in their country of normal legal residence. Certificates of Sponsorship are available for jobs at graduate level or above (at least NFQ 6) and where the employee will be paid UK market rate salary (including some allowances).

Tier 2 Intra Company transfers

If the employee has already been employed by the company for at least 12 months in a different commonly owned or linked entity, an Intra Company Transfer application may be most appropriate. Newly hired oversees employees required in the UK for a short time and high calibre employees on global graduate programmes may also be permitted to come to the UK via this route.

The English language requirement does not apply initially and this route will not lead to permanent residency. Employees can however bring their spouse or long term partner and children under 18 with them to the UK and the dependant adult can work freely.

Tier 2 General - Long term 'new hires'

This option under Tier 2 does allow the employee and their family to remain in the UK long term and in due course, settle permanently. With some limited exceptions, this option requires the UK employer to demonstrate there are no settled workers in the UK who are able to undertake the role in question, usually through an advertising process known as the "resident labour market test". Rules in respect of the minimum level of skill and salary required also apply to this immigration category and English language skills are also a prerequisite.

Settlement

As stated above, the Tier 2 General option can lead to settlement after 5 years. Residence requirements (i.e. actual time spent in the UK) apply and require that applicants should not have been outside the UK for more than 180 days in any 12 consecutive months. Additionally, absences must be for a reason that relates to the employment or a reason such as serious illness. From 6th April 2016 onwards, those who entered Tier 2 under rules in force from the 6th April 2011 must be paid a minimum of £35,000 per year or the minimum rate of pay specified by the UK Border Agency as being usual for their role, whichever is the higher amount. As with all settlement applications, the requirement to show sufficient English language ability and knowledge of life in the UK also exists within this immigration category.

Restrictions

It is important to note that changes to the Immigration Rules introduced in 2011 and 2012 have limited the length of time many Tier 2 migrants may remain in the UK. Moreover, the changes also specifically prohibit some from returning for further employment within the Tier 2 category (known as the "cooling off period"). The Rules in respect of Tier 2 status are complex and we would advise expert guidance is sought by those seeking to employ staff in their start-up business via this immigration category.

Sole representatives

If an overseas company is seeking to establish a UK presence, the 'sole representative of an overseas company' visa is an option. This type of visa will allow a senior level employee to come to the UK without a certificate of sponsorship, as a sole representative of an overseas company to set up a wholly owned subsidiary or register a UK branch for an overseas parent company. Such an employee would represent the company's interests only. This category has regained prominence in the UK as start-up companies sometimes seek to combine this with a longer-term strategy of registering as sponsors; once a sole representative visa is granted and once the employee is in the UK, a sponsor licence application can be made.

There are several requirements of sole representatives, which include:

- the applicant is a senior employee (but not a majority shareholder in the company) who intends to establish a commercial presence for the company in the UK
- the company has no branch, subsidiary or other representative in the UK
- the representative has full authority to take operational decisions on the company's behalf and be able to demonstrate a very good track record in the same business
- the applicant can demonstrate English language ability.

The initial visa is for three years with an option to extend by a further two years (so long as the conditions for extension are met) and allows immediate dependants (spouse / long term partner or children under 18) to join the applicant in the UK.

Settlement

To qualify for settlement as a Sole Representative, an applicant must have maintained and accommodated themselves and dependents without public funds throughout the 5 years, still be required as the representative in the UK of the business and meet the requirement to have sufficient knowledge of language and life in the UK. The requirements in respect of absences are as within the Tier 2 category referred to above.

Visitors

The final option start-up companies could consider is the visitor option. Close attention should be given to exactly what activities will be undertaken in the UK to ensure compliance with the Rules but in practice, this option can be quite attractive to those coming to the UK as, for certain nationals, there is no requirement to apply for a visa in advance of travel and such a strategy is likely to align well with tax planning.

The potential issue with those seeking to start a company in the UK is that visitors are prohibited from working in the UK. Whilst there are business-related activities which are allowed to visitors, such as attending meetings and conducting negotiations, these are tightly defined and, in practice, we find judgements of whether a specific individual is conducting such permissible activities can often be arbitrary.

There are circumstances in which a business may be started by an individual conducting permissible activities only in the UK and for the minority of the year. In some such circumstances, obtaining a business visit visa can be a sensible precaution as it can allow assessment of the application in advance by a visa officer and reduces considerably the prospect of unexpected refusal on entering the UK.

Most visitors to the UK are permitted to stay for up to six month at a time, though they should not stay for a period of more than six months cumulatively in any 12 month period.

Some key questions

The different categories of Tier 1 Investor and Entrepreneur visas, Tier 2 Sponsorship, Sole Representative visas and Visitor visas require careful consideration, with the correct choice of application being determined by a range of factors. We would suggest some key considerations include:

What is the goal of the transfer? Is this to establish a permanent presence in the UK to meet an ongoing need for services, or is it to achieve a specific, time-limited objective? The structure of the entity being created in the UK and the tax planning surrounding the investment will be key criteria in determining which visa category is the most appropriate.

Are there alternatives? Two of the options outlined above require the individual transferee to show evidence of funds, so it would be necessary for these to be under the applicant's control. That is not generally how start-ups operate in the UK unless the transferee to the UK is also an owner of the business. It should also be noted that most, but not all, of the above categories require some element of English language knowledge to be demonstrated. It may be that the requirements of the categories are such that one visa category strongly suggests itself.

What are the assignee's intentions? A common experience we have noted in discussing such matters is that the business' objectives are often interlinked with the individual applicant's personal circumstances. A desire to service a market within the UK, for example, may also be matched by the individual's intention that his children should be educated in the country also; this would indicate a visa which allows permanent migration would be appropriate.

Will there be future transfers to the UK? The Investor, Entrepreneur and Sole Representative categories effectively only allow for one individual plus dependants to travel to the UK. Whilst that may be acceptable initially, a need to bring other staff to the UK in the longer term would indicate making a Sponsor Licence application is likely to be the way forward. The organisation may need to define a strategy at the outset to ensure that it is able to make suitable transfers in future.

Something which is noteworthy from the Home Office statistics within Figure 1 above is that applications within the Investor, Entrepreneur and Sole Representative category remain relatively few in comparison to those seeking to transfer to the UK with the orthodox Tier 2 visa for employment. It should also be noted, however, that there has been growth in each of these categories in the past twelve months and longer term growth when assessed against such applications over the last ten years.

Conclusion

It is clear from the above that there is no straightforward answer to the question: "which visa do I need?" from entrepreneurs seeking to start new businesses in the UK. There are a series of potential options. It could be as straightforward as entering the UK without a visa as a business visitor. At the other end of that scale, a significant investment may be required, with substantial supporting documentation necessary to support a prior visa application. The most appropriate starting point is to assess what the purpose of the start-up is and what the longer term intentions of the individual and company are. These do vary considerably and the intentions of the individuals concerned can be at least as important as the business need the UK entity is to serve.

A final point to note is that, whilst most of these immigration categories have existed for several years, the requirements of each do change regularly and often without notice. A useful example of this is the comprehensive changes to the Tier 1 Entrepreneur category, introduced in February 2013 with minimal notice. From being an immigration category in which, essentially, a cash investment and an idea were required, this transformed into one which allowed immigration officials to make assessments of the likely success of businesses in the UK and the business records of the potential proprietors; there is now a significant element of subjectivity to the decision-making process in that immigration category, making the outcome of such applications unpredictable. Whilst we hope this summary is a useful one to provide general information about the potential choices, it should not be a substitute for the relevant professional advice.

Figure 2.6.2: Comparison of potential immigration applications for individuals starting a company in the UK.

Please see the above paragraphs for full information and commentary in respect of each category

	Investor	Tier 2	Entrepreneur	Sole Representative	Visitor
Investment required	Yes, £1 million, £5 million or £10 million .	No.	Yes, £200,000, or £50,000 if relying on the graduate provisions or alternative funding described above.	No.	No.
Permission to stay	Three years and four months initial permission, with extensions of two years.	Between one month and nine years depending on the relevant category and proposed length of assignment	Three years and four months initial permission, with extensions of two years.	Three years initial permission, with extensions of two years.	Six months maximum.

	Investor	Tier 2	Entrepreneur	Sole Representative	Visitor
Restrictions on stay	Minor.	Employment with sponsor (some additions).	Business activity.	Employment elsewhere not permitted.	No "employment" – specifically defined activity only.
Time to obtain visa	Documents will take time to collate, but processing time tends to be between ten and fifteen days once the application is submitted.	Visas are often issued within two - fifteen working days of application	Usually within 10-15 working days.	Usually within 10-15 working days	Visas, if required, are often issued fairly quickly Formal expedited processing is available in several countries.
Any compliance risk?	Yes, if the investment value drops or if funds are invested in the wrong types of products.	Borne by employer, who has extensive duties to report changes and maintain compliance.	Unable to work elsewhere as an employee. Must be actively involved in the business.	Potential risk is ceasing to be the only employee or failing to establish the UK entity.	Yes, activities are limited to those deemed as "permissible" and are very restrictive.
Settlement available?	Yes. Expedited settlement after three or two years is possible for investments of £5 million and £10 million respectively.	Only for new hires in the 'General' sub category.	Yes, after 5 years with accelerated options available	Yes, after 5 years.	No.

	Investor	Tier 2	Entrepreneur	Sole Representative	Visitor
Recommended for....	Those seeking a quick category which allows flexibility who a can invest minimum of £1 million.	Those wishing to employ non-EEA workers with atrading presence in UK and one UK based employee. Companies who may need to bring multiple assignesss to the UK	Those intending to establish and drive a company with some limited capital.	Senior employees of overseas companies seeking to establish themselves in the UK.	Short term travellers who will visit rather than work.

2.7 COMPLYING WITH THE UK'S MONEY LAUNDERING REGULATIONS

Donald Plane, Mazars

The UK's Money Laundering Regulations came into force in December 2007, replacing and updating the existing regulations; their purpose is to protect the UK financial system. Any business covered by the regulations must implement controls to prevent it being used by criminals or terrorists for money laundering activities. Failure to comply with the law could have serious consequences.

WHICH BUSINESSES ARE COVERED BY MONEY LAUNDERING REGULATIONS?

Regulations apply to a number of business sectors, including:

- most UK financial and credit businesses such as banks, currency exchange offices, cheque cashers or money transmitters;
- independent legal professionals;
- accountants, tax advisers, auditors and insolvency practitioners;
- estate agents;
- casinos;
- 'High Value Dealers' - businesses that accept cash payments for goods worth 15,000 Euros or more either in a single transaction or in installments;
- Trust or Company Service Providers.

If your business falls into one of these business sectors there is a requirement for it to be monitored by a supervisory authority. It may be the case that your business is already monitored, for example by a professional body, such as the Law Society, or by the Financial Conduct Authority, but if it is not you will probably need to register with the UK Revenue & Customs (HMRC).

To register with HMRC under Money Laundering Regulations you must complete an application form (MLR100) to register each place where you carry on business activities that require supervision. There is a fee for registering each business premises and a subsequent annual renewal fee.

If your business is a Money Service Business or a Trust or Company Service Provider, you are also required to apply for the 'fit and proper' test (form MLR101) in addition to registering with HMRC. The 'fit and proper' test must be taken by all those people who are involved in the running of the business.

CRIMINAL OFFENCES UNDER THE ANTI-MONEY LAUNDERING LEGISLATION

Money Laundering is the term used for a number of offences involving the proceeds of crime or terrorist funds. It includes possessing, or in any way dealing with, or concealing, the proceeds of any crime. It also involves similar activities in relation to terrorist funds, which include funds that are likely to be used for terrorism, as well as the proceeds of terrorism.

Someone is engaged in Money Laundering if they:

- Conceal, disguise, convert, transfer or remove (from the United Kingdom) criminal property;
- Enter into or become concerned in an arrangement which they know or suspect facilitates (by whatever means) the acquisition, retention, use or control of criminal property by or on behalf of another person;
- Acquire, use or have possession of criminal property.

Criminal Property is very widely defined, but, in summary, property is Criminal Property if it:

- Constitutes a person's benefit in whole or in part (including pecuniary and proprietary benefit) from criminal conduct; or
- Represents such a benefit directly or indirectly, in whole or in part; and
- The alleged offender knows or suspects that it constitutes or represents such a benefit.

Criminal Conduct is conduct that constitutes an offence in any part of the United Kingdom or would constitute an offence in any part of the United Kingdom, if it occurred there (subject to the exemptions listed below). This includes tax offences committed abroad if the action would have been an offence were it to have taken place in the United Kingdom. There is no need for there to be any consequential effect on the United Kingdom's tax system.

However, no offence is committed in any of the following circumstances:

- Where the persons involved did not know or suspect that they were dealing with the proceeds of crime;
- Where the act is committed by someone carrying out a law enforcement or judicial function;
- Where the conduct giving rise to the criminal property was reasonably believed to have taken place outside the UK, and the conduct was in fact lawful under the criminal law of the place where it occurred, and the maximum sentence if the conduct had occurred in the UK would have been less than 12 months (except in the case of an act which would be an offence under the Gaming Act 1968, the Lotteries and Amusements Act 1976 or under sections 23 or 25 of the Financial Services and Markets Act 2000, which will fall within the exemption even if the relevant sentence would be in excess of 12 months).

It is a general rule that an element of intent is required before many criminal offences can be committed. For example, theft can only be committed where the offender is dishonest and has intent to deprive permanently. In some cases, where the monetary proceeds of a suspected theft or tax fraud are small, it may be that the perpetrators were acting in error or in the mistaken impression that they had permission to act as they did.

It is also important to note that for indirect tax, section 167(3) Customs & Excise Management Act 1979 provides that a wide range of innocent/accidental errors are criminal offences (although they are in practice generally dealt with under the civil penalty regime).

For the avoidance of doubt, Criminal Property includes (but is by no means limited to):

- The proceeds of tax (direct or indirect) evasion including the under declaring of income and the over claiming of expenses.
- A benefit obtained through bribery and corruption (including both the receipt

of a bribe and the profits earned from a contract obtained through bribery or the promise of a bribe).

- Benefits obtained through the operation of a cartel.
- Benefits (in the form of saved costs) arising from a failure to comply with a regulatory requirement, where that failure is a criminal offence, e.g. a breach of health and safety regulations.
- Property, even of minimal value, acquired by theft (including, for example, not telling a customer that they have erroneously paid twice or an overdrawn director's current account in a relevant company).

The following can constitute a criminal offence:

- Providing assistance to a money launderer to obtain, conceal, retain or invest funds if you knew, or in some cases, if you should have known that the funds were the proceeds of serious criminal conduct. Making a report precludes a charge of assisting a money launderer.
- Tipping off a person, or any third party, in connection with an investigation into money laundering. This could include, for example, informing someone of your money laundering suspicions.
- Failing to report a suspicion of money laundering if the suspicion was acquired in the course of your employment (or, as the case may be, your profession). It is a criminal offence not to comply with the Regulations and a criminal offence may also be committed by anyone who has consented to or connived at non-compliance with the Regulations, including where such non-compliance is attributable to their neglect.

There are thousands of criminal offences in the United Kingdom that, if committed, are likely to result in a person benefiting from an offence and thereby having Criminal Property. The key point to note is that Proceeds of Crime Act (POCA) introduced an 'all crime' reporting regime. That is, Money Laundering offences can relate to the proceeds of any criminal activity not just, for example, drug trafficking.

In addition to the offences under the POCA, there is also an obligation for businesses to report belief or suspicion of the proceeds from, or finance likely to be used for, terrorism, or its laundering, based on information which came to them in the course of its business or employment.

MONEY LAUNDERING CONTROLS AND PROCEDURES

Businesses covered by the Money Laundering Regulations must put controls in place to prevent them being used by criminals or terrorists for money laundering purposes. The controls include:

- Assessing the risk of the business being used by criminals to launder money
- Appointing a 'nominated officer'
- Implementing a procedure to check the identity of customers and 'beneficial owners' of corporate bodies and partnerships and keeping all relevant documents
- Ensuring employees are aware of money laundering regulations.

The 'nominated officer' must be a person in the business; they cannot be an external consultant. As it is an important role, it must be undertaken by a person who:

- Has access to all customer records and documentation;
- Can make the decision, without reference to others, whether or not to report suspicious activities;
- Can be trusted with the responsibility.

If you are a sole trader in a regulated business with no employees, you must act as the 'nominated officer' yourself.

The duties of the 'nominated officer' include:

- being the first point of contact for reports of suspicious activity from any employee in the business;
- considering all information and assessing whether evidence of money laundering or terrorist financing exists;
- reporting any suspicious activities or transactions to the Serious Organised Crime Agency (SOCA);
- requesting permission from SOCA to continue with any transactions that they have reported, and ensure that no transactions are continued illegally.

All employees, particularly those in customer-facing positions, must receive regular training to ensure that they are aware of the money laundering laws, understand how the business' procedures affect them and appreciate the penalties of non-compliance. They should also be able to recognise suspicious activity and know what to do about it.

WHAT ARE THE PENALTIES FOR NOT COMPLYING WITH THE MONEY LAUNDERING REGULATIONS?

If you do not comply with Money Laundering Regulations there are various measures that can be taken, from warning letters to criminal prosecution. Although criminal prosecution is a last resort, the penalty may be harsh; depending on the severity of the offence, the courts can impose penalties ranging from unlimited fines to lengthy imprisonment, or both.

Part Three:

Infrastructure and Key Investment Locations

3.1 RENEWABLE ENERGY: A UK PERSPECTIVE

Sophie Yule, Kristina Cavanna,
Watson, Farley & Williams LLP

INTRODUCTION

When the coalition Government took office in 2010, the Prime Minister announced his intention that this would be the "greenest government ever". This objective coincides with the UK's obligation under the EU Renewables Directive to increase its reliance on energy from renewable sources to 15% of its final energy consumption by 2020. As electricity generation is one of the more mature and efficient areas to increase reliance on renewable sources, it is expected that the UK will have to increase renewable penetration to 30% of the electricity market. Consequently, there have been a wide range of opportunities, and accompanying incentives, to invest in renewable energy projects. Over £4.7 billions' worth of new renewables projects were announced between 2011 and 2012.

Although the UK's reliance on renewable energy increased by 27% in 2009 and 2010, by the end of 2010 energy from renewable sources still only accounted for 3.3% of the UK's total energy consumption. Therefore, whilst progress is being made towards hitting the 2020 target, greater investment is needed over the next eight years. The UK Government has placed great emphasis on incentives to stimulate further investment in the renewables (and wider low carbon) sector. These incentives include: an ambitious electricity market reform package; a renewables heat subsidy scheme; and measures to drive down the cost of offshore wind. As explained in greater detail in the 'Clean Tech and Low Carbon Economy' chapter, a UK Green Investment Bank has been established. Steps are also being taken to put in place a legally binding target for decarbonising UK electricity generation by 2030.

OVERVIEW OF THE REGULATORY FRAMEWORK

Under the Electricity Act 1989 (the "Act"), any person carrying on one of the five electricity 'regulated activities' must hold a either a licence or an exemption from the requirement to hold a licence. Participation in a regulated activity without such authority constitutes a criminal offence.

The regulated activities are: generating electricity; participating in the transmission (i.e. high voltage conveyance) of electricity; distribution (conveyance along local low voltage line) - where such generation, transmission or distribution is for the purpose of giving a supply to premises (or enabling a supply to be so given); supplying electricity to premises; or participating in the operation of an electricity interconnector.

All electricity licences in Great Britain are granted by the Office of the Gas and Electricity Markets ("Ofgem"). Ofgem is the executive arm of the energy regulator, the Gas and Electricity Markets Authority ("GEMA"). For most regulated activities, licences are granted at Ofgem's discretion, on application by the licensee. The exception is offshore transmission ("OFTO") licences, which are awarded through competitive tender exercises, run by Ofgem in accordance with a statutory procedure. The OFTO regime is explained further below.

The Secretary of State for Energy and Climate Change ("SoS") has the power under section 5 of the Act to grant a statutory exemption from the requirement to hold a licence to any individual or any class of individuals. In practice, applications for exemptions are dealt with by the Department of Energy and Climate Change ("DECC").

The electricity class exemptions are set out in the Electricity (Class Exemptions from the Requirement for a Licence) Order 2001 ("CEO"), as amended. The CEO contains various classes of exemption in respect of generation, distribution and supply activities. There are, for the most part, exemptions for on-site, offshore or small-scale activities. For example, Schedule 2 to the Order contains an exemption for "small generators" i.e. generators exporting no more than 50MW where declared net capacity is no more than 100MW. Class exemptions are 'self-certifying' in the sense that parties do not receive explicit confirmation that they are exempt, but must simply satisfy themselves that they are covered by one of the class descriptions.

From time to time, and in accordance with the policy of the government of the day, DECC also grants individual exemptions. Although each individual exemption is subject to public consultation, exemptions have consistently been granted, for example, in respect of generating stations which do not export more than 100MW of electrical power to the national transmission system. There are, at the time of writing, no individual or class exemptions in respect of electricity transmission or participation in an interconnector.

The regulatory regime in Northern Ireland follows a similar structure, albeit with different authorities. The Northern Irish Authority for Utility Regulation ("NIAUR") grants electricity licences, whilst exemptions are granted by the Department of Enterprise, Trade and Investment in Northern Ireland ("DETINI").

REFORM OF THE ELECTRICITY MARKET

Policy Overview

In July 2011, the Government published a consultation document entitled "Planning our electric future: a White Paper for secure, affordable and low-carbon electricity". This was followed by a Technical Update Paper in December 2011. Together, the Papers set out proposals for an overhaul of the electricity market (referred to as the "Electricity Market Reform" or "EMR"), in order to address security of supply concerns associated with the closure of existing plant and the increased electrification of sectors that have traditionally been carbon-intensive, such as transport and heat.

In addition to the broad objectives described above, the EMR is designed to put in place the requisite institutional and market arrangements to deliver the scale of change in the power sector needed to meet the UK's legally enforceable renewable and low-carbon targets (15% energy from renewable sources by 2020 and 80% reduction in carbon emissions by 2050, respectively).

The key difference between "renewable" and "low-carbon" energy, in this context, is that the low carbon bracket includes carbon capture and storage (CCS) technology and nuclear energy. The Government is conscious of the need to provide comfort to the renewable industries that renewable energy will not be prejudiced by nuclear support. It has therefore made a commitment that "there will be no levy, direct payment or market support for electricity supplied or capacity provided by a private sector new nuclear operator, unless similar support is also made available more widely to other types of generation[1]". In order for this promise to be met, any Government subsidy for nuclear power arising out of the

1 Chris Huhne's Written Ministerial statement of 18 October 2010: https://www.gov.uk/government/news/written-ministerial-statement-on-energy-policy-the-rt-hon-chris-huhne-mp-18-october-2010

EMR will oblige the Government to provide at least the equivalent level of support in respect of renewable technologies.

Draft Energy Bill

The draft Energy Bill 2013, which was first published in May 2012, contains proposed primary powers for the Government to amend the regulatory framework, via future secondary legislation, in order to create the mechanisms needed for EMR. The contents of the draft Bill and all suggested amendments tabled by the Government or Opposition parties are currently being debated by the House of Commons and House of Lords Committees. The draft Bill is expected to receive Royal Assent, and therefore become a final Act of Parliament, by the end of 2013. The Government will then have the legal power to pass the secondary legislation needed for implementation, which it intends to achieve in 2014.

The EMR provisions of the draft Bill introduce two key new mechanisms, namely a feed-in-tariff with a Contract for Difference ("CfDs") element and arrangements for Capacity Agreements:

CfDs

Under the proposals, any eligible generator will have the option of signing up to a CfD, which is contract to pay or be paid the difference between a notional market "reference price" and an agreed "strike price" for the electricity generated by it. Where the strike price is above the reference price, the generator will receive a top up payment from a Government-owned counterparty body. However, if the reference price is above the strike price, the generator must pay the counterparty body the difference. This means that, if the generator can sell its electricity into the wholesale market at the reference market price, it will receive in aggregate a revenue stream equal to the strike price. This removes price volatility for the generator and is therefore intended to reduce the cost of capital.

When renewable power is sold to a supplier under a Power Purchase Agreement (PPA), the generator usually offers a discount on power price in exchange for the supplier taking on certain risks (e.g. weather forecasting and balancing risks). In circumstances where power is being sold at a discount, the generator will still receive the difference between the strike price and the reference price, rather than the difference between the strike price and the actual price at which it is selling the power. In order to compensate for this DECC has, in setting the draft strike prices, endeavoured to set the prices high enough to account for this discount[2].

CfDs will replace the Renewables Obligation ("RO") regime (see below) when it closes in 2037. The draft Bill sets out transitional arrangements for the transition

2 https://www.gov.uk/government/uploads/system/uploads/attachment_data/file/223652/emr_consultation_annex_b.pdf

from the RO to CfDs, which are explained further below. The draft Bill also includes powers for DECC to make Regulations establishing CfDs, including eligibility, terms, and the strike price level, as well as powers to set maximum costs and targets relating to CfDs. It also includes powers for DECC to issue "investment instruments" (with similar terms to CfDs) in advance of implementation of CfDs and 'back-stop' power for market intervention to help independent renewable generators find a 'route to market' for their power.

The renewable technology categories that will be entitled to apply for a CfD are broadly similar to the RO, but with a few exceptions. There are several technologies which currently fall within the RO but which are not supported by CfDs; either by the Government setting a strike price or by the offer of bespoke negotiations. These are: biomass co-firing; dedicated biomass; standard bioliquids; and geopressure. In addition, a minimum capacity threshold of 5MW has been introduced for many technologies. Projects beneath that threshold will still be able to apply for the small-scale 'Feed in Tariff' ("FiT") support scheme, which is described below.

Unlike RO accreditations, which will only be made once the project is constructed and the developer can demonstrate that it is capable of generating electricity, CfD accreditations will be available at the pre-construction phase. Current proposals suggest that CfD accreditation will require developers to have obtained development consent and a grid connection offer. The CfD contract length will be 15 years (5 years shorter than the RO, though draft strike prices have been set in a way which attempts to make up for this difference) and will start to run from the point at which the project starts generating.

When applying for a CfD, developers will be required to set a target date for generation commencement, around which a "target commissioning window" will be established. Projects that miss the window due to delays will still be entitled to receive CfD payments once the generation commences (subject to a "long-stop" cut-off date). The 15 year contract term will begin to run from the end of the target commissioning window.

Capacity Agreements (within a Capacity Market)

These are contracts for payments to generators in return for guaranteeing reliable capacity to be available when needed, helping to ensure security of supply. Capacity Agreements will be awarded through a centrally run auction process, from 2014. Those successful in the auction will enter into capacity agreements, committing to provide electricity when needed in the delivery year (in return for a steady capacity payment) or else face penalties. In the delivery year, providers will be paid for their capacity. The Bill contains broad enabling powers for DECC to design and introduce the Capacity Market.

In order to prevent overcompensation, generators will not be permitted to receive payments under a CfD and a Capacity Agreement at the same time.

These regimes will be supplemented by two supporting mechanisms:

(a) a "Carbon Price Floor" – a tax to underpin the carbon price in the Emissions Trading Scheme; and
(b) an "Emissions Performance Standard" – a regulatory measure which provides a back-stop to limit emissions from unabated power stations.

More information about these supporting mechanisms is contained in the Clean Technology and Low Carbon Economy Chapter of this Guide.

The costs of CfDs and Capacity Agreements will be shared between electricity suppliers and, ultimately, consumers. National Grid, as the national electricity System Operator, is intended to be the delivery body for both mechanisms. Notwithstanding that the contents of the Bill may vary as it progresses through Parliament, at the time of writing the draft Bill contains powers to amend National Grid's licence in order bring this into effect. There is also a mechanism for the SoS to transfer delivery functions to another body should this be necessary. Finally, the draft Bill contains reserve powers to deal with potential conflicts of interest within National Grid, in the context of its role as Delivery Body. Ofgem will be consulting on potential conflicts later this year.

A consultation on the first EMR "Delivery Plan" was published in July 2013. The consultation includes the draft CfD strike prices and further information on how the CfD regime and Capacity Market will operate. The final versions of the first Delivery Plan and strikes are due to be published in December 2013. The detail of the CfD terms and allocation rules is due to be published in August 2013.

THE RENEWABLES OBLIGATION

Overview of the RO Scheme

The Renewables Obligation (RO), governed in accordance with the Renewables Obligation Order 2009[3] (the "Order") as amended, is currently the main public support mechanism for medium and large-scale renewable energy projects. (Small scale projects, i.e. under 50kW, fall into the domain of FiT regime instead).

The RO is an obligation on licensed electricity suppliers to hold a certain number of Renewable Obligation Certificates ("ROCs"). Suppliers must demonstrate their compliance with the Obligation by submitting ROCs to the regulator

3 Renewables Obligation Order 2009 (SI 2009 No 785) as amended.

(Ofgem). Accredited generators are entitled to be granted ROCs by Ofgem, for a period of 20 years in respect of any net renewable electricity that they generate. Suppliers often purchase ROCs from the renewable generators from whom they purchase the electricity, as part of a "Power Purchase Agreement" or "PPA". However, ROCs are separately tradable from the electricity to which they relate and ROCs can be bought from ROC traders.

If a supplier fails to provide to Ofgem with the requisite number of ROCs to demonstrate its compliance with the RO, it must pay a penalty known as the 'buy-out payment'. The buy-out payment is of an amount set periodically by Ofgem[4] and has the effect of providing a cap on the ROC price. Buy-out payments go into a buy-out fund administered by Ofgem and this fund is recycled back to ROC-holders in proportion to the number of ROCs they hold. This payment (known as a "smear-back payment") is factored into the ROC price that a supplier would negotiate with a renewable generator.

Renewable generators will receive, in addition to the price for the electricity that they generate, a price for each ROC sold which will include an element for the smear back payment. It is in this way that generators raise funds through ROCs.

The level of the RO is set on a "guaranteed headroom" basis. This means that each year the DECC will review the amount of ROCs in circulation and, if it appears likely that the total number of ROCs will exceed the Renewables Obligation (calculated in ROCs), the Obligation will be increased. The purpose of this is to maintain the stability of the system and ensure that ROCs retain their value, which is vital for the economics of renewable energy projects.

ROC Banding Review

A system of 'ROC banding' is in place under the Order, which entitles generators to different numbers of ROCs per MWh of electricity generated, depending on the renewable technology used to generate that electricity. This enables DECC to target the highest levels of support on the technologies which need it the most. The Order gives the SoS the power to review the ROC bandings every four years.

In July 2012 the Government published its response to a consultation on the bandings for different renewable technologies (although as part of this response it was decided that a further consultation was needed specifically on solar projects, the outcome of which is discussed below). Amongst the various banding rates announced, the key standouts were the confirmation that offshore wind generators will retain their 2 ROCs per MW banding until March 2015 (dropping to 1.9 on 1 April 2015 and then 1.8 on 1 April 2016), whilst onshore wind and biomass will

4 The buy-out price from April 1 2011 to March 31 2012 stands at £38.69 per MWh (see Ofgem's website: www.ofgem.gov.uk).

only receive modest reductions in their support (from 1 ROC per megawatt to 0.9 for onshore wind and from 0.25 ROCs per MW to 0.2 for landfill gas).

In December 2012 the Government published its response to a further consultation dealing with (amongst other things) the banding for solar technologies. In the response DECC announced that it now intends to provide support for solar under the RO and under the FiT systems on separate basis rather than on an equivalent basis. It has also decided to provide different bandings for building mounted (i.e. commercial) and ground mounted (i.e. industrial) solar projects.

When DECC amends the ROC banding for a given renewable technology, there is a general principle of "grandfathering" in place, which means that projects accredited before the banding rate change are not affected by the change but rather, are able to receive the ROC banding that was in place at the time of accreditation, for the full 20 year life of that ROC agreement.

Transition from RO to CfDs

As mentioned above, in the longer term, DECC proposes to replace the RO (and therefore ROCs) with a system of CfDs under the EMR.

The first CfDs will not be signed until mid-2014 at the earliest. Between then and 31 March 2017 (the "transitional period"), it is intended that generators will be able to choose between the RO and the new CfD. During the transitional period, generators that have opted for the RO will also be able to accredit additional capacity under the CfD (if the additional capacity is over 5MW) or the RO. An application for a CfD will not be successful if there is an RO application pending for the same capacity[5], and vice versa.

After 31 March 2017, the RO will close to new accreditations (including in respect of additional capacity to existing stations). The last RO schemes will run until 2037 (this is referred to as the "vintaged period").

Under the EMR proposals at the time of writing, between 1 April 2017 and 31 March 2027, the RO will continue to be calculated annually on a "headroom" basis. All projects will be grandfathered at the support level for which they are eligible on the 31 March 2017 cut off date, in order to provide certainty in relation to the ROC banding. Moreover, because no new projects will be signing up to the RO, Ofgem and DECC should, on the face of it, be in a strong position to accurately predict the amount of renewable generation (and therefore the number of ROCs issued) over the course of a given year, which should make it possible to set the Obligation a level which maintains ROC prices.

The draft Energy Bill contains transitional powers to transfer the RO to a "certificate purchase scheme" from 1 April 2027 (although DECC's July 2013

5 Application for preliminary RO accreditation will be permitted.

Consultation on the Transition from the Renewables Obligation to Contracts for Difference seeks views on the earlier date of 1 April 2017). After this date, it is proposed that a central body (probably either DECC or Ofgem) will purchase ROCS, rather than suppliers being obliged to obtain them under the RO. This is known as the "fixed ROC scheme". Secondary legislation to implement the fixed ROC scheme will be consulted on in spring 2014.

The fixed ROC scheme was chosen specifically to provide maximum certainty for investors. Indeed, generators will have the advantage of knowing the exact value of each ROC in advance (rather than simply knowing how many ROCs they will get per MWh and the value of each ROC being determined by the market). Of course, this advantage will need to be weighed against the loss of the ability to use ROCs to entice suppliers into signing PPAs with them. DECC has promised further announcements on measures to address this PPA market concern.

FEED-IN TARIFFS

Overview

Currently, generators of electricity from renewable sources with a total installed capacity between 50kW and 5MW can register their installation under the Feed-in tariff ("FiT") scheme rather than the RO scheme. Generators may only exercise this option once; installations cannot be transferred between the ROC scheme and the FiT scheme.

FiTs were introduced by the Government to incentivise small scale electricity generation from renewable sources. Generators that are eligible for the scheme have guaranteed grid access and enter into long term contracts for the electricity that they produce.

The broad powers relating to the FiT scheme are set out in the Energy Act 2008. The SoS sets out the rules of the FiT scheme through the Feed-in Tariffs (Specified Maximum Capacity and Functions) Order 2010 (as amended). The FiT scheme is administered by Ofgem.

At present FiTs are available for:

- solar photovoltaic (PV) installations with total capacity less than 5MW;
- wind installations with total capacity less than 5MW;
- micro combined heat and power (CHP) installations with total capacity less than 2MW (up to a maximum of 30,000 installations);
- hydro installations with total capacity less than 5MW;
- anaerobic digestion installations with total capacity less than 5MW.

In relation to smaller-scale projects, a Government amendment to the Energy Bill was tabled in July 2013, by which the Energy Act 2008 would be amended to empower the Secretary of State to raise the FiT capacity thresholds to a maximum of 10MW[6] for community energy projects. It is not yet known whether this amendment will ultimately be adopted into the Bill, which is currently undergoing Parliamentary scrutiny.

PV, wind and micro CHP installations with total capacity less than 50kw and micro CHP installations with a total capacity less than 2kW must be accredited through the microgeneration certification scheme (MCS) prior to being eligible for FiTs.

Installations which have a declared net capacity greater than 50kW and up to and including 5MW (or all AD and hydro up to 5MW) need to apply to Ofgem for 'ROO-FIT' accreditation.

Persons with eligible installations receive FiT payments from their energy supplier. Each year the energy suppliers that make FiT payments go through a "levelisation" process whereby their FiT payments to generators are balanced so that each supplier pays an amount of the total outgoing FiT payments that is proportionate to the supplier's share of the domestic electricity supply customers.

FiT payments

FiT payments are set by Ofgem. These payments are comprised of:

- A generation payment for the amount of electricity that the installation generates. The generation payment varies according to the type of technology used, the total installed capacity and the "eligibility date" (which is explained below). The FiT tariff tables are published by Ofgem[7].
- An export payment for any surplus electricity that is not used by the generator but is exported back to the grid. Historically, the export payment has been fixed regardless of type of technology or total installed capacity. However, as of 1 August 2012, solar PV projects, for which the eligibility date fell on or after 1 August 2012 benefit from a higher export rate of 4.5p/kWh (compared to 3.2p/kWh for other technologies).

One of the three factors relevant for determining the amount of the generation payment and, in respect of PV installations, export payment, is the eligibility date. The eligibility date of the installation is the later of when an accredited supplier receives a written request for FiT registration, the ROO-FiT application is received by Ofgem or the commissioning date of the installation. FiT payments start on the

6 https://www.gov.uk/government/news/more-community-energy-projects-to-get-support-under-feed-in-tariffs

7 http://www.ofgem.gov.uk/Sustainability/Environment/fits/tariff-tables/Pages/index.aspx

eligibility date and continue for 20 years. There are two exceptions to this 20 year limit: PV installations whose eligibility date was 1 August 2012 or earlier are eligible for 25 years; and micro CHP installations are eligible for only 10 years.

The generation payment for installations for which the eligibility date fell before 1 November 2012 is set at a fixed rate for the duration that the installation is eligible. The government has introduced a "degression" rate for PV installations with an eligibility date of 1 November 2012 or later. This means that the generation tariff can be changed every three months. The amount that FiTs degress will depend on deployment of PV installations. The baseline degression rate will be 3.5% every three months. This rate can be increased up to 28% if the rate of eligible PV installations is very high. Conversely, Ofgem can freeze the FiT rate for up to 9 months (i.e. a degression rate of 0%) if the installation rate is low. In determining whether the rate of installations is high or low, the Government will consider three types of installation distinctly: domestic; small commercial; and large commercial/utility.

FiT Comprehensive Review

DECC recently undertook a comprehensive review of the FiT scheme to determine the efficiency of the FiT scheme. Phase 1A related to small scale solar PV and Phase 2A to solar PV cost control measures. These phases resulted in a discount to the tariff rates for person with multiple small-scale solar PV installations, reducing the duration of FiT eligibility for solar PV installations from 25 years to 20 years and introducing degression rates.

The final phase of the spending review, Phase 2B, considered all other technologies; namely wind, anaerobic digestion and micro CHP. DECC's response to its consultation on Phase 2B was published on 20 July 2012. The response confirmed new tariff levels for anaerobic digestion, hydro, micro CHP and wind and a tariff degression mechanism for those technologies, which will be effective from 1 April 2014. It also announced the introduction of "preliminary accreditation" system for solar and wind installations of greater than 50kW capacity, and all anaerobic digestion and hydro installations that meet the relevant criteria. In addition, it set out a package of changes designed to support community energy projects.

Renewable Heat Incentive

The Renewable Heating Incentive (the "RHI") is a tariff scheme which pays participants who generate and use renewable energy to heat their buildings. The RHI scheme is currently being implemented by the Government in order to encourage installation of "renewable heat" systems to reduce both energy bills and reliance on fossil fuels. DECC develops the overarching framework for the RHI scheme and sets the tariffs for different technologies. The scheme is administered by Ofgem, which is also the competent body for accrediting installations.

At present, the RHI scheme, which has been in place since November 2011, covers non-domestic sectors (for example, the industrial and commercial, public and not-for-profit sectors) and is expected to open up to provide long term support for domestic premises. According to the consultation by DECC "Domestic Renewable Heat Incentive: the first step towards transforming the way we heat our homes", published on 12 July 2013, the scheme will be administered by OFGEM and be open for applications from spring 2014. In the meantime, for domestic customers the Renewable Heat Premium Payment Scheme, a voucher scheme is available and has been extended for a further year to March 2014 to support households until the new domestic scheme is introduced.

The current RHI scheme applies to a range of renewable heat technologies including solid biomass technology (such as biomass boilers and waste combustion), ground source, water heat pumps, geo-thermal systems, solar collectors, and biomethane injection and biogas combustion. In September 2012 the Government consulted on plans for extending the non-domestic RHI scheme to new technologies and DECC is currently finalising these for publication in autumn this year. The relevant tariffs for any given installation will depend on the technology used and the size of the installation (i.e. how much heat it generates). Following industry feedback the Government launched the Non-Domestic Scheme Early Tariff Review consultation in June 2013, in order to respond to low up take of certain technologies in the scheme so far. The outcomes are due to be announced in autumn 2013.

The RHI scheme is expected to cost £42m over 2012/2013. In order to control costs and ensure the sustainability of the RHI scheme, the scheme is capped at £70m in its first year. Therefore, if the scheme reaches 97% of its annual budget, DECC will give one week's notice of its intention to suspend the scheme. The suspension will only affect applications for the scheme made after the suspension date.

In February 2013, the Government announced the implementation of a long-term budget mechanism, the "degression mechanism", for the non-domestic RHI scheme. This is intended to make sure the RHI continues to be economically sustainable as certain tariffs paid to new RHI recipients can be reduced if uptake onto the scheme is greater than required to achieve the heat objectives of the UK's 2020 renewable energy targets.

OFFSHORE WIND

Offshore Wind – Generation

Successive governments have been keen to promote the development of offshore wind projects in the UK which are recognised as offering the potential for much larger-scale projects than onshore wind.

The London Array project is one such example at 1,000 MW. More recently, on 11 July 2013, DECC gave development consent to the 1.2 GW Triton Knoll Offshore wind farm, the largest project for which consent has been granted so far. In addition to creating potential for larger projects than can be accommodated onshore, offshore wind farms, particularly those far out to sea, are also generally less likely to encounter the same level of objections on planning grounds as onshore wind farms.

In 2001 the former Government organised the first round of tenders for offshore wind projects (known as 'Round 1'). Eighteen projects were awarded for sites within the twelve nautical mile territorial limit around the UK. Each site had to have a minimum generating capacity of 20 MW. Successful developers were granted agreements for leases which would be followed by the grant of the leases once the relevant consents had been obtained. The developers were given a three year period to obtain the consents.

Round 2 followed in 2003 and was on a much more ambitious scale. Sites were grouped in three strategic areas both in territorial waters and in the Renewable Energy Zone created by the Government which extends two hundred miles into international waters. Fifteen projects with a combined capacity of 7.2 GW were awarded but the Round 2 agreements for leases allow developers seven years in which to obtain the necessary consents, before leases will be awarded.

In June 2008 the Crown Estate announced proposals for a Round 3 programme designed to deliver up to 25 GW of additional offshore capacity by 2020. This announcement sparked significant interest and following the closure of the competitive bid process for licensing of the wind farms in March 2009, the Crown Estate had received 40 bids relating to the nine Round 3 development zones from 18 different companies/consortia, originating from at least nine different countries.

In January 2010 the Crown Estate announced the successful bidders for each of the nine Round 3 offshore wind zones within UK waters. Each of these bidders have signed exclusive zone development agreements with the Crown Estate who will assist them in taking these proposals through the planning and consenting phases.

The former Government's plan to reach 32 GW of offshore wind by 2020 is largely dependent on the level of financial support the Government allows through the Renewables Obligation mechanism. In April 2009, DECC received information regarding the high costs faced by current offshore wind projects arising for various reasons, including immature supply chains, increased foreign exchange costs and the increased cost of risk in the current financial climate. Subsequently, an increase to 2 ROCs per MWh was accepted by DECC.

All offshore wind projects that receive full accreditation between 1 April 2010 and 31 March 2014 will receive 2 ROCs per MWh subject to specific requirements. It is estimated that these changes will provide £525 million of support from 2011 to 2014, which will protect 3 GW of proposed investment over the next four years. This higher level of support is only guaranteed up until 2014 which is a year before construction on many of the Round 3 projects is scheduled to begin.

Offshore wind – Transmission

The former Government introduced a new regime for construction and operation of transmission assets for offshore wind farms. With effect from June 2010, the offshore transmission assets (i.e. cables, offshore substation, etc.) of larger existing offshore wind farms and some wind farms which are in the course of construction must be transferred to independent offshore transmission owners. These new owners (offshore transmission operators or "OFTOs") are appointed under a competitive tender process to carry out operation and maintenance of those assets.

Ofgem established two transitional rounds of tenders for transmission assets of thirteen offshore wind farms. Following these transitional stages, Ofgem is now operating an "enduring regime" for offshore wind projects qualifying after 31 March 2012. The enduring regime is expected to provide an investment opportunity up to £14 billion up to 2020 (with further investment opportunities continuing beyond 2020).

There are two build options for transmission assets under the enduring regime: the Generator Build option; and the OFTO Build option.

Under the Generator Build option, the generator is responsible for the design, pre-construction, procurement and construction of the transmission infrastructure. After the generator has completed construction, the transmission assets are transferred to the OFTO, which will operate, maintain and decommission the assets. It is proposed in the Energy Bill, which was tabled in May 2012, that the generator should also be permitted to operate the transmission assets for testing and whilst commissioning the transmission assets.

Under the OFTO Build option, the generator will obtain the connection agreement and have a high level of involvement in design and preconstruction. The OFTO will then undertake the detailed design work and procure that the construction is completed. Once operational, the OFTO will operate, maintain and decommission the assets.

3.2 CLEAN TECH AND LOW CARBON ECONOMY

Emanuela Lecchi, Sophie Yule, & Nick Payne,
Watson, Farley & Williams LLP

INTRODUCTION

There has been a focus in recent years on trying to make the UK a "low carbon economy", using subsidies and fiscal incentives in an attempt to boost the development and deployment of clean technology (often abbreviated to "clean tech").

The Climate Change Act 2008 imposed a legally binding requirement on the Government to reduce greenhouse gas emissions in the UK by 80% (compared to the level for 1990) by 2050. It also created the Carbon Reduction Commitment ("CRC"), which imposed emissions limits and introduced emissions trading for businesses in the UK which are not heavy pollutants and are thus not covered by the existing emissions trading scheme for power plants and other heavy industry which came into effect in 2005. The CRC is discussed further below.

In 2009 the Department of Energy and Climate Change ("DECC") brought out a White Paper entitled The UK Low Carbon Transition Plan which set out a number of policy proposals designed to make the UK a low carbon economy and to "lead the clean industries of the future". In the electricity sector, this meant increasing the drive for renewable energy, encouraging nuclear energy, development of a "smart grid" and encouraging carbon capture and storage (CCS) by providing a support mechanism for demonstration CCS installations and by requiring new coal-fired power plants to incorporate a CCS facility. For homes and businesses, it meant encouraging energy efficiency and reduction of carbon emissions through various schemes. With regard to transport, the proposals included encouraging low-carbon cars and buses and the development of electric cars and the infrastructure for charging them. In relation to agriculture, the plan to 2020 is intended to cut emissions from farming and waste through more efficient use of fertiliser and better management of livestock and manure, support for anaerobic digestion (a technology that turns waste and manure into renewable energy), reducing the amount of waste sent to landfill and better capture of landfill emissions.

Alongside the White Paper, the Department for Business, Innovation and Skills ("BIS") and DECC produced The UK Low Carbon Industrial Strategy. This strategy document addressed business opportunities in clean technology. Based on an industry analysis, it stated that the global market for low carbon and environmental goods and services was worth £3 trillion in 2007/8 and could grow to £4.3 trillion by 2015. Further, the UK low carbon and environmental goods and services market "is worth £106 billion and employs 880,000 people directly or through the supply chain". Key policies would include development of the UK offshore wind industry and wave and tidal industry, investing in nuclear power, developing low carbon vehicles and vehicle-charging infrastructure and developing renewable construction materials, chemical and low carbon manufacturing.

The Energy Act 2010, passed by the previous Government shortly before it left office, introduced a new CCS incentive to support the construction of four commercial-scale CCS demonstration projects in the UK and the retrofit of additional CCS capacity if required. It also required regular reports to be prepared by the Government on the progress made on the decarbonisation of electricity generation and the development and use of CCS.

The present Government's first Annual Energy Statement, issued in July 2010, identifies certain policy objectives including its delivering energy efficiency in homes and business through the "Green Deal" and introduction of smart meters, developing renewable heat and developing CCS. It is also proposed a "green investment bank" to support investment in low carbon projects.

In March 2011, the Government issued a Carbon Plan to implement these objectives. The Carbon Plan sets out actions and deadlines for energy efficiency in homes and communities, reducing emissions from business and industry, encouraging low-carbon transport, cutting emissions from waste and managing land sustainability.

In May 2012, the Green Investment Bank ("GIB") was formed as a public company, with the Government as its sole shareholder. The GIB became fully operational in October 2012 when it was granted state aid approval by the European Commission to make investments on commercial terms. More detail on the GIB is set out in the next section.

At the time of writing, the latest energy bill ("the Bill") (which will become the Energy Act 2013) is progressing through Parliament. Further detail on the contents of the Bill is contained in the Renewable Energy chapter. However, it is worth noting here that it is currently intended that statutory provision to be made in the Bill for the Secretary of State to set, by 2016, a target for decarbonising UK electricity generation by 2030 ("the 2030 decarbonisation target").

Clean technology embraces a number of elements, in various sectors, which have common themes of benefitting the environment and being energy efficient and covers sectors as diffuse as energy, water, waste, transportation, manufacturing, agriculture and homes and businesses generally. However, as can be seen from the recent developments described above, the current political and regulatory climate places the emphasis not only on developing efficient clean technologies, but specifically on creating a fertile investment environment for 'green growth'.

GREEN INVESTMENT BANK

The GIB (whose website declares it to be the first bank of its kind in the world) was formed with the intention of financing projects that will help develop the UK's low carbon economy, and in particular the development of "green infrastructure assets".[1] To that end, it is expected to utilise at least 80% of its capital in the following priority sectors:

- offshore wind
- waste recycling and energy from waste
- non-domestic energy efficiency, and
- support for the Government's 'Green Deal' (see next section).

However, the GIB describes itself as working towards a "double bottom line", as it is expected to achieve both a substantial "green impact" and make financial returns.[2] The GIB has made it clear that it is "unashamedly and unambiguously a 'for profit' bank", and expected to make investments that are commercially as well as environmentally sound.

In October 2012 the GIB received EU state aid approval, meaning that it was deemed not to be an anti-competitive from of Government aid. In November 2012

1 Drawn from BIS's "Update on the design of the Green Investment Bank", published 2011
2 See the Green Investment Bank's Investment Approach document, available at: http://www.greeninvestmentbank.com/what-we-do/our-investment-approach.html

the GIB was opened for business as UK Green Investment Bank plc (a public limited company with the UK Government as its sole shareholder), and funded with £3 billion in capital for investment. The goals, independence and capitalisation of the GIB were enshrined in law on 25 April 2013 when the Enterprise and Regulatory Reform Bill received Royal Assent.[3]

The GIB has currently made £635 million of investments in 11 different projects around the UK.[4] The GIB will be limited to this £3 billion in capital until April 2015, when it is intended that it will be given powers to borrow further money to invest (subject to public sector debt falling as a percentage of GDP).

GREEN DEAL/EMISSIONS PERFORMANCE STANDARD

The Green Deal and the Energy Company Obligation

The Energy Act 2011 established a number of measures to promote energy efficiency measures in homes and businesses. The Act established the legal framework for the Green Deal and the Energy Company Obligation ("ECO"), which have replaced the existing Carbon Emissions Reduction Target ("CERT") and the Community Energy Saving Programme ("CESP") following their expiration in 2012. CESP provided funding for the installation of modern insulation, wood pellet boilers and solar water heaters in households that would not be able to afford such measures privately. CERT put requirements on energy providers of a certain size to cut the emissions of the households that they supply, incentivising them to encourage their customers to make energy efficiency improvements to their properties.

The Green Deal and ECO are designed to further encourage the improvement of the energy efficiency of the UK's existing and future building stock. The Green Deal gives individual and business property owners access to Government funded credit through their energy providers in order to pay for improvements to their property and improvements to their heating systems that will lower their energy usage (and as a result their energy bills). Repayments are recovered from the owners' savings in energy usage (the so-called "golden rule" is that monthly savings must be greater than monthly repayments for the improvements to be eligible) by allowing the energy provider to charge the owner the same monthly or annual price for their energy, and use the difference between the amount charged and the actual cost of the energy used (which should be substantially lower than the total bill due to the efficiency improvements made) to pay off the credit.

Meanwhile, the ECO places obligations on energy companies to provide credit to their customers themselves to facilitate the installation of energy efficiency measures in their homes. The ECO is intended to fit within the Green Deal

3 See http://news.bis.gov.uk/content/detail.aspx?ReleaseID=428955&NewsAreaId=2

4 See http://www.greeninvestmentbank.com/userfiles/files/Press-releases/GIB-transactions.pdf for further details.

framework supporting its role in the domestic sector where Green Deal finance alone is not sufficient.

In November 2011, the Government launched a public consultation in respect of the Green Deal and the ECO. The Government Response[5] to the consultation, published on 11 June 2012, set out their next steps and confirmed that Ofgem would be responsible for administrating the ECO. On the same day, the Secretary of State for Energy & Climate Change Edward Davey announced secondary legislation, designed to provide the foundations of the Green Deal and ECO[6].

In October 2012 the statutory provisions implementing the Green Deal (for example, enabling Green Deal assessors and providers and installers of Green Deal products to become accredited) came into force. From 28 January 2013 customers have been able to apply for Green Deal finance. In February 2013 the EU Commission granted State Aid Approval to the Green Deal, meaning that it will not be held to be anti-competitive or anti-free movement of goods. To support the Green Deal the Government has published a number of "quick guides", and it has also produced a Green Deal code of practice, a second version of which was published in January 2013.

Energy Performance Certificates

In 2007 Energy Performance Certificates (EPC) were introduced as part of the (now defunct) Home Information Pack ("HIP") programme. EPCs rate the energy efficiency of buildings as being between A and G, with A being the most and G the least energy efficient. When the HIPs requirement was removed the EPCs were kept as a requirement for all buildings, and they are now being tied into the feed-in tariffs system by virtue of the fact that to qualify for any of the renewables based feed-in tariffs a building must hold an EPC and be rated band D or higher.[7]

A building's banding depends on its Standard Assessment Procedure ("SAP") rating, which is determined by how many SAP Points the building scores. Points are allocated based on what energy efficiency related improvements or features it incorporates, such as double glazing, low energy lighting and cavity and roof insulation.

The 2012 draft Energy Bill[8] contained powers to introduce an Emissions Performance Standard (EPS). This will be a regulatory cap on the carbon emissions permitted to be released from new power stations. The Government has announced its intention to initially set the level at 450g CO2/kWh, aimed at delivering the Government's commitment to prevent coal-fired power stations being built unless they are equipped with CCS, whilst allowing the desired short-term investment in gas (needed to ensure security of energy supply) to take place.

5 This document is available at: http://www.decc.gov.uk/en/content/cms/consultations/green_deal/green_deal.aspx
6 See http://www.decc.gov.uk/en/content/cms/news/gdeco_wms/gdeco_wms.aspx for the full text of the statement.
7 For more information of Feed-In Tariffs, see the Renewables chapter.
8 See Renewables Chapter 2.1 for more information on the Draft Energy Bill.

In order to ensure sufficient certainty for investors, the Government has announced its intention that power stations consented under the 450g/kWh-based level would then be subject to that level until 2045[9]. Power stations which have consented before the EPS comes into effect will not be subject to the cap.

CARBON PRICE FLOOR

Setting a price for carbon is at the centre of the UK Government's strategy to reduce future emissions[10], and the UK is the first country to implement a carbon price floor in its power sector. Creation of a so-called Carbon Price Floor in the UK means that companies are required to pay a top-up charge if the market price for carbon falls below a level set by the Government.

The rationale behind the introduction of the Carbon Price Floor is to increase the cost of pollution and similarly increase the rewards for low carbon projects. The Carbon Price Floor would ensure that companies would be paying a minimum price for producing carbon at all times. It would also go some way towards helping the UK meet its targets for reducing emissions in the medium to long term[11].

The Government has also emphasised that the Carbon Price Floor will supplement the CfD regime under EMR, by putting electricity generated from low-carbon sources at a competitive advantage, as compared to electricity generated from fossil fuels. Under the current Climate Change Levy ("CCL") (a levy placed on all power sold by electricity suppliers) arrangements, there are exemptions in place for electricity generated by certain fossil fuels (as well as electricity generated by renewable sources). The new Carbon Price Floor will be implemented by removing these exemptions from the CCL (and certain other fuel duty exemptions). It is also worth noting that from 1 April 2013 the CCL rates will increase in line with the RPI.

The Carbon Price Floor is thus also designed to incentivise investment in low-carbon electricity generation in the UK, as the Government is of the view that the carbon price set by the market under the EU Emissions Trading Scheme (EU ETS) has not been stable, certain or high enough to encourage sufficient renewable generation.

In the current carbon market the price of carbon is relatively low, as the demand for permits is high relative to their supply. Such low price levels do not create an ideal environment to dissuade polluters from creating emissions, and when coupled with a fair amount of price uncertainty, will not provide an attractive forecast for returns for potential investors into low carbon solutions.

Investment in low carbon generation is a key step towards transformation of the UK power sector towards a greener future, and complements the decarbonisation[12]

9 DECC Press Release 17 March 2012.
http://www.decc.gov.uk/en/content/cms/news/pn12_025/pn12_025.aspx
10 Carbon Price Floor Consultation: the Government response (March 2011)
11 Ibid.
12 Ibid.

of the power sector in general, supplementing the EU Emissions Trading System (EU ETS), which was previously known as the EU Emissions Trading Scheme. The UK introduced the Carbon Price Floor from April at around £9.55/tCO2 and is forecasted to rise to £30/tCO2 in 2020, rising to £70/tCO2 in 2030 (real 2009 prices).[13]

EMISSIONS TRADING

The EU ETS was introduced across the EU to help it meet its greenhouse gas emissions reduction target under the Kyoto Protocol. The EU ETS commenced in 2005 and is the largest multi-country, multi-sector greenhouse gas emissions trading system in the world. It includes around 11,000 installations (excluding aviation which has been recently added to the system) accounting for about 45 per cent of EU carbon dioxide (CO2) emissions.

Each year the UK reports its analysis of UK annual emissions and places them in context by looking at the EU-wide picture. In the UK, the Environment Agency is the body that enforces the EU ETS and issues Greenhouse Gas Emissions Permits.

The EU ETS operates by the allocation and trading of greenhouse gas emissions allowances throughout the EU - one allowance represents one tonne of carbon dioxide equivalent. An overall limit, or 'cap', is set by Member States' Governments on the total amount of emissions allowed from all the installations covered by the scheme. The allowances are then distributed to the installations in the scheme.

At the end of each year, operators are required to ensure they have enough allowances to cover their installation's emissions. They have the flexibility to buy additional allowances (on top of their free allocation), or to sell any surplus allowances generated from reducing their emissions.

The scheme currently has four operating phases:

- Phase I ran from 1 January 2005 to 31 December 2007 and was a 'learning by doing phase';
- Phase II ran from 1 January 2008 to 31 December 2012 and included revised monitoring and reporting rules, more stringent emissions caps and additional combustion sources;
- Phase III currently in progress, will run from 1 January 2013 to 31 December 2020, and brings major changes including harmonised allocation methodologies, an EU-wide cap on allowances, increased allowance auctioning and additional greenhouse gases and emission sources. The EU

13 (Electricity Market Reform: policy overview) http://www.decc.gov.uk/assets/decc/11/policy-legislation/emr/5349-electricity-market-reform-policy-overview.pdf

cap will reduce the number of available allowances by 1.74% each year, delivering an overall reduction of 21% below 2005 verified emissions by 2020;

- Phase IV is anticipated to begin in 2021,[14] and DECC is beginning to consider what this should consist of.[15]

The EU ETS covers electricity generation and the main energy-intensive industries – power stations, refineries and offshore, iron and steel, cement and lime, paper, food and drink, glass, ceramics, engineering and the manufacture of vehicles, and now aviation operators.

The EU ETS has been expanded so as to include aviation operators because a study undertaken on behalf of the European Commission demonstrated that whilst the EU's total greenhouse gas emissions fell by 5.3 per cent from 1990 to 2003, carbon dioxide emissions from international aviation activities of the 25 member states increased by 73 per cent during the same period.

The study concluded that without due policy intervention, the growth in emissions is expected to continue in the coming decades. Following consultation on the Commission's proposals, a Directive (2008/101/EC) to include aviation within the EU ETS was published on the 13 January 2009.

The Directive and the UK Regulations require aviation operators to monitor their CO2 emissions according to approved guidelines. On 28th February 2012, the UK issued allowances for 2012 to those aviation operators that successfully applied. However, on 12 November 2012 the EU Commission announced that it intended to implement a temporary suspension of the Aviation EU ETS in respect of international flights in April 2013 (which has now come into force). The UK Government launched a consultation on whether to implement this decision in the UK on 18 March 2013 and published its response in May 2013. In its response the Government confirmed its intention to implement this decision in the UK.[16]

There has been speculation that the EU ETS will be expanded so as to include shipping. The EU has been consulting on the number of options for reducing shipping emissions, including a market-based mechanism that would apply to ships' emissions from the port they left to any EU port, and then on to the next port of call. This could mean bringing shipping into the EU ETS, a move that would require carriers to purchase carbon allowances to cover the CO2 they emit. According to the Europa Website "*The European Commission is currently considering possible European action in 2013 to introduce monitoring, reporting and verification of greenhouse gas emissions from maritime transport as a first step towards measures to reduce these emissions*."[16]

14 https://www.gov.uk/participating-in-the-eu-ets#delivery-phases-of-the-emissions-trading-system
15 A report on an informal stakeholder event held by DECC in April 2013 can be found at: https://www.gov.uk/government/uploads/system/uploads/attachment_data/file/192571/asha future_of_eu_ets_april_2013_event_report.pdf

Wave/Tidal

Tidal and wave power are two of the less developed forms of renewable energy production in the UK. However, the consistency and predictability of tidal energy and the fact that wave energy is at its greatest during the winter (when energy demands are at their peak) make both attractive propositions, and the Government is keen to encourage development of wave and tidal energy projects. DECC estimates that the UK has "*around 50% of Europe's tidal energy resource*"[17] and that "*generating energy from the power of waves or tides could provide up to 20% of current UK electricity*"[18], as well as helping to cut carbon emissions and create green jobs. According to RenewableUK, although the sector is in its infancy, it could still create 19,500 jobs by 2035 and generate revenue in the region of £6.1 billion.[19]

As a result, DECC has put in place what it terms "*the most comprehensive marine energy support programme in the world*."[20] Early stage marine energy research is funded through the SuperGen Research Marine Programme (run by the Research Council), and later stage research is funded through a range of programmes and organisations, including the Technology Standards Board, the Carbon Trust and the Energy Technologies Institute, as well as smaller schemes aimed specifically at marine energy programmes.

On 5 April 2012 the Government launched the £20 million Marine Energy Array Demonstrator ("MEAD") Scheme. This scheme funds two pre-commercial projects that demonstrate the long term energy generation capabilities of wave and tidal energy technologies. This is one of a series of schemes being organised by the Low Carbon Innovation Co-ordination Group in order to promote innovation in marine technology. DECC also considered possible efforts to further encourage marine energy development in the UK in its recent consultation on the Renewables Obligation.[21] Following this consultation the Government has decided to provide support for wave and tidal stream generators at a rate of 5 ROCs per MWh for generators of up to 30MW capacity, and 2 ROCs per MWh for larger generators for all generators accredited before 1 April 2017.

The Government has also set the level of support for tidal range schemes below 1 GW (barrages/lagoons etc) at 2 ROCs per MWh for new accreditations and additional capacity added in 2013/14 and 2014/15, stepping down to 1.9 ROCs per MWh for new accreditations and additional capacity added in 2015/16 and 1.8 ROCs per MWh for new accreditations and additional capacity added in 2016/17.

16 http://ec.europa.eu/clima/policies/transport/shipping/index_en.htm

17 https://www.gov.uk/wave-and-tidal-energy-part-of-the-uks-energy-mix

18 See: http://www.decc.gov.uk/en/content/cms/news/pn12_043/pn12_043.aspx

19 "Wave and Tidal Energy in the UK: State of the Industry Report", March 2011

20 http://www.decc.gov.uk/en/content/cms/news/pn12_043/pn12_043.aspx

21 More information on the Renewables Obligation is contained in Chapter 3.1, page 127.

Carbon Capture Storage

Carbon Capture and Storage (CCS) is a process by which the carbon dioxide (CO2) from fossil fuel power stations is captured and safely stored, rather than being emitted into the atmosphere. The first stage of the process can occur either before or after combustion at the power plant. The captured CO2 is then transported via pipeline and stored safely in a designated storage area, such as depleted oil and gas reservoirs.[22] CCS can be applied not only to the generation of power, but also to a range of industrial processes such as petroleum engineering and process engineering. The UK is particularly suited to the deployment of CCS due to the large storage capacity it has in the North Sea.

Up to $40 billion worldwide has already been committed by Governments to CCS technology, with UK-based firms set to benefit from an estimated £3-6.5 billion per year by the 2020s.[23] The scale of this investment level demonstrates the global commitment to CCS, and cements its position as one of the key clean technologies going forward.

This continuing Government commitment was shown in their announcement on the 3rd April 2012 of the Commercialisation Programme and CCS Roadmap, which set out the future strategy of this growing sector.

The Commercialisation Programme makes available up to £1 billion funding for commercial-scale CCS projects, with the aim of trying to reduce the cost of the technology to make it viable on a large scale by the 2020s.[24] As at 16 May 2012 several companies had registered a strong interest in the programme, such as Centrica, Shell and National Grid.[25] The Programme also makes available the possibility of Contracts for Difference[26]. A competition was run between April and July 2012 for projects that wished to receive financing under this scheme, and on 20 March 2013 the Government announced their two preferred. Negotiations are being undertaken in relation to the testing phase, and a final investment decision will be made by the Government in early 2015 on whether to construct one or both of these projects.

As well as this Commercialisation Programme, the Government Roadmap puts forward a series of interventions designed to make the UK the a focal point for the global CCS industry. The main aspects of this Roadmap include making available £125 million over 4 years for research and development, intervention to address key barriers to the commercial deployment of CCS (such as supply chain difficulties), development of a market for low carbon electricity, and international engagement aimed at sharing knowledge.[27]

22 http://www.decc.gov.uk/en/content/cms/emissions/ccs/what_is/what_is.aspx

23 http://www.decc.gov.uk/assets/decc/11/cutting-emissions/carbon-capture-storage/4899-the-ccs-roadmap.pdf

24 Full press release: http://www.decc.gov.uk/en/content/cms/news/pn12_040/pn12_040.aspx

25 Full press release: http://www.decc.gov.uk/en/content/cms/news/pn12_060/pn12_060.aspx

26 Please see [ref to renewables Chapter] for more information on Contracts for Difference.

27 Full details of the Government Roadmap can be found here: http://www.decc.gov.uk/assets/decc/11/cutting-emissions/carbon-capture-storage/4899-the-ccs-roadmap.pdf

Smart grids and smart meters

The existing national grid that supplies UK homes and businesses with gas and electricity will be replaced by a smart grid to allow for greater energy efficiency by taking advantages of developments in digital technology. For example, a smart grid, combined with smart meters in customer premises, would mean that domestic appliances such as washing machines could be turned on remotely during times of low energy demand and off in times of peak demand. This could provide the consumer with significant financial savings over the long term as energy providers would charge less for off-peak consumption.

Furthermore, a smart grid would expand the capacity of the national grid and increase connections to renewable energy sources such as wind farms and tidal generators. The *UK Low Carbon Transition Plan* provided for £30 million[28] of direct funding for network related research in order to accelerate the development of smart grid technology within the UK. The importance of the implementation of a smart grid was reiterated in the *Carbon Plan* published in March 2011[29]. In addition DECC have established the Smart Grids Forum which is focusing on the importance of network development as part of the low carbon transition.[30]

A further technical development initially outlined in the *UK Low Carbon Transition Plan* is that of smart meters. These devices will allow consumers to manage their energy consumption by displaying how much energy is being consumed at different times and the cost of consumption. The UK Government's vision is for every home in the UK to have smart energy meters, with businesses having smart technology implemented that is suited to their needs by 2019[31]. Energy providers will be replacing traditional gas and electricity meters and offering users more detailed and accurate information as to how much electricity and gas is used by their household. Subsequently, smart meters will allow suppliers to produce more flexible price plans based on the times when most electricity and gas are used – rewarding customers for consumption in off-peak times and will allow consumers with generator facilities (such as solar photovoltaic panels) to sell electricity back to the grid.

Smart meters continue to be regarded as playing an important role in saving energy in homes and communities. The Government is currently engaged in consultation on the licensing, marketing codes and technical standards with a view to rollout commencing in 2014. Notwithstanding that the legal framework surrounding smart meters has not been finalised, several energy suppliers are already responding to consumer demand and installing some form of smart meter. Once rollout does commence formally, it is estimated that over 53 million smart gas and electricity meters will be installed, commencing in 2014 to be completed

28 p.10, The UK Low Carbon Transition Plan (DECC, 2009).

29 Para 2.16, Carbon Plan (The UK Government, March 2011).

30 DECC/Ofgem Smart Grid Forum (http://www.ofgem.gov.uk/Networks/SGF/Pages/SGF.aspx)

31 http://www.decc.gov.uk/en/content/cms/tackling/smart_meters/smart_meters.aspx

by 2019[32]. Suppliers rolling out smart meters will have to offer meters to consumers at no additional upfront cost, although there will be no legal requirement for consumers to have a smart meter fitted and nor will the suppliers be required to force their customers to have a smart meter fitted. They may however cover the cost of smart meters through regular utility billing.

Low carbon vehicles

Promotion and encouragement of the use of low carbon and electric vehicles lies at the core of the current government's philosophy to tackle the problems of carbon emissions in the transport sector. A Carbon Price Floor (see above) will provide clear economic signals to move away from high carbon technologies, by increasing the price paid for emitting carbon dioxide.[33] Moreover, the Government has set itself the target of having "almost every car and van to be a zero emission vehicle by 2050."[34] Through the Office for Low Emission Vehicles the government has committed to providing over £400 million in funding over the life of this Parliament in order to encourage the development of ultra-low emission vehicle technologies and the purchase of such vehicles. The Government has implemented the Low Carbon Vehicle Procurement Plan which provides funding for public procurement of low carbon vehicle fleets.

A key aspect to the development of electric vehicles is to have an infrastructure in place to charge them. The Department of Transport launched the Plugged-In-Places Scheme in November 2009 to provide seed funding of up to £30 million to support installation of charging infrastructure in various urban locations. By the end of 2010, Greater Manchester was the only city in the country to benefit from the scheme. On 26 May 2011, the Mayor of London announced that a single scheme "Source London" would be launched to operate the largest city-wide electric point recharging network which will comprise 150 new charge points in the city.[35] The scheme also aims to deliver 1,300 publicly accessible charge points by 2013[36] and is also exploring the possibility of cooperating with the proposed East of England charge point network so that members of both schemes can have cross-access to the facilities at an annual membership fee. In February 2013 the government also announced a £37 million funding package for home and on-street charging and for new charge points for people parking plug-in vehicles at railway stations under which the coalition government will provide 75% of the cost of installing new charge points.

32 Ibid.
33 Ibid.
34 https://www.gov.uk/government/policies/reducing-greenhouse-gases-and-other-emissions-from-transport/supporting-pages/ultra-low-emission-vehicles
35 London announces 'go live' of 150 EV recharging points in the capital (http://www.lowcvp.org.uk/news/1640/london-announces-go-live-of-150-ev-recharging-points-in-the-capital/); Source London (https://www.sourcelondon.net)
36 https://www.sourcelondon.net/mayor-switches-new-electric-vehicle-scheme-source-london

There are currently government grants available in relation to:

- Plug-in Cars;
- Plug-in Vans;
- domestic chargepoints;
- residential on-street charge points;
- residential on-street and rapid chargepoints for local authorities;
- train station car park chargepoints; and
- chargepoints on the public sector estate.

However, the charging infrastructure will to a large extent be determined by how people decide to use and charge their electric cars. For example, if there is strong demand for fast charging, that may require a particular type of charging infrastructure whereas other types of infrastructure may be possible for people who are willing to leave their vehicles for long periods to be charged. Taking this into consideration, under the Source London Scheme, a balance of both needs can be achieved in that, while most of the charge points will allow vehicles to charge over a number of hours, a small number of points in the network will be rapid chargers which can top up a battery within 20 minutes and provide a full charge in around 30 minutes.[37]

The type of journeys that people make may determine whether all-electric cars or hybrid cars become more prevalent: all-electric cars would be suitable for people who only drive short distances and can then charge their cars whereas hybrid cars are going to be more suitable for drivers who want to drive long distances and do not want to have to charge their cars during the journey.

Source London will bring together London's new and existing public charge points into one network. This will be operated by Transport for London working in partnership with Siemens, who are sponsoring Source London.[38]

The Government also specified a desire in the *Carbon Plan* to further develop high speed rails and electrify certain rail lines between cities in England, as well as to promote the use of sustainable biofuels as part of the strategies to lower carbon emission in the transport sector.[39]

37 https://www.sourcelondon.net/charge-points
38 https://www.sourcelondon.net/source-london
39 Chapter 5, The Carbon Plan.

3.3 ISSUES FOR INVESTORS IN THE UK UPSTREAM OIL AND GAS SECTOR

Heike Trischmann, Watson, Farley & Williams LLP

INTRODUCTION

Oil production on the United Kingdom Continental Shelf (UKCS) commenced in the 1960s and today the area is regarded as a mature oil & gas producing region. Production peaked in 1999 but is now in decline as easily accessible reserves are depleted. However, recent data shows that substantial reserves remain. For example, EnCore Oil plc (now Premier Oil plc[1]) announced that the Catcher, Catcher North and Catcher East fields in the North Sea hold possible reserves of between 40 and 80 million barrels of oil equivalent (**boe**)[2] while Premier Oil expects that the Solan field, in which it has a 60% share, alone could produce as much as 40 million boe. The current best estimate published by the Department of Energy and Climate Change (**DECC**), the body within the UK Government responsible for upstream oil and gas activities, of total remaining recoverable oil is approximately 5.9 billion barrels of oil and 3 billion boe of gas from the UKCS[3].

By comparison, the UK onshore oil & gas industry started back in the early 1900s but so far has yielded much more episodic success. The productive basins from conventional oil and gas sources are now also considered to be at a mature stage[4]. However, the UK is said to have significant unconventional oil & gas reserves and the extent of those is constantly being updated and currently stands at approximately 1,300

1 Following Premier Oil plc's acquisition of EnCore Oil plc in 2012 http://www.premier-oil.com/premieroil/about/history

2 This represents a downward correction from an initial estimate of 300million boe. See: http://www.premier-oil.com/premieroil/media/press/drilling-update-catcher-north for further details. Information last updated 8 February 2011.

3 See: https://www.gov.uk/oil-and-gas-uk-field-data for estimates of UK additional potential resources 2012

4 See: https://www.gov.uk/government/uploads/system/uploads/attachment_data/file/66170/uk-onshore-prospectivity.pdf

trillion cubic feet (approximately 2.4 trillion boe)[5].

Although the UK Government is committed to a lower carbon future[6], it recognises the importance of security of supply in relation to its energy policy during the transitional period i.e. within the context of moving towards a low-carbon economy[7]. The economic extraction of remaining UK oil and gas reserves, to avoid over-reliance on imports and excessive movement in the price of hydrocarbons, is a key element in ensuring security of supply. This has led to, among other things, the UK Government licensing acreage in the challenging and as yet unexplored deep waters west of Shetland.

UK legislation relating to both onshore and offshore licences provides that all rights of "searching and boring for and getting" petroleum are vested in the Crown[8]. The Secretary of State for Energy and Climate Change (the **Secretary of State**) is empowered, on behalf of the Crown, to grant licences to such persons and on such terms and conditions as he thinks fit.[9] The legislative structure giving discretion to the Secretary of State in this manner has remained unchanged throughout the active life of the oil and gas industry in the UK, and certainly in relation to the UKCS. Although this has led to some historical complexity, it has also allowed the licensing regime to adapt quickly to commercial change.

Ongoing economic extraction will require both exploration of new areas and further development of existing fields by employing new and more efficient technologies. While the UK Government recognises that the scope of future UK activity will be dictated by "geological inheritance" (that is, the amount and accessibility of oil and gas remaining) and global oil prices, it is conscious of the need to present flexible, attractive and predictable regulatory and fiscal regimes to encourage new investment from existing and potential participants, for example, in onshore unconventional hydrocarbon reserves.

This chapter presents an overview of the main regulatory requirements for investment, focusing on the UK offshore conventional and UK onshore unconventional oil and gas sectors.

OFFSHORE – SEAWARD LICENCES

Types of licences

There are currently four types of Seaward Licences allowing for intrusive exploration and production of licence areas (known as "blocks"). There is also one type of offshore licence allowing for non-intrusive exploration of areas not currently covered by any

5 See: http://www.bgs.ac.uk/shalegas/#ad-image-0

6 See: http://webarchive.nationalarchives.gov.uk/20100509134746/http:/www.decc.gov.uk/en/content/cms/publications/lc_trans_plan/lc_trans_plan.aspx for a copy of the UK Low Carbon Transition Plan.

7 See paragraph 2 of the Government's response dated 19 October 2009 to the House of Common's Energy and Climate Change Committee's first Report of Session 2008-09, *UK offshore oil and gas*, HC 341-I, published 17 June 2009 at: http://www.publications.parliament.uk/pa/cm200809/cmselect/cmenergy/1010/101002.htm

8 Section 2(1) Petroleum Act 1998. The "Crown" is an imprecise concept but in this context means the UK State. http://www.legislation.gov.uk/ukpga/1998/17/section/2

9 Sections 3(1) and (3) Petroleum Act 1998.

other production licence. However, for the purposes of this article we are concentrating on Seaward Production Licences, just touching on Seaward Exploration Licences further below.

Seaward Production Licences are split into three successive periods, known as "terms", the duration of which depends on the type of licence. During each term the licensee is required to carry out its activities pursuant to "Minimum Work Programmes" that must be pre-agreed with DECC. The initial term usually involves exploration of the relevant licence area, including obtaining seismic data and drilling or another similarly substantive activity. If the Minimum Work Programme for the first term has been completed and the prescribed proportion of the licence area relinquished (i.e. handed back to the UK Government, see column 3 below), the licence may continue into the second term. If during the second term a commercial discovery has been made and a development plan approved for it, and provided that all areas not included in the development plan have been relinquished, the licence will normally continue into its (extended) third term that is intended for the production phase.

The main features of the four types of Seaward Production Licences are set out in Table 3.4.1 below:

Table 3.4.1 Main features of the four types of Seaward Production Licences

1. Licence	**2. Duration of Term**			**3. Relinquishment**	**4. Comments**
	1	**2**	**3**		
Traditional Licence	4	4	18	50% (term 1)	Most common form of licence. In use since 1960s. Competence of licensee(s) proved before grant.
Promote Licence	4	4	18	50% (term 1)	Aimed at small and start-up companies. Applicants awarded licence before proving their competence within 2 years of the start of the licence.

1. Licence	2. Duration of Term 1	2	3	3. Relinquishment	4. Comments
					Annual rental rate (see below) reduced by 90% in first two years.
Six-Year Frontier Licence	6	6	18	75% (3 years) then 50% of remainder (term 1)	Extended first term allows extensive exploration in large areas with numerous potential prospects. Competence of licensee(s) proved before grant.
Nine-Year Frontier Licence then	9	6	18	75% (3 years) then 50% of remainder (term 1)	Designed for harsh areas such as West of Scotland. Requires "drill or drop[10]" decision after six years and extensive seismic acquisition. Competence of licensee(s) proved before grant.

On all licences, licensees are required to pay an annual rental rate based on the area covered by the licence (per square kilometre). The rate increases over time as the field moves towards production, which provides an incentive for licensees to relinquish unused or unexplored areas.

Seaward Exploration Licences

Companies which do not intend to drill for or produce oil and gas can apply for a Seaward Exploration Licence, which will allow them to carry out non-intrusive exploration in any acreage not covered by a Seaward Production Licence at any particular time. Seaward Exploration Licences are aimed primarily at companies which collect seismic data for sale. Seaward Exploration Licence holders are able to explore acreage covered by Seaward Production Licences with the consent of the Production Licence holders.

10 A "drill or drop" licence requires a licensee to commence operations by a specific date or to surrender the licence.

Model Clauses

The standard terms applicable to petroleum licences, known as "Model Clauses", are set out in secondary legislation made under the Petroleum Act 1998 (the **Petroleum Act**) and incorporated (historically by reference but now set out in full) into each licence. The Model Clauses which apply to a licence are those that were in effect on the date of the grant of the licence (so the terms of a licence do not change during its term by amendments to the underlying legislation).

There is one set of Model Clauses for all four types of Seaward Production Licences[11], and one set for Seaward Exploration Licences[12].

Licence application process

The majority of Seaward Production Licences are awarded through competitive licensing rounds. Applications are invited on an annual basis and the latest round (the 27th Seaward Licensing Round) closed on 1 May 2012[13]. Very few companies are willing or able to take on the entire risk and expense of being the sole licensee on a Seaward Production Licence, so companies often bid for licences together as a group (the bid is usually coordinated by the intended operator (see below)). Regardless of whether applications are made on an individual or group basis, all licensees share joint and several liability vis-à-vis the UK Government for all operations under a licence. That is to say that the Government may pursue each licensee for the total cost of any liability that may arise from such operations.

From time to time, DECC will also consider "Out of Round" applications for Seaward Production Licences. A company wishing to apply for a licence "Out of Round" must make submissions to DECC, persuading it to invite such an application. Such applications are only considered in situations where there is some urgency for a company to acquire a licence and where there is little chance that there would be any competition for it, for example where the only company that would have a genuine interest in acquiring a licence would be the licensee of an adjoining licence.

"Out of Round" applications for Seaward Exploration Licences can be made at any time.

Acquisition of licence interests

Parties can also acquire interests in Seaward Production Licences by buying an undivided percentage interest in the licence from an existing licensee.

Companies acting together on a Seaward Production Licence usually do so by way of an unincorporated joint venture pursuant to a joint operating agreement

11 The Petroleum Licensing (Production) (Seaward Areas) Regulations 2008 (SI 2008/225)

12 The Petroleum Licensing (Exploration and Production) (Seaward and Landward Areas) Regulations 2004 (SI 2004/352)

13 See: https://www.gov.uk/oil-and-gas-licensing-rounds#timing-of-the-28th-seaward-licensing-round DECC declared that it may publish, in January 2014, a notice in the Official Journal of the European Union inviting applications under the 28th Seaward Licensing Round.

(**JOA**). The JOA will specify the undivided percentage interest that each party has in the licence and will regulate the relationship between the relevant parties[14]. Subject to consent from DECC, each party is entitled to assign part or all of its interest to a third party, which provides opportunities for new parties to enter the licence agreement. Interests may be sold at every stage of the life of a licence, which allows incoming companies to assess the appropriate level of risk.

DECC regards a large volume of transfers of licence interests as a positive stimulus, both to enable new parties to enter the market and to allow existing participants to realign their interests. The offshore oil and gas operators have, in conjunction with DECC, taken steps to facilitate licence transfers. Standard transfer documents such as the Master Deed[15] and the Approved Model Deed of Assignment[16] are aimed at cutting costs of external advisors and providing transferors and transferees with certainty. DECC expects, however, that companies will acquire their licence interests for the purposes of development and does not intend that they become tradable assets.[17]

Competencies

Given the different types of operations which are necessary to fully exploit the remaining UKCS reserves, DECC is keen for a wide range of companies to participate in UKCS activities. There are, however, minimum criteria for participants (whether applying for a licence or acquiring a licence interest by way of assignment) to ensure that they are financially and technically capable of operating in the UKCS, and to ensure that the UK can benefit from any resulting tax revenue.

(a) Financial capacity

All companies seeking to be included on a licence must demonstrate that they have sufficient financial capacity to meet the actual costs which may reasonably be expected to arise under a licence (although note that for a Promote Licence, the requirement on the grant of the licence is to show financial viability (a lower threshold) only – financial capacity need only be demonstrated within two years of the start of the licence (see Table 3.4.1 above)).

The level of financial capacity required is not prescribed and will depend on a number of factors. DECC's primary concern is that the presence of a particular

14 It is worth mentioning that under English law an undivided percentage interest in a JOA is considered to be held by the relevant party as a "tenant in common", which, as a land law concept, differs from a contractual share in a joint venture (JV).
15 The Master Deed provides a voluntary mechanism for licensees to transfer licence interests on pro-forma terms and without the need to collect signatures from all licensees on all transfer documents.
See: http://www.masterdeed.com/masterdeed.cfm for further details.
16 See: https://www.gov.uk/government/uploads/system/uploads/attachment_data/file/15109/licguideapp4-1.doc
17 Applications for approval of licence assignment can now be made to DECC through its new e-licence administration system (PEARS: The Petroleum E-Licensing Assignment and Relinquishments System).

licensee will not prevent or delay work being carried out pursuant to a licence.

The evidence required for a particular licensee will depend entirely on its funding strategy, and the net worth of larger companies may be sufficient in itself to demonstrate financial capacity. Where the potential licensee is small, any larger parent company with significant assets will be required to provide a standard form parent company guarantee.

(b) Technical capacity

One of the parties to a JOA must be designated as the operator under the licence, whose role it will be to exercise day-to-day control of the exploration or production activities under the licence. DECC requires that as well as demonstrating financial capacity, the party acting as operator also needs to demonstrate the necessary technical capacity to carry out the role on behalf of the other participants. DECC will review the track record of potential operators, including in other jurisdictions, in deciding whether a particular company is a suitable operator[18].

Each other licensee must demonstrate the technical capacity that will enable it to exercise responsible oversight of operations (through decisions made under the JOA), although this standard is lower than that required of the operator.

(c) Environmental capacity

Licensees are also required to show environmental competence in relation to their proposed operations through detailed submissions to DECC in relation to, among other things, arrangements for pollution liability and environmental management. The timing of such submissions depends in each case on the type of licence and stage of development of the field.

Oil and gas operators are subject to extensive environmental regulation[19]. Following the major oil spill caused by the explosion of BP's Deepwater Horizon rig in the Gulf of Mexico, the UK Government announced a doubling of annual environmental rig inspections and a further review of deep water procedures prior to the commencement of deep water drilling west of Shetland[20].

The UK has also set up an Oil Spill Prevention and Response Advisory Group to assess the findings of the US investigation into the Gulf of Mexico spill, which provided two interim reports followed by a final report in September 2011[21]. Following publication of the OSPRAG Technical Review Group Interim Report, the UK Health and Safety Executive has written to all offshore duty holders to ensure that the lessons from the Deepwater Horizon accident are being fully considered by the UK industry[22]. Although the UKCS has a good safety record and robust

18 This will be done through PEARS.

19 See: https://www.gov.uk/oil-and-gas-offshore-environmental-legislation

20 See: http://www.publications.parliament.uk/pa/cm201011/cmhansrd/cm100614/debtext/100614-0008.htm

21 See: http://www.oilandgasuk.co.uk/knowledgecentre/Progressreports.cfm

22 See: http://www.hse.gov.uk/offshore/deepwater.htm

regulation (largely introduced in response to the Piper Alpha disaster in 1988), it is possible that further regulation may result from the recent Gulf of Mexico incident. Already, contingency plans have been strengthened and existing forums made permanent in an effort to drive the industry on to further improvements.

The EU Commission has also taken steps by adopting a Directive on safety in offshore oil and gas operations in June 2013[23] in an effort to set an EU-wide minimum standard in health and safety and environmental protection in the offshore oil and gas industry. The Directive addresses eight main issues, including obligatory ex ante emergency planning, which "operators" of offshore installations will have to comply with in order to commence and continue operations.

(d) Corporate capacity

All companies with interests in the UKCS must have a place of business within the UK, which means (i) it is a UK registered company, or (ii) it is a UK registered branch of a foreign company, or (iii) it has a staffed presence in the UK[24].

Licensees in producing fields must have a staffed presence in the UK or be a UK registered company. Operators must also demonstrate that they have sufficient proximity to the licence area to adequately control operations.

Decommissioning

The UK Government is required, under international law[25], to remove all offshore installations or structures on the UKCS which are abandoned or disused in accordance with generally accepted international standards[26]. The UK Government is permitted some discretion as to whether installations are removed in their entirety, but OSPAR Decision 98/3[27] clarified that derogations from the basic principle would be limited to concrete installations, concrete anchor bases and the footings of large steel installations that are heavier than 10,000 tonnes, or other exceptional cases. The categories of disused offshore installations which attract such derogations are to be reviewed in 2013[28].

These obligations rest with the UK Government, which passes them on to UKCS licensees through Part IV of the Petroleum Act. The Petroleum Act empowers the Secretary of State, by written notice, to demand an "abandonment programme"[29] for

23 See: http://ec.europa.eu/energy/oil/offshore/standards_en.htm

24 See: https://www.gov.uk/oil-and-gas-petroleum-licensing-guidance

25 Arts. 60(3) and 80 of the UN Law of the Sea Convention 1982 21 I.L.M. 1261 (UNCLOS) www.un.org/depts/los/convention_agreements/texts/unclos/unclos_e.pdf and the Oslo and Paris Convention for the Protection of the Marine Environment of the North East Atlantic 1992 (OSPAR)

26 The standards adopted are the draft Guidelines and Standards for the Removal of Offshore Installations and Structures on the Continental Shelf and in the Exclusive Economic Zone, as adopted by the Assembly of the International Maritime Organisation on 19 October 1989. See: http://www.imo.org/blast/mainframe.asp?topic_id=1026

27 A decision of the signatories (including the UK) to OSPAR

28 See: https://www.gov.uk/government/uploads/system/uploads/attachment_data/file/42782/1471-consultation-oil-gas-installation-charges.pdf

each offshore installation setting out the measures to be taken to decommission an installation, along with projected costs and timing and any continuing maintenance that may be necessary[30]. The notice can be served on a number of parties, including the operator of the installation, licensees of the area in which the installation is located, parties to the JOA or parties with any other interest in the installation, and associates of any of the above[31].

In practice, DECC usually serves this notice on the licensees shortly after grant of the licence, requesting an abandonment programme at a time to be determined by it at a later date. Where licensees change through the life of the licence, the Secretary of State reserves the discretionary right to withdraw this notice, although such discretion will not be exercised where DECC judges that any remaining licence holders would be unacceptably weakened by the departure of a company from the group of licensees.

Once approved, all parties who submitted the abandonment programme bear joint and several liability for carrying it out, as mentioned above. If the parties fail to do so, the Secretary of State can himself arrange for abandonment work to be carried out and recover the cost (plus interest) from the defaulting parties. The Secretary of State also has the power, whether before or after approval of the abandonment programme, to take such security as is necessary to ensure that sufficient funds are available[32].

Parties to a JOA are understandably concerned that all other parties have made financial provision for what can be fairly onerous obligations. It is therefore common practice for parties to enter into a decommissioning security agreement, under which parties make regular payments to a separate trust fund (protected from creditors as far as possible) as security for future decommissioning costs[33].

Taxation

Taxation of offshore oil and gas activities is complex and specialist advice should be taken prior to any investment. This complexity is derived largely from successive governments seeking to find a balance between providing financial incentives for exploration and development while ensuring the UK economy as a whole derives significant benefit from the country's natural resources.

Further details of applicable rates and reliefs can be found on HMRC's website[34].

29 The term "abandonment" is used interchangeably with "decommissioning" in this context, although the latter is the preferred term, as stipulated by the Guidance Notes to the Decommissioning of Offshore Oil and Gas Installations and Pipelines under the Petroleum Act 2008.

30 Section 29 Petroleum Act 1998

31 Section 30(1) Petroleum Act 1998, as amended by the Energy Act 2008.

32 See: https://www.gov.uk/government/uploads/system/uploads/attachment_data/file/69754/Guidance_Notes_v6_07.01.2013.pdf

33 See: https://www.gov.uk/oil-and-gas-decommissioning-of-offshore-installations-and-pipelines for examples of approved decommissioning programmes

ONSHORE – LANDWARD LICENCES

Types of Licence

Petroleum Exploration and Development Licence (**PEDL**) is the full name of the UK Landward Production Licence. If the operator of a PEDL wants to shoot a seismic survey near the boundary of its existing licence area, and to the extent that that will require the operation of survey equipment outside that area, the operator can apply for a Supplementary Seismic Survey Licence.

A PEDL is similar to the traditional Seaward Production Licence (although for historical and practical reasons there are many differences in detail which, for the purposes of this article, we will ignore). Like with a Seaward Production Licence, applicants must prove technical, financial and corporate competence as well as awareness of environmental issues before an offer of a PEDL will be made. The rules concerning application for and assignment applicable to Seaward Production Licences also apply to PEDLs.

Once granted/acquired, PEDLs confer a similar right to search for, bore for and get hydrocarbons, but, contrary to Seaward Production Licences, PEDLs do not confer any exemption from other legal/regulatory requirements such as any need to gain access rights from a private landowner, health and safety regulations and planning permission from relevant local authorities, which must be obtained independently[35]. Decommissioning will also be dealt with as part of the relevant planning regime rather than through DECC.

As mentioned above, the onshore oil and gas industry has been operating in the UK for well over 100 years. There are currently some 28 onshore oil fields and 10 onshore gas fields in production in the UK; all of them from conventional hydrocarbon sources. However, this type of onshore production currently only contributes approximately 1.5% of overall UK oil and gas production and increasingly the attention is focused on unconventional petroleum sources.

Onshore shale gas exploration and production

Shale gas production has been of increasing importance in the US for some years but exploration only just started in the UK. In 2008, the 13th Round of Onshore Licensing resulted in the award of several blocks for shale gas exploration, though bids were often based on a quest for conventional and unconventional prospects as the regulatory regime was identical for both.

Cuadrilla Resources' Preese Hall No. 1 well drilled in 2010 was the first exploration well drilled to specifically test for UK shale gas. However, all operations on that licence had to be suspended in May 2011, pending the investigation of two seismic tremors experienced in the area during initial drilling operations.

35 See: http://www.gove.uk/oil-and-gas-petroleum-licensing-guidance

This incident and the fact that the use of those drilling and fracturing techniques that led to the shale gas renaissance in the US is now being extended to the extraction of oil from shale, led DECC to commission a thorough review of the suitability of the current UK regulatory regime applicable to onshore petroleum exploration and production from unconventional sources.

In light of the recommendations of a panel of independent experts, comments received in response to a public consultation, and the recommendations of an authoritative review of the scientific and engineering evidence on shale gas extraction made by the UK's science and engineering academies, the Royal Society and the Royal Academy of Engineering, the Secretary of State announced the introduction of new regulatory requirements to ensure that any risk of increased seismic tremors by such operations can be effectively mitigated[36].

Subject to these new requirements, in December 2012 DECC declared that it was prepared in principle to consider new applications for consent to exploration and production activities for hydrocarbons from unconventional sources, and, as a result, the suspension of Cuadrilla's operations near Preese Hall was also lifted.

The new controls do not remove any of the existing regulatory controls and requirements but were introduced to supplement the current regulation of onshore oil and gas (including from unconventional sources) exploration. The controls principally relate to the management by operators of potential seismic activity triggered by the specific methods employed in shale oil and gas exploration activities.

Accordingly, operators have to, amongst other things, more carefully review available information on geological faults in the relevant area and monitor background seismicity before operations commence as well as in real time during the life of such operations. These operations will be subject to a "traffic light" regime so that operations can be quickly paused and data reviewed if unusual levels of seismic activity are observed. Operators will also have to submit a "fracking plan" before consent can be given by DECC to any such activities[37].

DECC also announced the establishment of a new Office of Unconventional Gas and Oil to maintain and strengthen the coordination between the regulatory bodies currently involved in overseeing activities in this area, this mainly being DECC, the Environment Agency and the UK Health and Safety Executive[38].

CONCLUSION

Although being considered mature, the UK oil and gas sector still offers a wide range of investment opportunities. The experience gained during the last few

36 See: https://www.gov.uk/oil-and-gas-onshore-exploration-and-production#resumption-of-shale-gas-exploration

37 See: https://www.gov.uk/government/news/new-controls-announced-for-shale-gas-exploration

38 See: https://www.gov.uk/government/policy-teams/office-of-unconventional-gas-and-oil-ougo

decades of oil and gas exploration and production in the UK has given it a dependable regulatory system and a responsive and efficient regulator. The UK Government's stated aim[39] to ensure security of supply through economic extraction of remaining reserves should give confidence to new and existing participants that the environment for further investment will remain favourable for the remaining life of the resource. Interested investors are encouraged to consult their advisers and DECC for further information.

39 See: https://www.gov.uk/government/uploads/system/uploads/attachment_data/file/65643/7101-energy-security-strategy.pdf

3.4 ISSUES FOR INVESTORS IN THE UK OFFSHORE OIL AND GAS SECTOR: LNG, GAS STORAGE AND ACCESS TO INFRASTRUCTURE

Heike Trischmann, Watson, Farley & Williams LLP

INTRODUCTION

Total gas demand in the UK in 2010 reached 1,093TWh, which represented an 8.4% increase compared to 2009. Gas consumption in the UK in 2010 was split roughly equally in thirds between electricity generation (371TWh), domestic consumption (390TWh) and the remainder (332TWh) being used by a combination of (energy) industry/services. That gas demand was satisfied by a mixture of domestic gas production and imports: gas imports to the UK were up 29% to 590TWh, and North Sea gas production was down 4% to 664TWh when compared to 2009.

Until 2004 the UK was a net exporter of gas, with production peaking in 2000 at 1260TWh, since then production has been declining at a rate of around 6% each year. At the same time, UK gas demand is steadily increasing each year, forcing the UK to import more and more of the gas it uses. Some reports suggest that the UK will be importing 80% of its gas needs by 2020[1].

Accordingly, liquefied natural gas (LNG) and piped gas imports became the

1 See: http://www.europeanoilandgas.co.uk/article-page.php?contentid=11530&issueid=352 Although total gas demand decreased by almost a fifth in 2011, dropping from 1,093 TWh to 906 TWh, the reasons (mainly the mild weather in that year and a reduction of the use of gas for power generation due to the economic downturn and high gas prices in comparison to coal) are considered temporary in nature and the general trend of increased gas demand to continue in the future.

major sources of gas to fill the growing gap between demand and the UK's domestic supply capabilities. LNG's share of total gas imports rose from 25% in 2009 to 35% in 2010 and 47% in 2011[2]. In 2010, most of the imported gas came in the form of LNG into the three existing UK onshore terminals[3] and the offshore import terminal at Teesside[4] as well as through the Langeled pipeline from Norway[5], the Interconnector[6] from Belgium and the BBL[7] from The Netherlands. However, in September 2010, LNG imports into the UK exceeded pipeline imports for the first time[8]. LNG was mainly imported from Qatar, Trinidad and Algeria. In 2011, Qatar accounted for over 80% of LNG imports[9].

Concerns about security of energy supply mean that the UK Government has to focus on a coherent legal framework to attract the necessary investment in increased gas import and storage and associated infrastructure. However, while the regulatory regime regarding such activities and infrastructure onshore is well developed in the UK, the regime concerning offshore activities and infrastructure was, until recently, mostly targeted at oil and gas exploration and production and therefore not appropriate to cover storage and gas importation.

This chapter focuses on the recent changes to the UK regulatory framework regarding offshore energy activities, including their licensing requirements, decommissioning and third party access to the relevant infrastructure. It does not cover the various environmental consents that also need to be obtained.

THE ENERGY ACT 2008 (THE ACT)

The provisions of the Act apply to England and Wales, Scotland and, for most parts, to Northern Ireland.

Activities covered by the Act

The Act covers three main activities: (i) offshore LNG regasification and

2 See: https://www.gov.uk/government/uploads/system/uploads/attachment_data/file/65881/5949-dukes-2012-exc-cover.pdf

3 The 3 terminals are the LNG import terminal at the Isle of Grain in Kent (total annual import capacity of 118.8TWh), the South Hook LNG import terminal (total capacity of 125.4TWh) and the Dragon LNG terminal (total annual capacity 66Twh) both of which are located at Milford Haven, South Wales. The South Hook and Dragon LNG terminals together are capable of supplying up to 30% of the UK's current gas requirements.

4 The Teesside Gasport has a peak unloading capacity of 0.187TWh/day using the Energy Bridge floating regasification technology.

5 The Langeled pipeline is a forward flow gas pipeline only with an annual capacity of 280.5TWh which represents 20% of Britain's current peak gas demand.

6 The Interconnector is a forward flow and reverse flow gas pipeline between Bacton in the UK and Zeebrugge in Belgium with an export capacity from the UK of 220TWh per annum and an import capacity into the UK of 280.5TWh per annum.

7 The Balgzand Bacton Line (BBL) is a forward and non-physical interruptible reverse flow gas pipeline between Balgzand in The Netherlands and Bacton in the UK with an annual import capacity of 211.2TWh.

8 See: https://www.gov.uk/government/uploads/system/uploads/attachment_data/file/65800/5954-dukes-2012-chapter-4-gas.pdf

9 See http://www.eia.gov/todayinenergy/detail.cfm?id=6770

unloading, (ii) offshore gas storage, and (iii) offshore carbon capture and storage (**CCS**), each of which the UK Government expects will increase in importance over time in ensuring security of energy supply and at the same time reducing carbon emissions.

Each activity and its importance is briefly explained below.

(a) Offshore gas storage

Traditionally, gas is stored in depleted or near depleted oil and gas fields, salt caverns and aquifers as well as LNG peak shaving facilities. Gas storage provides obvious benefits: gas can be injected (or liquefied) during periods of low demand, when the gas is cheap, and can be withdrawn during periods of high demand when the gas is more expensive. The UK currently has approximately 44TWh of onshore (including LNG peak shaving) and offshore gas storage capacity, which approximates 14 days' worth of gas supply at average winter gas demand rates. By contrast, Germany has 77 and France 91 days' worth of strategic gas storage.

By 2021, UK gas storage capacity is set to increase almost five-fold, to 209TWh. More than three-quarters of this increase will be achieved by more cost-effective gas storage in depleted/near depleted oil and gas fields[10], most of which will be located offshore on the UK Continental Shelf (**UKCS**).

(b) Offshore LNG regasification and unloading

The advantages of Floating Storage and Regasification Units (**FSRUs**) over conventional onshore LNG regasification terminals include their short implementation time (18 to 24 months), cost-effectiveness and reduced upfront capital requirements, and enhanced delivery flexibility. Using FSRUs, LNG can be loaded conventionally at LNG liquefaction plants and then either (i) shipped to an offshore unloading facility (such as the Teesside Gasport) where it is regasified onboard the unit and the regasified LNG (mostly methane) delivered through a high pressure gas connection to, for example, a subsea buoy moored in the hull of the unit or (ii) discharged as a liquid at any conventional onshore LNG receiving terminal.

(c) Carbon Capture and Storage

Gas is the predominant fuel used for power generation in the UK: 44.2% of electricity generated in the period from 1 April 2010 to 31 March 2011 was generated by gas-fired power plants. The other energy sources are coal, which accounted for 28.9%, nuclear 17.3% and renewables 7.9% of total UK electricity production during the same period.[11] However in 2012, power generation from

10 See: http://www.gie.eu.com/download/maps/GSE_STOR_MAPDATA_MAY2012_UPDATED.xls
11 See: http://www.decc.gov.uk/en/content/cms/statistics/energy_stats/source/total/total.aspx

gas was down by 32.1% (or 47 TWh), to its lowest level since 1996. This was mainly due to high gas prices in comparison to coal. Power generation from coal was therefore up by 31.5 %(or 34 TWh)[12].

Given these trends and the fact that the UK has committed to at least an 80% cut in greenhouse gas emissions by 2050 against a 1990 baseline, CCS is seen both domestically in the UK and internationally as a cornerstone method of reducing greenhouse gas emissions from the continued use of fossil fuels, particularly the use of coal in power generation. In March 2012, Günther Oettinger (Head of Energy of the European Commission) even suggested that the European Union should consider making mandatory the use of carbon capture technology in an effort to reach its 2050 emissions targets as this would allow further consumption of fossil fuels without worsening Europe's carbon foot print. However, this would first require the cost of the relevant technology to drop significantly (see also below)[13].

Carbon dioxide (**CO2**) storage is the final stage in the disposal of CO2 captured from power plants and industrial facilities. Currently, the industrial scale capture and subsurface geological disposal of CO2 only occurs at a very small number of natural gas production and processing operations internationally. Cost is a central issue when planning to develop viable CCS projects along with the large scale demonstration of the integrated capture, transport and storage technologies. The UK Low Carbon Transition Plan[14], and the Framework for the Development of Clean Coal[15], initiated a programme of CCS demonstration with public financial backing to 2020. It is clear, therefore, that the role of the UK Government (and the European Union[16], see below) in supporting the industrial scale demonstration of CCS is essential.

The UK Government is committed to the construction of a CCS demonstration plant in the UK by 2014 and in May 2011 submitted seven projects to the European Investment Bank (EIB) for consideration in the EU's New Entrant Reserve (NER) Scheme of funding[17]. The EIB completed its technical and financial due diligence of all project proposals in early February 2012, and submitted a list of projects, ranked by their cost-per-unit performance, to the European Commission. On 12 July 2012, the Commission published a first list of candidates for award decisions,

12 See: https://www.gov.uk/government/publications/electricity-section-5-energy-trends

13 See: http://www.energia.gr/article_en.asp?art_id=25798

14 See: http://webarchive.nationalarchives.gov.uk/20121217150421/http://www.decc.gov.uk/assets/decc/white%20papers/uk%20low%20carbon%20transition%20plan%20wp09/1_20090724153238_e_@@_lowcarbontransitionplan.pdf

15 See: www.ukccsrc.ac.uk/system/files/09D606_0.pdf?

16 The CCS European Industrial Implementation Plan 2010-2012 was launched in June 2010 and aims to enable the cost competitive deployment of CCS after 2020. See: http://ec.europa.eu/energy/technology/initiatives/initiatives_en.htm

17 The NER is a fund set up to support CCS and innovative renewable energy projects across the EU. Up to 3 projects may be supported per EU Member State. See also: https://www.gov.uk/government/uploads/system/uploads/attachment_data/file/190227/130409_NER_UK_Guidance_-_DRAFT_-_FINAL.pdf.

including four CCS projects from the UK[18].

On 30 October 2012, the UK Government announced that it had also shortlisted four bidders for the next phase of the UK's CCS competition, however, the list of those shortlisted bidders did not coincide with that shortlisted by the European Commission[19]. Although the UK CCS competition was originally organised to dovetail with the EU NER Scheme, by now, the UK selection process had become out of sync with the European process and at the end of 2012, the European Commission announced that it would not fund any CCS projects in its first round of the NER Scheme, partly due to member states' funding gaps and partly due to a lack of sufficient technical advancement of the projects.

Nevertheless, on 20 March 2013 the UK Government announced the two preferred bidders in the UK CCS competition. The two projects are the Peterhead Project in Aberdeenshire, Scotland, developed by Shell UK and Scottish and Southern Energy (SSE) and the White Rose Project in Yorkshire, England, developed by Capture Power and National Grid[20]. In April 2013, the European Commission launched the second call for proposals under the NER Scheme and it is expected that the 2 shortlisted UK projects will be submitted for additional EU funding[21].

Offshore licensing regime

The Act provides for a licensing regime governing offshore gas storage and unloading of regasified LNG (natural gas consisting mainly of methane) as well as the permanent subsurface storage of CO2. The regime applies to storage and unloading within the offshore area comprising both the UK territorial waters[22], and the area extending beyond the territorial sea that has been designated under the Act[23] as a Gas Importation and Storage Zone (**GISZ**)[24].

(a) Offshore gas storage

Anyone who wants to explore or drill for or use a natural gas storage site in the UK's offshore area must hold a gas storage licence[25] issued by the Secretary of State for Energy and Climate Change (the **Secretary**). The gas storage licence will provide the framework for regulatory consent to the physical activities at the

18 See: http://ec.europa.eu/clima/funding/ner300/docs/2012071201_swd_ner300.pdf

19 See: https://www.gov.uk/government/news/short-list-for-uk-s-1bn-ccs-competition-announced

20 See: https://www.gov.uk/government/news/preferred-bidders-announced-in-uk-s-1bn-ccs-competition

21 See: http://ec.europa.eu/clima/policies/lowcarbon/ner300/index_en.htm

22 Territorial waters are defined as that part of the sea that is located within 12 nautical miles from the coast line.

23 As set out in section 1(5) of the Act. See also Gas Storage and Importation Zone (Designation of Area) Order 2009 (SI 2009/223). This is in addition to the rights granted under the Energy Act 2004 concerning the Renewable Energy Zone (REZ) in this area.

24 The GISZ includes the waters beyond the territorial sea to 200 nautical miles from the coast line.

25 See: http://www.opsi.gov.uk/si/si2009/pdf/uksi_20092813_en.pdf

relevant site[26] and the subsequent submission of a Gas Storage Development Plan (**GSDP**) for approval by the Secretary. The Secretary will assess each applicant's operating competence (technical and environmental) and financial viability. The Secretary has discretion to decide whether or not to issue a gas storage licence, and if so, to whom and on what conditions.

If the gas is stored in a depleted/near depleted offshore oil and gas reservoir, a developer will also have to apply to the Secretary for a seaward production licence[27]. This is because native gas from the relevant reservoir will co-mingle with any non-native gas injected into the reservoir for storage and will inevitably be produced from the reservoir when the gas is recovered from storage. Frequently, the developer of an offshore gas storage facility from a depleted/near depleted reservoir will be the developer of the underlying oil and gas reservoir and therefore already hold the relevant seaward production licence.

In addition, a lease from The Crown Estate[28] is required for storage activities for all offshore areas as the right to store gas in these areas is vested in the Crown by virtue of the Act. An initial Agreement for Lease will contain defined 2D geographical boundaries and will allow for exploration and appraisal activities to be undertaken within these boundaries. The grant by The Crown Estate of the actual gas storage lease is dependent on the Secretary having granted the relevant gas storage licence(s) and approved the GSDP. The gas storage lease from The Crown Estate will define the formation within which the gas may be stored, as a three-dimensional space.

The Crown Estate and the Department of Energy and Climate Change (**DECC**) endeavour to deal with the applications broadly in parallel until both are ready to issue their respective documents.

In relation to a proposed gas storage facility in a subsurface feature that is not subject to a current seaward production licence, The Crown Estate's grant of rights will be subject to compliance with competition requirements, which are likely to seek an open, transparent and potentially competitive process prior to the grant of an Agreement for Lease. However, in the case of a depleted/near depleted oil and gas reservoir that is subject to a current seaward production licence, DECC will most likely have run a competitive licensing round that is considered sufficient to avoid the need for further tender processes.

(b) Offshore unloading of regasified LNG/methane

The provisions of the Act and secondary legislation relating to offshore unloading

26 The Offshore Exploration (Petroleum, and Gas Storage and Unloading) (Model Clauses) Regulations 2009 set out the model clauses for exploration licences for gas storage (and regasified LNG unloading activities), using non-intrusive methods such as seismic data gathering and shallow drilling. The Offshore Gas Storage and Unloading (Licensing) Regulations 2009 set out the model clauses for gas storage (and unloading) licences and cover the relevant activities themselves.

27 See: https://www.gov.uk/oil-and-gas-petroleum-licensing-guidance#types-of-licence

28 The Crown Estate is a statutory body which acts on behalf of the Crown in its role as landowner within the area of the territorial sea and as owner of the sovereign rights of the UK seabed beyond the territorial waters. The Crown Estate operates as a commercial landowner under the provisions of the Crown Estate Act 1961.

activities are very similar to those relating to offshore gas storage activities. Accordingly, anyone who wants to construct and operate a regasified LNG/methane unloading platform in the UK's offshore area must hold an unloading licence[29] issued by the Secretary and an unloading lease from The Crown Estate acting in the capacity of a landlord (see before). However, unloading gas into an apparatus that is part of a submerged pipeline with no surface installation does not require such a licence.

In addition to the same conditions that need to be satisfied for a gas storage licence, the Secretary has to ensure that the offshore unloading development will not cause unacceptable conflicts with other users of the sea such as fishermen, oil and gas licensees, gas storage and CCS licensees (see below), the shipping industry, or other UK Government departments.

(c) CCS

The Act also provides a licensing regime for the permanent storage of CO2 below the seabed within the territorial waters and the GISZ[30,31].

Again, the Secretary is the licensing authority for offshore CO2 storage, except in relation to the territorial sea adjacent to Scotland for which Scottish Ministers have authority to grant the relevant licence[32]. Once any exploration activities, as may be required by the CO2 storage licence, have been completed and all other relevant Licence terms have been complied with, the licence holder may apply to the Secretary for a storage permit concerning the storage site covered by the CO2 storage licence[33,34].

As with offshore gas storage and unloading activities, the developer will need to obtain a grant of the appropriate proprietary rights from The Crown Estate. As with the other activities, The Crown Estate will award those rights through two documents: an Agreement for Lease and the CO2 storage lease itself. The Agreement for Lease for CO2 storage provides time and rights for the developer to appraise the prospective storage site and develop the detailed storage plan. The lease provides the rights to install, commission, operate and maintain storage infrastructure, and store CO2 permanently in the permitted storage site. It also provides the time for the tenant to carry out its closure, decommissioning and post closure monitoring obligations.

For storage projects involving a depleted/near depleted hydrocarbon reservoir

29 See: http://www.opsi.gov.uk/si/si2009/pdf/uksi_20092813_en.pdf
30 There is currently no framework legislation in the UK dealing with the storage of carbon dioxide onshore. Also, the provisions of the Act do not apply to CO2 being used for enhanced petroleum recovery.
31 These provisions form part of the transposition into UK law of EU Directive 2009/31/EC on the geological storage of carbon dioxide. The Storage of Carbon Dioxide (Licensing etc) Regulations 2010 (SI 2010/2221), which transpose many other requirements of the Directive, came into force on 1st October 2010 and were subsequently amended by the Storage of Carbon Dioxide (Inspections etc.) Regulations 2012 (SI 2012/461).
32 Energy Act 2008, s 18.
33 The Storage of Carbon Dioxide (Licensing etc) Regulations 2010 (SI 2010/2221)
34 Please note that there is no pro forma CO2 storage licence available yet.

that is operated under an existing seaward production licence, The Crown Estate will only grant CO2 storage rights to existing holders of that seaward production licence unless the developer of the CO2 storage project has entered into an agreement with the holder(s) of that seaward production licence which allows the development of the site in a timely manner.

The competitive selection process through which UK Government funding is being awarded to CCS demonstration projects is considered sufficient to meet the competition requirements that apply to The Crown Estate's grant of storage rights.

CABLES AND PIPELINES

If any of the developments referred to above require the laying of cables or oil and gas pipelines that will cross the UK seabed within the UK territorial waters or transit the GISZ, additional consents will be required as mineral rights or offshore wind farm developments may be affected.

Under Part 3 of the Petroleum Act 1998, a "Pipeline Works Authorisation" is required for the construction and/or use of a "pipeline" in the UK territorial sea or GISZ. The Act extended the original Petroleum Act definition of "pipeline" and now includes any pipeline and associated apparatus, as well as certain associated services.

Permission in the form of a lease or a licence is also needed from The Crown Estate as the relevant landlord to obtain the rights to lay, maintain and operate cables and pipelines on the seabed. However, The Crown Estate will only grant this once all the necessary statutory consents have been obtained from the relevant Governmental authorities. Care needs to be taken as The Crown Estate owns some, but not all, of the UK offshore areas and consents may therefore be required from the Welsh or Scottish Assembly/Parliament.

DECOMMISSIONING - PART IV PETROLEUM ACT 1998 (PART IV)

Decommissioning requirements impose significant financial obligations on those with interests in any infrastructure but particularly when such infrastructure is located offshore.

Decommissioning of offshore oil and gas installations and pipelines covered by the Part IV decommissioning regime is regulated by DECC under powers given to it by the Petroleum Act 1998, as amended by the Act. The Act extended the definition of "offshore installation" to include installations associated with the conversion, storage or unloading of gas[35] (which would include gas storage, CCS and LNG importation) as further discussed in the relevant article on this subject contained in this publication.

35 Petroleum Act 1998, Part IV, s. 44.

Accordingly, the Secretary is empowered to serve notice on a wide range of persons, which may specify the date on which a decommissioning programme for each installation or pipeline is to be submitted. The persons such notice may be served on will, in the first instance, include licensees in respect of installations and owners in respect of pipelines.

Part IV requires all offshore installations to be removed to the extent possible after the permanent cessation of the relevant operations. The decommissioning programme sets out the measures proposed to be taken in connection with the decommissioning of disused installations and/or pipelines and will describe in detail the methods employed.

Recent years have seen a significant and increasing number of seaward production licence assignments (particularly to smaller entrants) and while such transactions are generally welcome because they can extend field life and maximise economic recovery of the hydrocarbon resources, the UK Government has a duty to ensure that the taxpayer is not exposed to an unacceptable risk of default in meeting the costs associated with decommissioning. As a result, the UK Government has developed a policy to ensure that adequate security for decommissioning costs is maintained on a field-by-field basis and may require financial security to be provided at any time during the life of the installation or pipeline.

THIRD PARTY ACCESS (TPA) TO INFRASTRUCTURE

The evolution of offshore infrastructure on the UKCS has been characterised by field owners developing pipelines and processing plants for sole usage, but, as production levels started to decline, ullage (spare capacity) was progressively made available to third parties on payment of a tariff. Field-dedicated infrastructure is economically viable when fields are relatively large but become less so as fields get smaller. To ensure that new and smaller players in the UKCS can develop and bring on stream discoveries that require third party infrastructure, in 2004 industry participants adopted a Code of Practice for TPA to offshore infrastructure (the **Code**)[36].

The Code is voluntary in nature and sets out principles and best practice procedures to guide all those involved in negotiating TPA to upstream oil and gas infrastructure on the UKCS. Under the Code, companies seeking access for their hydrocarbons to such infrastructure must apply in the first instance to the owner of the infrastructure in question.

However, if by following the Code a third party is unable to agree satisfactory terms of access with the owner of the relevant offshore infrastructure, legislation[37] gives that third party the right to make an application to the Secretary to require

36 See: http://www.oilandgasuk.co.uk/publications/viewpub.cfm?frmPubID=243

37 The first and second Gas Directives (98/30/EC and 2003/55/EC) introduced provisions for TPA to pipelines, LNG importation and other essential facilities by providing a choice between negotiated and regulated TPA. The UK adopted a regime of negotiated TPA to such infrastructure by amending the Petroleum Act 1998 in respect of offshore downstream gas pipelines (section 17B). The TPA regime to submarine pipelines is administered by the Secretary. In accordance with Article 22 of the second Gas Directive 2003/55/EC, section 17A of the Petroleum Act

access, and to determine the terms on which such access is to be granted. The Energy Act 2011 strengthens the Secretary's powers in this regard by giving him the right to require, on its own initiative, from the infrastructure owner the necessary access to, and, under certain circumstances, the necessary expansion of, that infrastructure[38].

While the Code applies to offshore pipelines, processing facilities and other infrastructure, it does not apply to the actual offshore gas storage or unloading facilities, or CO2 storage facilities. Provisions concerning negotiated TPA to offshore gas storage facilities are contained within sections 17C and 17D of the Petroleum Act 1998, which follows the TPA regime applicable to onshore gas storage facilities as set out in the Gas Act 1986.

The EU's Third Energy Package[39], among other measures, introduced a mandatory regulated TPA regime to LNG import facilities. These provisions were introduced into UK law in November 2011[40] and apply to offshore (and onshore) LNG unloading facilities. It is worth pointing out that this remains the only access regime in the UK that works on a regulated rather than negotiated basis. For this reason Ofgem[41] who administers this regime has recently produced guidance notes on how it will apply this regime in practice[42].

As far as CO2 storage facilities are concerned, the Environmental Protection - Storage of Carbon Dioxide (Access to Infrastructure) Regulations 2011 extend the regime of negotiated TPA that applies to pipelines and oil and gas processing facilities, to CCS infrastructure.

CONCLUSION

The regulatory regime governing different types of UK offshore activities is complex and this chapter can only touch upon its various aspects. Investors in the sector are encouraged to obtain detailed advice.

now also provides that the Secretary may under certain circumstances grant an exemption from the requirement to offer negotiated TPA to offshore downstream gas pipelines. The right of negotiated TPA to downstream gas processing facilities is set out in section 12 of the Gas Act 1995, as amended by the Act and further amended by the Energy Act 2011. The provisions granting negotiated TPA to upstream gas processing and oil processing plants are contained in section 82 of the Energy Act 2011. The right of negotiated TPA to (offshore) upstream petroleum pipelines is also set out in section 82 of the Energy Act 2011 but rights of negotiated TPA to other (offshore) pipelines continue to be covered by section 9 of the Pipe-lines Act 1962 and section 17 of the Petroleum Act 1998, both as amended by the Energy Act 2011.

38 See Part 2, Chapter 3, sections 83 and 84 of the Energy Act 2011

39 For the purposes of this article, the relevant parts of the Third Energy Package are Gas Directive 2009/73/EC, and Gas Regulation 715/2009.

40 See: http://www.legislation.gov.uk/ukdsi/2011/9780111513965/contents

41 The Office of the Gas and Electricity Markets Authority (the regulator of the gas and electricity markets of Great Britain). See: http://www.ofgem.gov.uk/Pages/OfgemHome.aspx

42 See: http://www.ofgem.gov.uk/Markets/WhlMkts/CompandEff/Documents1/Guidance%20on%20the%20regulated%20Third%20Party%20Access%20regime%20for%20Liquefied%20Natural%20Gas%20Facilities%20in%20GB.pdf

3.5 SCIENCE PARKS AND BUSINESS INCUBATORS

Nick Hood, Carter Jonas

THE INVESTMENT RATIONALE FOR SCIENCE PARKS

In our opinion Science Parks should be considered as a separate sector within the property investment market. Factors for investors to consider include:

- consistently high occupancy rates leading to reduced void costs for investors;
- new opportunities for investors to enter the market with the pressure on public sector investment into the sector;
- tenants often willing to take long leases leading to security of income;
- technology companies perform well at different times within the wider economic cycle diversifying the risk;
- preliminary evidence that investment returns have been better than office parks over one, three and five years.

These issues and the importance of Incubators are discussed in greater detail in this chapter.

SCIENCE PARKS

The Science Park movement in the United Kingdom is now over 40 years old;

Cambridge Science Park has celebrated its 40th birthday and Herriot Watt Science Park was established when the University relocated from central Edinburgh to a green field site to the west of Edinburgh in 1971. The movement started slowly but gathered momentum in the 1980s and the United Kingdom Science Park Association was founded in 1984.

Today there are now over 100 members of UKSPA including business affiliates and the Parks vary in size and composition but all contribute to the promotion of the 'knowledge based economy' in the United Kingdom. UKSPA provides a useful definition of a Science Park as:

"A Science Park is essentially a cluster of knowledge-based businesses, where support and advice are supplied to assist in the growth of the companies. In most instances Science Parks are associated with a centre of technology such as a university or research institute."

All Science Parks will comply with some aspects of the definition but it is perhaps the human activities in the promotion of business support and interaction, coupled with the proximity and links to a centre of technology, which is the principal differentiator between a Science Park and a more conventional business park. The cluster effect is important and extends beyond the boundaries of an individual park. It is not therefore surprising that the more successful and prosperous Science Parks are located in cities with strong universities and research organisations. Edinburgh, Cambridge, Manchester and Oxford all have strong Science Parks.

Some of the important characteristics of these clusters are:

- Strong academic base in science
- Skilled workforce
- Effective research and development networks in the region
- Entrepreneurial culture
- Attractive environment so people wish to live in the area
- Good local schools
- Good local support infrastructure; access to finance, legal teams, accountants etc.

BUSINESS INCUBATORS AND INNOVATION CENTRES

Most Science Parks, but not all, will have a Business Incubator or Innovation Centre as part of their model. A Business Incubator or Innovation Centre does not necessarily need to be on a Science Park but where it is, it will often be considered a generator of tenants for the wider Science Park. The term Business Incubator,

Innovation Centre or Enterprise Centre is widely used but they vary considerably in terms of what they seek to provide and some are actually no more than managed work space.

A Science Park, a Business Incubator or Innovation Centre will provide small business suites with units of normally less than 100m2 (1,000 sq ft) on short term 'easy in easy out' agreements with common services and meeting rooms as with most business centres. Space will normally be let at market rates but there will be additional business support services provided either directly or through third party partners at often minimal or low cost to the recipient. Indeed, a good Innovation Centre will be delivering these services to a wider area so that tenants do not need to be in the Centre or even on the Park which contributes to the marketing of the Park. The Centre will interact with the local business community and regional higher education institutes and research organisations to provide a catalyst for the growth of new and early stage business opportunities in their region. This activity will often be supported by the local authority but some parks will see this activity as the pipeline for future tenants not only for the Incubator/Innovation Centre but also for the park. A good Innovation Centre or Incubator will act as a Flagship in terms of generating activity and publicity for the benefit of the wider Science Park and will usually be focused on a particular sector or sectors of the technology market place.

The majority of Incubators and Innovation Centres will provide basic workshop or office specification space, usually with good high speed internet connectivity. A few will offer more specialised space for biotechnology or other laboratory users. Some have been in response to the closure of a research organisation, such as Boots in Nottingham or Roche in Welwyn Garden City. The availability of specialised laboratory space at low or reduced cost, coupled with a skilled workforce, can provide a unique opportunity to create a new broader business base at a time when the potential job losses in the local market place is seen as a major problem.

In contrast, managed workspace will provide simple offices or workshops for small businesses without any additional management support or advice and while they may well serve a useful local need they are not Incubators or Innovation Centres. Business centres provide an additional level of service and provide active support to their tenants and seek to create a business community within the centre but will not be actively looking to promote economic activity. They are often supported by local authorities and well run centres can thrive in private ownership within a vibrant local economy but are unlikely to be actively supporting business incubation.

Incubators are often considered high risk investments given the short term nature of their agreements and the comparatively poor covenant strength of their tenants. However, they generally charge inclusive rental packages and in well managed centres can, once established, achieve consistently high occupancy rates with the opportunity to generate additional revenue from other activities such that the net rent to the investor can often match or better the income from conventionally let buildings. In twenty years the occupancy of the St John's Innovation Centre in Cambridge very rarely fell below 90% and then usually only when a larger tenant matured and moved onto new premises. If this can generate leads to the wider park, both from indirect marketing and tenants expanding, the centres can provide a positive contribution to a park.

The new business Incubator, The Exchange, at Colworth Science Park near Bedford, a joint venture between Goodman and Unilever, provides conference and catering facilities in addition to fully serviced laboratories and offices on flexible terms on this 500,000 sq ft park which specialises in food health and wellness. The Exchange is already 75% let if the current applicants complete their agreements.

There are companies running Incubators who will take a direct investment stake into the businesses in their Incubators and will be actively involved in the business. This requires a different business model and is more closely akin to investment into a business rather than a property investment and has been successful in the USA.

OWNERSHIP

The Science Park movement is now reaching maturity and should be considered an investment sector in its own right. The original Science Parks were often funded by academic institutions seeking to promote the growth of businesses utilising the technologies within academia and to foster links between academia and the wider business communities. In general, while they were not considered on strict investment criteria, they were expected to deliver a return to their promoters in the longer term. These parks are generally found close to the major universities; The Surrey Research Park or Herriot Watt would be typical examples.

The success of these first parks encouraged others into the field and the public sector saw the potential benefits in the growth in knowledge based businesses. Local authorities started to encourage Incubators and Science Parks in association with their local higher education institutes and a number of publically funded research organisations also saw the benefit of promoting businesses alongside their own research. This support was further enhanced following the creation of the regional development agencies under the Labour Government. A number of leading Science Parks are joint developments between various stakeholders including local authorities and academic institutions such as Manchester Science Parks whereas Birmingham Science Park at Aston is a local authority initiative.

Today over 50% of Science Parks have a direct investment from an academic institution and a further 20% from publically funded research organisations and over 50% also have some aspect of funding from local authorities and development agencies. In the current economic climate and the demise of Regional Development Agencies it is difficult to see significant further public sector initiatives so it is a concern that there are few investment and development companies who have taken an interest in the Science Park movement. At present only about 20% of parks are controlled by the private sector and while some of these will also have public sector funding, they are expected to provide an economic return to their investors. These investment or development companies, such as Aviva or Goodman, have appreciated the potential from Science Parks and can see that proactive management of their parks, coupled with knowledge of the sector(s) in which they are investing, can improve investment performance. Unfortunately there are too few private sector companies who understand the sector or are perhaps even aware of the opportunities it presents.

The Technology Strategy Board (TSB) as the UK's national innovation agency is rolling out a network of world leading technology and innovation centres and seven Catapult Centres have been established with two more proposed. The TSB's website states:

"The seven chief executives and boards, together with the Technology Strategy Board, will continue to support the network of Catapults in their development and their mission to ensure cross-community engagement and innovation. Each Catapult will keep information and dialogue flowing through its website, connect groups, workshops and other engagement activities. The programme will also begin community engagement in order to implement the two newly determined Catapults; Diagnostics for Stratified Medicine Catapult and Energy Systems Catapult."

Sectors

Science Parks encompass a wide variety of uses and the building specifications will reflect this. Many technology companies are engaged in computing and software for which a standard office specification is appropriate, though possibly with enhanced cooling systems for server rooms and most investment companies or developers would be entirely comfortable with the specification. At the other extreme, a fully fitted biotechnology building will have an extensive fit out, probably costing rather more than the basic shell and core building. This requires a different approach by the developer/investor who may choose to simply provide a shell and core building, leaving the occupier to fund the fit out, usually on the basis of a 20 or 25 year lease with a rent geared to a proportion of an office rent. The basic shell and core will itself potentially be more expensive than a similar shell specification for a straightforward office use due to the requirement for the capacity for additional plant and equipment which might include an extra floor just for plant.

A more creative approach by a limited number of developers has been to split the package with a basic rent related to the shell and core building and a further 'rent' related to the fit out of the laboratory where the deal will be more related to a financial package than a traditional property one. Again the package may have different elements relating to the different elements of the fit out and the potential life expectancy of the components. This may give the occupier greater flexibility to modify the fit out as requirements change over time. Churchmanor Estates Company and Aviva Investors at Chesterford Research Park near Cambridge have successfully developed laboratory buildings and in October 2013 agreed a prelet of a 60,000 sq ft building to Biofocus which is now starting on site. They completed a speculative 28,000 sq ft flexible laboratory building at the end of 2012 capable of occupation in up to sixteen separate suites and have already let or have serious interest in 50% of the space.

The strength of the tenant covenant will play an important part in the negotiations as a specialised fit out may have limited value should a tenant vacate necessitating an expensive refit before the building is capable of occupation by another company.

Technology companies operate in growth markets often with higher margins than companies in more traditional markets. They are prepared to pay a premium for the right premises in the right location with the appropriate facilities to attract and retain their employees. Company failure rates on Science Parks are reputedly lower than average but this needs substantiation.

There are a few parks where laboratories are provided for early stage businesses but these will generally be to a fairly basic specification, in terms of the fit out, with further adaptation required to meet individual needs of tenants. Babraham Research Campus in Cambridge has successfully developed Bioincubator buildings for early stage biomedical enterprises and has received Government funding to build more.

FUNDING

The majority of existing Science Parks have been established through public sector funding in various forms, often working together and including universities, local authorities, regional development agencies and research organisations. While in some instances the initiative may have been in response to economic deprivation, in others it has been to exploit the economic potential of research within the local institutes. In the latter case the private sector can be involved in supporting the initiative as development can be economically viable.

Larger property investment funds will have an exposure to 'out of town business parks' and through these are already likely to have an exposure to science based tenants. These tenants will possibly have located to an area based on the potential 'cluster effect' and parts of the London market, the M4 corridor and Cambridge are typical. The companies are looking for the right environment for their employees and their business and the criteria that make a good business park are equally valid for a science based company. Larger companies will generate their own links with academia and research organisations and will therefore look for the best premises and terms to meet their requirements within a general geographical location. Science Parks should be seeking to provide a better environment to attract these businesses through the provision of services tailored to the specific needs of technology companies.

Technology companies will tend to be in growth sectors and, in our opinion, can often operate to slightly different economic cycles to the reminder of business in a region. If so they should also be considered as a separate asset class offering an opportunity to spread risk within the property sector. However, data is required to support this contention and at present, partly due to the nature of the ownership of a significant number of the parks, this is not available. With Parks which are in private ownership, or even where funds own an individual building on a Science Park, they will be assessing the performance of their assets by reference to the performance of other assets and, in particular, other property funds and as such are likely to provide information to the most widely used benchmark, the Investment Property Databank (IPD) Index. At present there is no IPD Index covering the Science Park sector and our attempts to find sponsorship for one has not been successful.

CONCLUSION

As part of their 30th birthday celebrations UKSPA are carrying out a Science Park and Innovation Centre Study to support their assertion of their catalytic role in supporting growth in the UK economy. This should help in attracting more funding from both the public and private sectors. At present only a small number of the property investment companies are aware of the sector and the potential it offers and it is essential that Science Parks promote themselves as a complimentary sector capable of offering competitive returns to investors and further spreading their risk from regional offices and business parks.

PART FOUR

Operating a Business and Employment in the UK

4.1 FINANCIAL REPORTING AND ACCOUNTING: AN OVERVIEW

Stephen Brown, Mazars

INTRODUCTION

All limited and unlimited companies in the UK, regardless of whether they are trading or not, are required to keep accounting records throughout the period. This chapter sets out the key financial reporting and accounting requirements for companies trading or investing in the UK.

GENERAL PRINCIPLES

Where formal accounts are required, in particular for limited companies, these must include:

- A trading profit and loss account;
- A balance sheet signed by the director;
- A directors' report signed by the director or the company secretary;
- Notes to the accounts;
- Cash flow statement (if applicable);
- Statement of Total Recognised Gains and Losses (if applicable);
- Group accounts (if applicable);
- An auditor's report signed by the auditor (if required).

In general, all private and public limited companies are required to send a full copy of their accounts to Companies House every year.

Once received, all accounts filed and held at Companies House are available to the general public on request. For this reason the option to file abbreviated accounts is attractive to some small companies.

Small companies are entitled to certain disclosure exemptions in relation to the accounts they must send their shareholders, and can, in addition, file abbreviated accounts with the Registrar of Companies. Medium-sized companies can also send abbreviated accounts to the Registrar but the reduction in disclosure in these accounts is negligible. They must, however, provide a full set of accounts for their shareholders. For both small and medium-sized companies, the production of abbreviated accounts is entirely voluntary.

A company filing small company abbreviated financial statements does not need to file a Directors' Report, Profit and Loss account and can include fewer notes to the financial statements.

For a company to qualify as small, at least two of the following conditions must be met:

- Turnover must be less than £6.5 million;
- Gross assets must be less than £3.26 million;
- Average number of employees must be less than 50.

A company filing medium abbreviated financial statements has a limited option to reduce disclosure but does need to include a Directors' Report, a Profit and Loss account and notes to the financial statements.

For a company to qualify as medium-sized, again, at least two of the conditions below must be met:

- Turnover must be less than £25.9 million;
- Gross assets less than £12.9 million;
- Average number of employees less than 250.

The time normally allowed for companies to deliver their accounts to Companies House is:

- 9 months from the ARD (Accounting Reference Date) for a private limited company
- 6 months from the ARD for a public limited company.

The ARD is the period-end date to which all accounts are prepared and normally covers a period of 12 months, although this can be extended to a maximum of 18 months. Filing of financial statements for a first year entity must be within 21 months of incorporation. Late delivery of accounts to Companies House will result in a late filing penalty, which is, technically, a criminal offence for which Directors can be prosecuted.

ACCOUNTING

Regulations regarding the presentation of the primary financial statements in the UK are found in several sources such as UK company law and UK and international accounting standards. Note that subsidiaries of overseas firms incorporated outside the UK are subject to the normal UK accounting practices. Branches or places of business of overseas firms have special registration procedures.

Accounting Principles

All accounts in the UK are prepared in accordance with two fundamental accounting concepts:

- Going concern – the accounts are prepared as if the company will be trading in the foreseeable future (at least 12 months from the date of signing the financial statements).
- Accruals basis – income and expenditure should relate to the period in which it occurred, not the period in which it was received/paid.

The use of historical cost values is widespread under UK GAAP (Generally Accepted Accounting Practice), although there is increased use of 'fair value' accounting as a result of convergence with International Financial Reporting Standards.

Whichever accounting policy is selected, they must be transparent and reflect industry and sector norms.

Financial Reporting

Every company is required to set out their accounts to specific standards. Currently, there are 30 FRS (Financial Reporting Standards) for companies to follow. There is a FRSSE (Financial Reporting Standard for Smaller Entities) specifically designed for small companies or groups, which basically is a single, more simple standard of financial reporting which makes it easier for smaller companies to produce their accounts.

Until relatively recently, Financial Reporting Standards were developed solely by the Accounting Standards Board (ASB). These standards, in conjunction with the requirements of UK companies legislation (principally the UK Companies Acts), helped make up what is known as UK GAAP, which gives guidance to companies and auditors on how UK accounts should be prepared to give a 'true and fair' view of the company's financial position.

However, due to increasing globalisation in the world economy, it became necessary to produce a set of International Financial Reporting Standards (IFRS) so that potential investors can compare firms on a global scale.

EU firms with securities that are publicly traded on a regulated stock exchange are required to apply EU-adopted IFRS when producing consolidated accounts. In the UK, this means any company listed on any of the markets of the London Stock Exchange. Individual subsidiary companies are not yet required to prepare financial statements under IFRS.

At present, only the types of company detailed above are required to adopt IFRS. However, even companies not required to do so can choose to adopt these new standards. A company that chooses to use IFRS to produce its accounts for one financial period cannot change back to UK standards in the following years. There are limited exceptions to this, such as if the company becomes a subsidiary of a group that uses UK standards as opposed to IFRS, in which case the company can revert back to using UK standards.

There has been an overall agreement that current UK GAAP will be updated to achieve greater convergence with international standards.

Under the proposals, UK companies will apply a new financial reporting framework, which would split UK entities into three tiers (defined by public accountability and size) for financial reporting purposes, the effective date for which is anticipated to be 1 January 2015.

As this new regime will require a full 18-month implementation process, companies should be considering the new rules from early 2013 to ensure they are suitably prepared for the transition.

AUDIT

Audits must be carried out by someone authorised to provide an audit, by:

- Being a member of a Recognised Supervisory Body (RSB); and
- Having the necessary qualifications/eligibility of that RSB to be an auditor.

An RSB can be a professional body such as the Institute of Chartered Accountants for England and Wales. UK companies are required to be audited unless they are designated as 'small' in size (and can satisfy 2 out of the three criteria), or are dormant. This 'small' exemption is subject to a number of detailed conditions which must be met in order for it to apply.

If a UK small company is part of a group of companies (UK or worldwide), the group in its entirety must meet the definition of 'small', otherwise the small UK company will be subject to an audit regardless of its individual size. There are circumstances where a parent company can guarantee the liabilities of a UK trading subsidiary and this can allow it to take advantage of an exemption from audit regardless of its size.

If a group of companies (UK or worldwide) contains a listed entity with its shares traded on a recognised stock exchange anywhere in the world, then any UK company which is part of that group will require an audit regardless of its own individual size.

Note here that exemption from the audit requirement does not exclude the company from having an audit if it so wishes.

Auditors are normally appointed in the following ways:

- They are appointed by a newly formed company, or by an existing company that requires a new auditor.
- They are reappointed by a company for which they are already existing auditors.
- They are ordered to be auditors of a firm by the Secretary of State.

This last case occurs when a company requiring an audit fails to agree to appoint an auditor.

The company's auditors are appointed/reappointed each year by either majority vote of the shareholders, or for a private company the provisions of deemed re-appointment of an existing auditor may apply. Directors have the authority to fill a vacancy that arose during the year but this will need to be later confirmed by the shareholders before the new auditor may continue in office for subsequent financial years.

Upon appointment, the auditor should send the company an engagement letter confirming their appointment as auditors, and setting out other items relating to the audit, such as the work they will carry out, confirmation of their independence and payment of audit fees.

An auditor ceases to audit a company in the following ways:

- They resign from the post of auditor of the company.
- They are removed by the company.

If an auditor resigns they must provide a written notice to the company and a statement of circumstances to the Registrar of Companies and anyone else entitled to copies of the company accounts.

If the members of a company wish to remove the existing auditor, the auditor has the right to have written circularisation to all members and the right to be seen and heard at the company's general meeting at which their removal is proposed.

4.2 BUSINESS TAXATION

Andrew Ross, Mazars

INTRODUCTION

This chapter is divided into the following parts:

- The key forms in which an overseas company could set up in the UK with a view to carrying on business.
- The basis of taxation in the UK, summarising the key taxes an investor needs to be aware of.
- Setting out the basis of calculation of taxable profits, noting the key rules on tax deductibility of expenditure and certain important tax reliefs and anti-avoidance provisions.

VEHICLES FOR DOING BUSINESS IN THE UK

There are several different vehicles that could be used when doing business in the UK, each with their own legal and commercial peculiarities. When considering the most suitable form of vehicle to use, investors would be recommended to consider such factors in addition to taking account of the differing tax treatment of each.

Representative office

It is important to distinguish between "trading in" and "trading with" the UK. An overseas person will not be subject to UK tax on profits simply because they are transacting with UK entities, even if the goods are delivered to UK locations or services are carried out within the UK.

This can be the case even if the overseas investor has set up an office within the UK, although this will depend on the nature of the activities carried out by that office. If, however, those activities cross a certain line, this could result in the creation of a taxable branch or permanent establishment.

Branch/"permanent establishment"

The UK branch (referred to for tax purposes as a "permanent establishment" or "PE") of a foreign company will be subject to tax in the UK on profits that are attributable to the branch. UK domestic legislation gives a definition of a PE which is broadly similar to that contained in many double tax treaties. Typically, a foreign company will have a UK PE if:

- it has a fixed place of business in the UK through which the business of the company is wholly or partly carried on, or
- an agent acting on behalf of the company has and habitually exercises in the UK authority to do business on behalf of the company (except where that agent is of independent status acting in the ordinary course of his business).

There are exceptions to this where, for example, the fixed place of business is for the storage of goods or purely for purchasing or information-gathering functions. In such a situation, the foreign company may not have a UK taxable presence.

Subsidiary

A UK incorporated subsidiary will be subject to UK tax on all of its trading profits, wherever those profits are earned (subject to the possibility of claiming an exemption from UK tax for profits within overseas branches).

A non-UK incorporated company can also be treated as UK tax resident (and so taxable in the UK on its worldwide profits) if its "central management and control" are located in the UK. Therefore care needs to be taken where a non-UK company is operating in the UK to ensure that the company as a whole does not become UK tax resident.

Branch v subsidiary

From a UK tax point of view, there is generally little difference in the basis of taxation between a branch and a subsidiary. UK corporation tax is charged at the same rates on branch or subsidiary profits and no withholding tax is charged on the remittance of funds by a branch to its head office or on dividends paid to its parent company.

Therefore, a decision on the most appropriate form will generally need to be based on commercial & legal factors and the non-UK tax implications.

One potential tax advantage of using a UK branch (particularly in start-up ventures) is that tax losses of the branch may (depending on the law of the relevant overseas country) be available to offset non-UK profits arising in the same foreign company. At the same time, those tax losses can also be carried forward to shelter future profits of the branch from UK tax (although the flip-side of this is that there may be less double tax relief to shelter those same future profits from tax in the overseas country).

Joint ventures

Where an investor wishes to enter into a UK joint venture-type arrangement with a 3rd party, the parties will likewise need to agree on the form of the joint venture, for example:

- Contractual joint venture: Each party (through its own legal entity) enters into a contract with a view to carrying out a business transaction or a project.
- Partnership: This is a more formal legal structure involving the carrying on of a business in common with a view to profit. Each party (again through its own legal entity) will enter into a formal partnership agreement. The basis for sharing profits will be set out in this partnership agreement.
- Company: A company is set up to carry out the joint venture business, with the joint venture parties owning shares in that company. The relationship between the joint venture parties may also be governed by a shareholders' agreement.

Again, commercial and legal considerations must be taken into account in determining the most appropriate vehicle. The tax treatment of each will also vary.

BASIS OF TAXATION

The main taxes payable in the UK may be summarised as follows.

Tax on company profits

Corporation tax is payable on the taxable profits (both income and capital) of a UK subsidiary or the UK branch of an overseas company. The rate of corporation tax is the same for both a branch and subsidiary.

Tax is calculated based on the profits of an "accounting period", which will normally coincide with the period for which the company prepares its financial statements.

There are two rates of corporation tax - the main rate and the "small profits rate".

To qualify for the small profits rate the company must be a UK-resident company with profits of less than £300,000 (the "lower limit"). There is a marginal rate when profits exceed that amount but are less than £1.5 million (the "upper limit"). However these upper and lower limits are reduced if the company has any "associated" companies at any time in the accounting period. For example, if worldwide there are 19 other associated companies (typically other members of a group), the upper and lower limits applicable to the UK company are reduced to £15,000 and £75,000 respectively (i.e. the limits are divided based on the 20 members of the group). As a result, for many groups, the small profits rate is unlikely to apply or, when it does, there is little benefit.

The current and proposed future rates of corporation tax are:

Profits arising in year from 1 April to 31 March:	2013/14	2014/15	2015/16
Main rate of corporation tax	23%	21%*	20%*
Small profits rate of corporation tax	20%	**	**

* *These rates are all enacted in Finance Act 2013*

** *small profits rate for these years yet to be announced*

In charging corporation tax on companies with year ends other than 31 March, a proportionate part of profits for an accounting period is taxed at each of the applicable rates. For example, the main rate of tax on taxable profits of a company with a 31 December 2014 year end is 22%.

From 1 April 2013 a new "Patent Box" regime was introduced giving a 10% corporation tax rate for "patent derived profits" for both new and existing patents.

For "large" companies (very broadly, being companies paying the main rate of corporation tax but subject to certain exceptions) the corporation tax liability for an accounting period is due and payable quarterly, the first instalment being seven months and 14 days after the beginning of the period (and hence estimates of the forecast tax for a particular year will need to be made for at least the first two quarterly payments). For companies not within the quarterly payment obligation, tax is due in a single payment, nine months after the end of the company's accounting period. Interest is payable to/receivable from HMRC on any under/over payment of tax.

Tax on individuals

Individuals are liable to income tax on trading profits, employment income, interest, dividends and other income and are subject to capital gains tax on chargeable gains. The rates for the tax year commencing 6 April 2013 are:

Taxable income (£)	Tax rate on income	Effective tax rate on UK/overseas dividends	Tax rate on capital gains*
up to 32,010	20%	Nil	18%
32,010 - 150,000	40%	25%	28%
over 150,000	45%	30.6%	28%

** A reduced rate of 10% is payable on the first £10m of gains made in a taxpayer's lifetime, on the disposal of qualifying business assets ("Entrepreneurs' relief").*

An individual who is trading in partnership is assessed to income tax on their share of the tax-adjusted trading profits for the accounting period of the partnership ending in the tax year. The basis of calculation of taxable trading profits is broadly the same as for a company.

The rules for the calculation of individuals' capital gains differ from the rules for companies in that "indexation allowance" (an allowance for inflation) is not available to individuals, whilst there are other reliefs available to individuals that are not available to companies (e.g. Entrepreneurs' relief).

Interest income is taxable when received. In most cases, UK interest is paid to individuals net of basic rate income tax. The gross income is taxable, with credit given against the tax liability in the tax year for the tax deducted. Where the tax liability is less than the tax deducted, the excess withholding tax is repayable.

Income tax on trading and other income that is not subject to PAYE (see below) is due in two instalments – on 31 January within the relevant tax year and 31 July following the end of the tax year.

Payroll taxes/national insurance contributions

An employer is obliged to make deductions from pay for employee income tax and employee national insurance contributions (NIC), using the "pay as you earn" (PAYE) system.

Employer NIC is an additional cost payable by the employer based on each employee's wages plus benefits in kind. The rates of employer NIC vary depending whether the employer offers a final salary pension scheme and has contracted out of the state earnings related pension scheme. The rates for the year commencing 6 April 2013 are:

Weekly earnings	Monthly earnings	Contracted in	Contracted out
Up to £144	Up to £624	Nil	Nil
£144 to £770	£624 to £3,337	13.8%	10.4%
Excess over £770	Excess over £3,337	13.8%	13.8%

The employer has to make monthly remittances to HMRC (by mandatory electronic funds transfer) of the amounts they deduct for employee income tax and NIC, along with the employer NIC.

VAT

All businesses investing or trading in the UK must register for UK VAT if they have a "business establishment" or usual place of residence in the UK. This test differs from the corporation tax tests of residence and it is therefore possible for an overseas investor to be required to register for UK VAT even though it may not have a branch that is liable to corporation tax.

VAT registered businesses are generally required to file VAT returns quarterly by way of electronic returns and therefore any VAT payable will usually be payable by not later than one month and seven days after the end of the relevant quarter. However, VAT-registered business with an annual VAT liability in excess of £2.3 million must make interim payments at the end of the second and third months of each VAT quarter as payments on account of the quarterly VAT liability. A balancing payment for the quarter is then made with the VAT return.

Stamp duty land tax ("SDLT")

SDLT is payable on the acquisition of any interest in land situated in the UK regardless of whether the acquirer is an individual, a partnership or a company or whether the acquirer is UK or non-UK resident.

The most common rate of SDLT when a capital sum is paid to acquire non-residential land or interest in such land (whether the acquisition is ownership of the land or on the grant or assignment of a lease) is 4%. Lower rates of SDLT apply if the purchase consideration is less than £500,000. Different rates of SDLT may apply to the acquisition of residential land. Caremust be taken, in particular, where residential land which was valued at more than £2 million on 1 April 2012 is to be acquired by a company (or other collective investment vehicle) since an Annual Tax on Enveloped Dwellings may also be payable.

On grant of a lease, in addition to the SDLT on any premium, the tenant is liable to pay SDLT at 1% of the net present value of the total rent payable under the lease, less a deduction of £150,000.

Stamp duty

Stamp duty, at 0.5%, is payable by the person acquiring shares or convertible loan notes of a UK registered company. There are exceptions for intra-group transfers. No duty is payable on the transfer of ownership of other assets, for example loan notes, goodwill or trade debtors. There is no duty on the issue of shares or convertible loan notes.

Withholding taxes

The UK does not impose withholding tax on dividends.

A 20% withholding tax is generally imposed on interest payments, although the rate may be reduced under an applicable double tax treaty or the EU Interest and Royalty Directive, provided that certain conditions & formalities are complied with prior to the payment of the interest.

There is no withholding from payments of interest by UK companies or to UK branches of overseas companies (which will include, in particular, UK branches of overseas banks), or on payments of interest on certain quoted loan stock (although HMRC has indicated that it is reviewing the future application of this rule). Where securities are issued at a discount, no withholding is applied on the discount element.

For royalties, a 20% income tax withholding applies, subject to lower rates in the relevant applicable double tax treaty or under the EU Interest and Royalty Directive.

Rent paid to a non-UK resident person is subject to a 20% withholding deduction, unless the landlord has met the requirements of HMRC's "non-resident landlords' scheme".

Under the construction industry scheme, there may be a withholding requirement on payments made by contractors to sub-contractors in relation to building projects.

No withholding tax is applied on service fees, technical fees or management charges.

DETERMINATION OF TAXABLE PROFITS OF A BRANCH/SUBSIDIARY

The rules for the calculation of the taxable profits of both a branch and subsidiary are essentially the same. The key issue for a branch is the extent to which profits of the relevant overseas legal entity should be allocated to the head office or the UK branch.

Taxable trading profits

The taxable result from trading is based on the profits for the year, as shown in the company's financial statements.

Costs that are not deductible for tax purposes include entertainment expenditure, fines and penalties, expenditure of a capital nature and non-specific provisions. Depreciation, amortisation and gains/losses from the disposal of fixed tangible assets are not allowed or taxed. For tax depreciation, there is a statutory relief for certain classes of assets (see capital allowances, below).

Tax relief is available on the cost of the acquisition of intangible fixed assets (for example goodwill) if acquired after 31 March 2002 from a non-connected person. The amount that is tax deductible is the charge in the profit and loss account or income statement. However, a company may instead elect to have tax relief of 4% per annum on the cost.

Remuneration paid to employees is deductible on an accruals basis providing payment to the employee is no later than nine months after the year end. Remuneration paid more than nine months after the year end is tax deductible in the period when payment is made.

Capital Allowances

Capital Allowances is the UK term for the statutory code for deducting the cost of capital expenditure from trading profits. The main class of asset that is eligible for capital allowances is plant and machinery. This includes plant within a building or structure (e.g. electrical, heating, water and air conditioning systems; lifts; escalators; sanitary ware). No allowances are given for the cost of buildings.

Eligible expenditure on plant and machinery qualifies for tax relief at one of two rates. Certain specified expenditure can obtain allowances at a rate of 8% per annum and all others at 18% per annum. For both, allowances are calculated on a reducing balance basis.

Assets in the 8% expenditure category include:

- Those with an expected life when new of more than 25 years
- Some plant within buildings
- Cars with emissions of more than 130 g/km (from 1 April 2013) of CO_2.

Up to £25,000 of a company's annual expenditure on eligible assets, other than cars or assets for leasing out, is subject to 100% tax relief in the year of purchase. This is known as the "annual investment allowance". When the company is a member of a group only one annual investment allowance is given to whole group.

Full relief is also available in the year in which it is incurred (100% tax allowances) for:

- Environmentally beneficial or energy saving plant (which includes cars with CO2 emissions of no more than 95 g/km (from 1 April 2013))
- Plant for research & developments activities
- Expenditure of up to 20 million euros on renovating empty commercial buildings until 11 April 2017.

On disposal of plant, the net sale proceeds, up to a maximum of cost, are deducted from the accumulated net pool of qualifying expenditure.

Interest and finance income and expense

In general, interest is taxed or relieved in accordance with the treatment in the company's financial statements.

Tax relief for finance expense in "large" (as defined) corporate groups may be restricted due to the "worldwide debt cap". This restriction is considered after making any transfer pricing (thin capitalisation) adjustments (on which, see below). Broadly speaking, the intention of the worldwide debt cap is that the tax deducible finance expense relieved against a group's UK profits should be no greater than the external finance expense in the consolidated results of the group. However this regime will not apply if the UK net debt is less than 75% of the group's consolidated gross debt. This is a complex area on which further advice should be sought. The rules are complex, so professional advice and guidance should be sought.

Dividends received

The UK has a comprehensive dividend received exemption which applies to dividends a UK-resident company receives from UK or non-UK companies. Various conditions must be met, although there is no minimum holding period or minimum ownership percentage.

Sale of capital assets

The taxable gain on the disposal of a capital asset is calculated as net proceeds received less the acquisition cost and costs incurred on improvements. "Indexation allowance" (an allowance for inflation) may also be given to disposals by companies. Gains on certain assets can also be deferred by reinvesting the proceeds in replacement assets ("rollover relief").

The UK has a form of participation exemption, which can exempt from tax the gain or loss on the disposal by a company of shares in a trading company or trading sub-group - the exemption is called the Substantial Shareholdings Exemption (SSE). SSE, along with the dividends received exemption, are core features that make the UK an attractive location for holding companies.

The SSE rules contain several detailed requirements and therefore professional guidance should be sought as to whether it applies, not least because a group's non-trading activities do not necessarily need to be substantial for the group not to be regarded as a "trading group" and hence not qualify for the relief. Advance clearance application can be made to HMRC where there is uncertainty as to whether SSE applies to a particular disposal.

Transfers of capital assets (including intangibles) between UK members of a group take place on a tax neutral basis regardless of the value of the asset or the price paid (see Chapter 4.3). However, if the transferee subsequently leaves the group still holding the asset within six years of the transfer, this can create a "de-grouping" tax charge based on a deemed disposal (and re-acquisition) of the asset at its market value at the date of the intra-group transfer.

Reliefs may apply to the transfer of a trading business to a company (a business incorporation) and to corporate acquisitions effected by a share-for-share exchange.

Losses

A company may claim to set a trading loss against all of its taxable profits within the same accounting period, and against the profits of the immediate preceding period, providing the company was carrying on the same trade in the previous period. Alternatively, or in addition, it may transfer some or all of a trading tax loss to another UK member, or UK members of a 75% group, for use against the other company/companies' profits within the same accounting period only. This is known as "group relief".

A trading loss not applied to the current or previous accounting period is carried forward and used against profits of the same trade arising in later periods, without time limit.

Tax relief for a non-trading company's finance expense in excess of the company's profits for an accounting period may be claimed against financial profits of the previous year. Alternatively, this expense can pass to another UK group member for use against that member's profits, in the same accounting period under the "group relief" provisions. Any unrelieved finance expense is carried forward, without time limit, to be used against future non-trading profits of the company.

Capital losses are set against gains of the company for the same period, with any excess being carried forward, without time limit, for use against net gains of subsequent periods.

There are several anti-avoidance provisions which may deny the carry forward of all types of tax losses when a group purchases a company with existing tax losses, and the main reason for the acquisition is to access these tax losses.

Research and Development Tax reliefs

Enhanced tax relief is available to companies which conduct R&D for the purposes of resolving scientific or technological uncertainty with a view to achieving an advancement in science or technology, or an appreciable improvement in existing technology.

There are two schemes of relief. One for small and medium sized companies (SME's) and one for larger companies.

An SME is broadly a company with less than 500 employees and not more than either 100m euros turnover or balance sheet total of 86m euros, taking into account certain linked and partner enterprises (e.g. group companies). SME's may claim an enhanced tax deduction of 225% of their qualifying R&D spend and, if loss making, trade in losses for a cash rebate of just under 25p in the £ of the actual qualifying spend, thereby creating an additional source of cash-flow for the company.

Large companies may claim a tax deduction of 130% of their qualifying spend and do not currently have the cash-back option. However, for accounting periods commencing on or after 1 April 2013 an "Above the Line" (ATL) credit scheme has been introduced. Under this scheme, in a large company's financial statements, the ATL credit will be recognised as a reduction in R&D expenditure in the Profit and Loss Account. For tax purposes, the ATL credit will be treated as a taxable receipt of the trade. For large companies with no corporation tax liability, or with a CT liability less than their ATL credit, the key advantage of this new scheme is that such companies can claim an immediate benefit from their R&D claim through a payable credit of 10% of qualifying R&D expenditure. ATL will operate as an alternative to the super-deduction scheme until April 2016 when the ATL scheme will become mandatory.

A UK R&D tax relief claim must be made via the company's tax return and must be made within 24 months of the accounting year end of a company.

Transfer pricing

The UK has transfer pricing rules, which substitute arm's length amounts to transactions with connected persons. These broadly are aligned to the OECD transfer pricing guidelines. The transfer pricing rules apply to both the interest rate (such that interest at a rate in excess of market value would not be deductible) and the amount of the borrowing (i.e. thin capitalisation, whereby a tax deduction will not be given for the whole of the interest on the element of debt in excess of that which would have been loaned by a 3rd party acting at arm's length).

Exemptions or reduced documentation requirements apply to small and medium sized enterprises.

There are no safe havens with regard to debt:equity ratios or interest cover ratios (e.g. EBIT:interest or EBITDA:interest). Each has to be negotiated separately with HMRC. In order to be non-discriminatory with regard to the EU, the transfer pricing rules apply to all connected party transactions, including those between UK enterprises.

The transfer pricing rules can also apply to the provision of finance by lenders who do not control (or even have no shareholding in) the borrower where those lenders are "acting together" with other persons who between them have control over the borrowing company

4.3 BUSINESS TAXATION & PLANNING

Andrew Ross, Mazars

INTRODUCTION

This chapter follows on from the overview of the UK business tax system set out in chapter 4.2 and covers various areas of UK tax planning that an investor should consider, both with a view to realising tax savings and also avoiding unnecessary tax costs.

ACQUISITION OF A BUSINESS: ASSETS v SHARES

Asset acquisitions

An asset (business) purchase could be effected using a new UK company or by a new UK branch of the overseas company. As discussed in Chapter 4.2, a UK branch of an overseas company and a UK company are subject to UK tax on profits in broadly the same way. Therefore, an overseas investor wishing to purchase a business in the form of an asset purchase will need to take into account commercial, legal and non-UK tax factors in deciding a preferred route.

One of the key non-tax advantages of an asset purchase is that any liabilities or exposures within the selling company do not automatically transfer across to the purchaser.

Share acquisitions

A company is a separate legal entity and, as such, when an investor acquires a company it is acquiring all of that company's history and liabilities. Therefore, any unknown or contingent liabilities (as well as those which the purchaser is aware of) will effectively be inherited by the purchaser. For this reason, a purchaser will normally seek to obtain from the vendor an indemnity against such liabilities, whether or not they had crystallised as at the date of the sale.

One of the first questions an investor will need to address is the vehicle to be used to make the acquisition, i.e. should the acquisition be made:

- directly by the overseas investor;
- by an intermediate holding company set up in the UK; or
- by an intermediate holding company set up in a 3rd territory.

Each investor will have their own specific fact pattern that may influence the choice and, as such, specific advice should be taken. But examples of factors that could, from a tax point of view, influence a purchaser towards one or other of these acquisition vehicles include:

- Where overseas tax rates are higher than UK rates, there could be an advantage to making the acquisition using the overseas investing company in order to benefit from any financing tax deductions in that territory.
- But where the overseas investor does not have sufficient profits to offset financing costs, a UK debt-financed acquisition vehicle may be preferable.
- If the investor wishes to create a sub-group to facilitate the cross-border expansion of the target business, it may be appropriate to set up an intermediate holding company (either in the UK or elsewhere).
- Whether the overseas territory has a favourable tax regime for the holding of shareholdings and how any local "controlled foreign company" rules may affect this.

Asset v share purchase

When acquiring shares in a company, the existing tax profile of the target company will remain and so the purchaser effectively inherits this.

From a buyer's point of view, the potential tax advantages of buying assets or shares include:

Assets

- Ability to obtain tax relief for the goodwill element of the deal price.

- Can claim capital allowances for plant & machinery and other qualifying fixed assets based on the consideration allocated under the Business Purchase Agreement rather than on the existing tax value of those assets within the target company (assuming the former is higher).
- Avoids 0.5% stamp duty (although stamp duty land tax would be payable if land is being acquired).

Shares

- Existing tax losses transfer across (but subject to anti-avoidance legislation aimed at preventing the acquisition of companies solely or mainly to enable the purchaser to benefit from these tax losses).
- If the current tax value of fixed assets is greater than the purchase price allocated to those assets, a share acquisition avoids a reduction in the amount on which capital allowances can be claimed.
- Avoids stamp duty land tax, which could be significant if there is valuable non-residential land within the target business (although there will be a 0.5% stamp duty charge on the consideration paid for the shares).
- Greater flexibility to enable the vendors to reduce or defer tax where the vendors are to retain a direct or indirect stake in the target business (e.g. by exchanging shares in the target company for new shares in the purchaser).

There will often be a conflict between the interests of the sellers and the buyers. Buyers typically prefer to purchase assets and sellers will often prefer to sell shares. See below for the tax aspects of a disposal.

Acquisition of a business: financing

The funding for an acquisition could be sourced in a number of different ways – e.g. existing cash resources within the investor, 3rd party borrowings, equity injection by the ultimate shareholder(s) – and this will need to be taken into account when determining the optimal financing structure from a tax point of view.

Likewise, a review will need to be carried out of the tax regimes of both the overseas territory and the UK in determining the optimal place for locating interest deductions if the funding is to be effected through loan finance.

Questions that may need to be considered include:

- *Is the acquisition to be made by the overseas investor directly or by a UK acquisition vehicle?* Clearly, if the investor is to make the acquisition directly, any external funding will need to be taken out by the investor (even if the assets of the target business are used as security, which has been possible over recent years following the relaxation of the "financial assistance" rules).

- *What capacity do the investor and the target company each have to utilise interest deductions against forecast taxable profits?* No benefit will accrue from deducting interest in a territory in which there are insufficient taxable profits against which those deductions can be offset.
- *Is the corporate tax rate in the investor's home territory higher or lower than the UK rate?* The preference may be to locate borrowings (and hence interest deductions) in the territory with the higher tax rate.
- *What restrictions apply to the deductibility of interest in the UK and the overseas territory?* In relation to the UK, for example, transfer pricing/thin capitalisation considerations and the "worldwide debt cap" will need to be taken into account even if all or some of the finance is being provided by a 3rd party.
- *Will the borrower be required to withhold tax on payment of interest?* 3rd party lenders will often include a gross-up clause such that any withholding tax will effectively be a cost to the borrower rather than a lender. Therefore the borrowing may need to be structured in such a form or location that avoids or minimises any withholding taxes.

Consideration will also need to be given to how interest payments are to be financed. Where the acquisition is funded out of existing cash resources provided by the investor, this may be less of an issue. But where 3rd party lenders are involved, the investor will need to have a clear plan on how payments of interest are to be funded. A UK company can remit cash to an overseas parent free of UK tax, whether by way of dividend or an upstream loan (although such a loan should itself be interest-bearing in order to meet transfer pricing rules), but the parent will need to consider the taxation of such receipts under its local tax regime. In this regard, it should not be assumed that an upstream loan would be tax-free in the investor, as some tax regimes can treat such loans as deemed dividends.

Repatriation of profits

No withholding taxes are charged on a repatriation of profits. This applies to dividends paid by a UK company, irrespective of the identity of the shareholders, as well as to repatriation of branch profits to head office.

As well as the use of dividends, groups should also consider the extent to which other charges should be levied on the UK business – for example, royalties, service fees and management charges. Provided that such charges relate to the UK business and are calculated on an arm's length basis (so that transfer pricing legislation is not applied), those charges can be deducted against UK taxable profits. The withholding tax position on such payments is covered in chapter 4.2.

Tax groups
Where an investor has an existing UK business, there will be advantages to structuring the acquisition so as to create a UK tax group. The main advantages are:

- Current period UK trading profits of one company can be sheltered from tax by using trading losses of another UK group company arising in the same accounting period. This is known as "group relief".
- Capital assets can be transferred between UK members of the tax group without crystallising a tax charge. This would enable the tax-neutral combination of two UK businesses, if commercially desirable.
- Capital gains arising in one company can effectively be offset against brought forward non-trading losses (including capital losses, expenses of management and non-trading loan relationship debits) of another company in the UK group.

Where investors are part of a consortium, it is also possible in certain scenarios to use some of the tax losses in the consortium-owned company to shelter taxable profits arising in one of the consortium members.

The definitions of "group relief" groups and capital gains groups differ and so care must be taken where companies are not 100% owned, since in some situations not all of the above benefits of tax grouping will be available.

"Group relief" group : Comprises companies in which a shareholding of at least 75% is held directly or indirectly by the parent company (provided that the shareholder is also entitled to at least 75% of profits available for distribution and assets on a winding up). Non UK resident companies can be taken into account when tracing 75% ownership. In Figure 4.3.1, tax losses can be surrendered between UK 1 (owned 80% directly) and UK 3 (owned 81% indirectly). However, UK 2 is owned only 72% by Overseas Parent and therefore UK 2 cannot surrender losses to UK 3 (or vice versa).

Figure 4,3,1 - Example of how "group" relief may be applied acording to levels of ownership

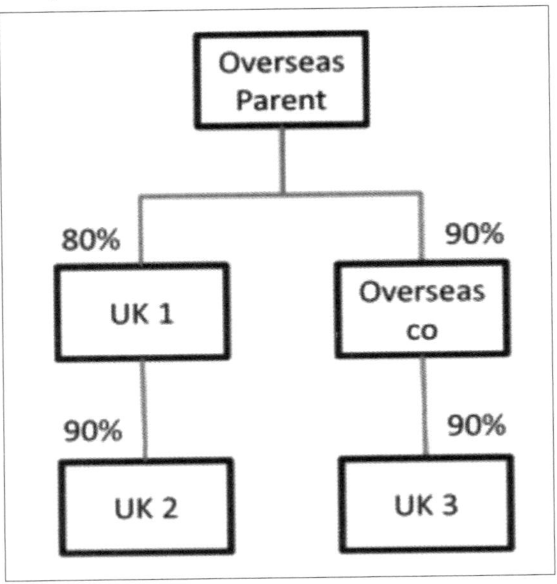

Capital gains group: This comprises companies which are held at least 75% by their immediate parent and which are indirectly held more than 50% by the top company in the group (provided also that the top group company is also entitled to more than 50% of profits available for distribution and assets on a winding up). Thus, in the above diagram UK 1, UK 2 and UK 3 are all part of the same capital gains group.

A tax group cannot be formed unless there is a common corporate parent company. Therefore, if an individual investor directly owns a number of UK companies, that investor will need to interpose a common holding company (which need not be a UK company) in order to create a tax group as illustrated in Figure 4.3,2:

Figure 4.3.2 - Creating a tax group

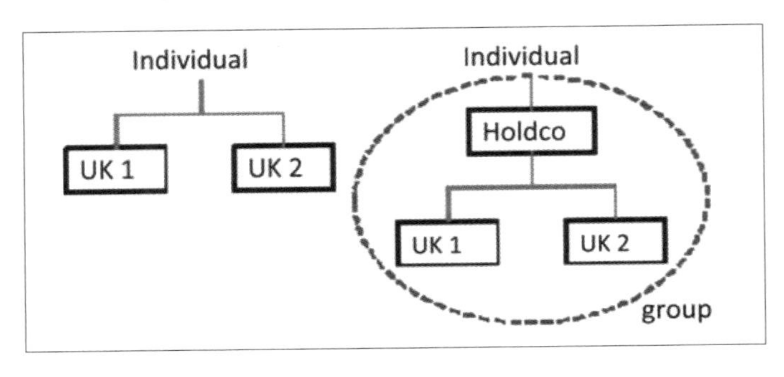

Even where there is no tax group in place, i.e. the individual holds both companies directly, the relationship between the two UK companies is such that they may still be regarded as associated or connected with each other for UK tax purposes. Hence:

- Transfer pricing rules can still apply to transactions or dealings between the two companies, to ensure that they are taxed on an arm's length basis.
- Transfers of assets must be for an arm's length consideration, failing which HMRC can substitute an arm's length value for the actual consideration.
- In determining the corporation tax rate payable by each company and, particularly, whether the small profits rate or marginal relief is available, both companies must be taken into account in calculating the number of "associated companies" – see Chapter 4.2 for the impact of this on the corporation tax rate payable.

Exit Considerations

When structuring an acquisition, an investor should also be mindful of the likelihood of a future exit, what form that exit might take and the tax implications of such an exit event.

Business held via a UK branch of an overseas company

- The disposal would need to be effected via an asset sale (assuming that a sale of the overseas company would not be feasible).
- This will trigger a UK tax liability, with any gains on the sale of chargeable assets being taxed at the prevailing corporation tax rate. Overseas tax may also be payable (subject to double tax relief for UK tax paid, depending on the tax regime in the overseas territory).
- The branch could be packaged up into a new UK company, with the overseas investor selling that new company. This is a more complex area and could give rise to both UK tax charges in the new company and overseas tax charges in the overseas company.

Business held within a UK company

- Gives the flexibility to sell via a sale of assets or sale of shares.
- A sale of shares would generally not give rise to a UK tax liability within the target company (although a "de-grouping charge" could arise if the UK company holds assets that were transferred into it from another UK group

company within the preceding six years). If the overseas parent company benefits from a "participation exemption" regime, this could enable a sale of the business, by way of a sale of shares, free of both UK and overseas tax.

- A sale of assets would generally be less tax effective, since a UK tax charge would arise in the UK company on any gains and an overseas tax charge could arise on a subsequent remittance of the disposal proceeds by the UK company.

Employee Incentivisation

Where an investor wishes to incentivise or recruit/retain key employees by means of the issuing of shares in the target business, there are a number of different share plans that can assist in achieving this objective in a tax efficient way. Ultimately, the most appropriate plan will be dependent on commercial requirements and the characteristics of the investors (e.g. UK v overseas; company v individual).

The area of share options and employee incentivisation is a complex one on which specialist advice should be sought.

Investor tax reliefs

There are also incentives aimed at encouraging UK resident individuals to invest in smaller, higher-risk trading companies, by offering tax reliefs for the purchase of new shares in such companies. So far as direct investment in companies is concerned, the main schemes are as follows.

Enterprise Investment Scheme (EIS) – Under EIS, an investor can claim income tax relief (i.e. a reduction in their income tax liability) of up to 30% of the amount invested (up to a maximum investment of £1,000,000 in a single tax year). The investor can also use the amount invested to defer other capital gains (whether or not on shares), with the deferred gain crystallising when the EIS shares are disposed of. In addition, disposals of EIS shares after three years may be free from capital gains tax. EIS is aimed at smaller, unquoted companies and enables such companies to raise up to £5m in any 12 month period.

Seed EIS (SEIS) – An individual subscribing for shares that qualify for SEIS can claim income tax relief of up to 50% of the amount invested. In addition, disposals of SEIS shares after three years may be free from capital gains tax. (For the tax years commencing 6 April 2012 and 6 April 2013 there is also an exemption from capital gains tax on gains realised from disposal of other assets, where the gains are reinvested through the SEIS in the same tax year.) SEIS is available for shares issued between 6 April 2012 to 5 April 2017 (although this period can be extended by Treasury Order) and is targeted at companies whose trade is less than two years old and whose assets (pre-subscription) do not exceed £200,000.

4.4 UK TAXATION FOR FOREIGN NATIONALS

Janet Pilborough-Skinner, Mazars

This chapter gives a brief overview of the UK tax considerations for a foreign national coming to the UK to work. By necessity, it only highlights the areas to consider and gives some indication of the current law. Advice should be sought in all respects, preferably before coming to the UK.

BASIS OF TAXATION

There are two concepts which need to be understood with regard to taxation in the UK. These are:

1. Residence
2. Domicile

Residence

Up until 5 April 2013, the question of residence in the UK was always a matter of case law and interpretation by the UK tax authorities, being broadly the number of days a person spends in the UK and their connections to the UK.

A new statutory residence test has been introduced from 6 April 2013. The legislation contains three parts detailing rules which will result in conclusive non residence, conclusive residence and a list of 'connecting factors' which will determine residence for the individuals who do not fall within the conclusive tests.

The tests are looked at in a certain order and only if a test is not satisfied do you move on to the next test. The order is the four automatic non residence tests, then the four automatic residence tests and finally, the "sufficient ties" tests which are based on connecting factors such as UK resident family, available accommodation, days spent in the UK and substantive employment.

The new rules are extensive and exhaustive but generally if a person comes here to work full time they will be resident in the UK for tax purposes. Although the tests are meant to give certainty, HMRC have issued substantial interpretation and guidance which indicates they are not necessarily as straightforward as they first look. There are also anti avoidance rules to ensure that the rules are not used in a way that the UK Government did not intend.

"Overseas workday relief" is available if certain conditions are satisfied. It only applies to non UK domiciled individuals (see below) and will, in limited circumstances give the "remittance basis" to foreign employment duties.

Domicile

The concept of domicile is relevant to taxation in the UK only if a person is not domiciled in the UK.

Domicile is a concept of general law; not a tax law and it is determined in a different way to residence and ordinary residence.

There are three types of domicile relevant to Income Tax ("IT") and Capital Gains Tax ("CGT"). These are:

- *Domicile of origin:* An individual will normally acquire a domicile of origin from their father at birth. An individual's domicile of origin need not be the country in which the individual was born. This is determined by the relevant parents' domicile at the child's birth.
- *Domicile of choice:* An individual has the legal capacity to acquire a new domicile at the age of 16. Whilst it is possible to acquire a domicile of choice, this means much more than simple residence and a person must settle in another country permanently and sever ties with the country of origin. It is extremely difficult to acquire a domicile of choice.
- *Domicile of dependence:* A child under 16 cannot have a domicile of choice. Whilst under 16 their domicile will follow that of the person on whom the individual is legally dependent.

UK TAXATION

In general, individuals resident in the UK will be liable on all their worldwide income and gains, known as the "arising basis" of taxation. This means that they will pay UK tax on all of their income as it arises and on their gains as they are realised, wherever that income and those gains are in the world.

Whilst an individual is non domiciled he can choose whether to use the "remittance basis" of taxation which is discussed later in this chapter.

Personal allowances

In general, individuals resident in the UK are entitled to an income tax personal allowance. This is set at £9,440 for the 2013/14 tax year and is the amount of income each individual can receive before they are liable to tax. For individuals with income over this amount, tax is only charged on income in excess of £9,440.

However, a personal allowance will not be available in certain circumstances, and so the individual will be chargeable to tax on all of their income. The allowances are withdrawn either where the income is in excess of £100,000 (and it is withdrawn gradually), or where the remittance basis is being claimed under certain circumstances.

There is also a CGT annual allowance available to reduce chargeable gains, which is currently set at £10,900 for the 2013/14 tax year.

UK Tax rates

Most forms of income are chargeable to tax at the following rates for the 2013/14 tax year:

£0 - £9,440	0%*
£9,441 - £41,450	20%
£41,451 - £150,000	40%
£150,000 +	45%

(If the personal allowances are still available).*

CGT for individuals is currently 18% if their marginal rate of income tax is 20% or below and 28% if their marginal rate of income tax is 40% or above.

Access to the remittance basis

Where an individual is resident in the UK, but not ordinarily resident or resident but not domiciled in the UK, they will have a choice whether to use the arising basis of taxation and therefore be taxed on their worldwide income or gains as they arise or to use the remittance basis of taxation.

If a claim for the remittance basis is made then the individual will only be liable to tax on income and gains arising in the UK and any overseas income and gains "remitted" (i.e. brought to or used to benefit the individual) in the UK.

Where an individual has been in the UK for less than 7 years, he can claim the remittance basis without paying for the privilege, however this will result in the loss of his personal allowance and CGT allowance.

Long term residents in the UK (broadly resident seven out of nine years) must pay a £30,000 remittance basis charge (RBC). Furthermore, where an individual has been in the UK for 12 out of the last 14 years, this RBC is increased to £50,000 per annum.

This is a particular area which needs specialist advice and would require a whole book to cover the rules, planning and anti avoidance in sufficient detail.

ON ARRIVAL

There are no specific tax forms which need to be completed on arrival in the UK, other than to register with HMRC as necessary. There are likely to be two registrations, one to obtain a National Insurance number and one to register with HMRC for tax purposes. Both of these are discussed briefly below.

National Insurance Contributions

Both employers and employees, including self-employed people, make compulsory national insurance contributions to HMRC in order to pay for a number of social benefits including the state pension and jobseeker's allowance. Men over the age of 65 and women over the age of 60 are exempt from making these contributions, although the age limit for women is in the process of rising from 60 to 65 to equalise with men. For employees, their employers will calculate their NIC and deduct this from their gross pay using PAYE; self-employed persons must work out their contributions themselves.

All UK residents over the age of 16 must have a National Insurance number if they wish to work in the UK and have their contributions credited to their "account".

So, before working in the UK, an individual will need to obtain a National Insurance number. This can be obtained by contacting HMRC and arranging for either an 'Evidence of Identity' interview or agreeing to submit a postal application in limited circumstances.

If an employee is being sent to the UK by his employer, the position in respect of social security will vary depending on the country from which the employee is being sent. It may be possible for the employee to continue paying social security in their home country or it may even be compulsory. Either way, agreement will need to be obtained from the tax authorities to ensure the appropriate compliance requirements are met.

In some circumstances, a 52 week NIC holiday may be appropriate, where the employee continues to pay social security in their home country for the first 52 weeks and then commences paying NIC in the UK.

National Insurance rates for 2013/14 are 12% for employees up to the higher rate of income tax and 2% thereafter, and for employers they are 13.8%. There is a small exemption broadly equivalent to the personal allowance.

UK tax return requirements

The UK tax year runs from the 6 April one year to 5 April of the next. The UK operates a "self assessment" system meaning that the responsibility to ensure the correct amount of tax is paid rests with the individual taxpayer. A UK tax return is likely to be required where the following circumstances apply:

- the individual is the director of a company in the UK; or
- he chooses to make a claim for the remittance basis; or
- he has income which is subject to tax (or a further tax liability) in the UK.

If an individual needs to be within the self assessment system he needs to complete form SA1 (obtainable from HMRC) to be registered.

HMRC does not generally assist an individual in the preparation of his tax return but they can ask questions and challenge certain items on the return. In general they are able to do this for up to a year after the return has been filed, though in certain cases this can be extended for up to 6 years.

HMRC may request that a return is prepared, but if they do not request a return, the individual is responsible for notifying HMRC that he is required to prepare a return for a particular tax year.

Completed tax returns need to be filed with HMRC by 31 October following the tax year end where the individual files a paper tax return. In most cases tax returns should be filed online as this provides a much more efficient service from HMRC and in addition, this extends the filing deadline to 31 January following the end of the tax year.

If the tax return is filed late, an automatic penalty of £100 will be charged which may be increased if the delay in filing is extended beyond 3 months.

Any additional tax liability will need to be paid to HMRC by 31 January following the end of the tax year. Provided the return has been processed by this time the taxpayer should receive a reminder from HMRC, providing details of how to pay and a payslip to use when making the payment.

If the individual's return has not been processed by this time, he is still liable to pay his tax by 31 January.

If the tax is paid late, interest will be charged from the day after the due date. In addition, if the tax has not been paid within a month of the due date, a surcharge of 5% of the outstanding balance will be levied. Further charges may be raised if the tax liability remains unpaid after this date.

For an individual coming to the UK, the date of arrival and some brief details on the individual intentions should be disclosed in the annual income tax return for the tax year of arrival.

OTHER TAXES

Capital Gains Tax

Mention has been made earlier of CGT with regard to the annual allowance and the tax rates at which it is charged. CGT is broadly charged on any gain made on holding an investment, such as shares or property.

There are several valuable exemptions, the most important one being an exemption for an individual's main residence. In addition, there are certain tax breaks which are available to encourage investment. One of those is Entrepreneurs' Relief, described below.

Entrepreneurs' relief

Entrepreneurs' Relief (ER) is available for "qualifying business disposals". The effect is to reduce the rate of Capital Gains Tax from 18% or 28% to 10%, for total lifetime gains of £10 million.

A claim for ER can be made more than once, but the total cumulative gains cannot exceed £10 million. If this is the case, any gains over this limit will be subject to the higher rates of CGT.

A "qualifying business disposal" includes a disposal of shares in a trading company, or the holding company of a trading group.

ER is normally available provided that, for a period of 12 months ending with the date of the sale, the individual holds at least 5% of the ordinary share capital; can exercise at least 5% of the voting rights and is an officer or employee of the company or of one or more of the companies which are members of the trading group.

Compliance with the rules should be checked carefully.

Business investment relief

A new relief aimed at UK resident non domiciled individuals has been introduced to encourage inward investment and subject to certain conditions, overseas income and gains can be remitted into the UK for investment into eligible trading companies, without triggering a tax charge on those funds being remitted to the UK. There is no limit to the investment and although there are some anti avoidance provisions, the rules appear to be relatively generous.

This relief is relatively new and advice should be taken to ensure any remitted funds qualify before investment.

Inheritance tax

The charge to Inheritance Tax ("IHT") is based on where the asset is situated and the domicile of the person concerned; the place of residence is irrelevant.

Deemed domicile

The concept of deemed domicile only applies for IHT purposes, and is essentially an anti-avoidance provision.

If an individual comes to the UK he will be deemed domiciled in the UK once he has been resident in the UK for seventeen out of twenty years. Certain Double Taxation Treaties may override these rules and should be checked carefully.

Basis of taxation

IHT is an integrated lifetime transfer and estates tax, and is a tax on capital transfers of value by an individual on certain lifetime gifts which are taxed immediately, lifetime gifts where the donor dies within seven years from the date of the gift and the chargeable estate upon the individual's death.

Each individual is entitled to a nil rate band (NRB) (currently £325,000 for 2013/14). Only transfers of value exceeding this band are liable to IHT. Any unused NRB can now be shared by spouses/civil partners on second death. The NRB is not an annual exemption. It is a seven year cumulative band which takes into account the previous seven years' chargeable transfers when determining whether a transfer has exceeded the NRB.

IHT is currently charged at rates of: 20% for lifetime transfers and 40% on death.

There are three types of lifetime gift: exempt transfers, potentially exempt transfers and chargeable lifetime transfers.

Upon death an individual is deemed to have made a transfer of value equal to the whole of their chargeable estate, which is the total value of all their capital assets less any amounts owing at the date of death.

Examples of the most common exempt transfers are transfers between spouses and civil partners, gifts to UK registered charities, the annual exemption – (the first £3,000 of gifts made each tax year) – and small gifts up to £250 de minimis. There are other valuable exemptions available.

The most common chargeable lifetime transfers (CLTs) are gifts to trusts. All gifts to trusts (except charitable trusts or trusts for the disabled) are CLTs.

Potentially exempt transfers are all lifetime gifts between individuals. During the donor's lifetime the transfers are treated as exempt from IHT and if the donor survives seven years from the date of the gift the transfer is completely exempt.

If the donor dies within seven years of the date of the gift the transfer becomes chargeable, although the amount chargeable depends on how many years have passed between the date of the gift and the date of death.

OTHER CONSIDERATIONS

Remuneration packages

Any benefits provided to an employee, either in the UK or in their home country, will need to be considered when calculating the UK tax position and some of the more popular benefits are mentioned briefly below.

It is also possible to use share schemes and incentives to remunerate in a tax efficient manner and these are discussed elsewhere in the book.

Common benefits

If accommodation is provided rent free or at a subsidised rate, the relevant benefit of that will be chargeable to both tax and NI. If the value of the property provided is in excess of £75,000, the tax benefit is particularly high and there are ways of minimising the tax liabilities.

If the employer helps with the move to the UK, there are some valuable reliefs worth up to £8,000 but it is important that advice and planning is undertaken before the move takes place.

If an employee is sent to the UK on a temporary secondment for less than 24 months it may be possible to claim tax relief in respect of the expenses in attending the "temporary workplace" in the UK. These expenses would include, but not restricted to accommodation costs, utilities, ordinary commuting to the temporary workplace and subsistence. This relief may extend to cover travel between the UK and their home country.

The taxable benefit of a car is generally calculated on its CO2 emissions and the list price before discounts. This has led to a move towards more fuel efficient cars and can make a difference to the overall taxable benefit.

Double taxation

It is always worthwhile to remember that there is a guiding principle that no one should suffer double taxation on the same income, gains or assets in more than one country. However, how this relief is given depends on the country of origin and any double taxation treaty which may be in force with the UK.

Taxation could be due in both countries, the country of origin only, or the country where the source is "arising". This changes depending on the type of income or gains and whether there is an old treaty, a new treaty or even no treaty at all.

Once again, the interaction between the countries should be checked before the foreign national arrives in the UK if at all possible.

4.5 EMPLOYMENT LAW

Asha Kumar, Watson, Farley & Williams LLP

INTRODUCTION

Employment law in the UK has changed over the decades to reflect social and political changes, and has also been affected by the UK's membership of the European Union (EU). This is an area of change and the UK Government is currently consulting on various amendments to the law in this area, with the aim of deregulating it and making the UK more competitive and a more attractive place to do business. However, any business considering the UK as a place of business needs to be aware of the employment and immigration laws that operate in the UK. Those investing in the UK will have to deal with different aspects of employment protection according to the mechanism used to invest in the UK, and it should also be noted that special protection is afforded to employees where there is a merger or acquisition of a business.

This chapter seeks to assist those unfamiliar with UK employment law by providing an overview of the rights and obligations afforded to individuals through the employment relationship.

EMPLOYMENT STATUS

In common with other European countries, UK employment law distinguishes between "employees", "workers" and the "self-employed". This status is important because it determines the statutory employment rights to which a person is entitled.

Significant rights are conferred upon employees who, traditionally, have been seen as individuals with full-time jobs working under indefinite employment contracts. However, as new working arrangements emerge, the UK has seen an increase in the number of individuals whose working arrangements fall outside the traditional pattern.

There is no statutory definition of "employee", and while case law has developed in this area, the actual finding of employment status depends upon the circumstances of each particular case. As a consequence, the growth of legislation that applies to "workers", a term wider than "employees", embraces certain types of self-employment. It should also be noted that there is also now limited employment law protection for qualifying temporary agency workers.

It should also be noted that from 1st September 2013, a new status of "employee shareholder" will be created. This is a new type of employment status, whereby employees give up certain employment rights, such as unfair dismissal and statutory redundancy payments, in return for an award of shares worth at least £2,000.

CONTRACTS OF EMPLOYMENT

A contract of employment comes into existence as soon as someone accepts an offer of employment in return for pay. It is legally binding between the employer and employee, and can be written or oral, express or implied, or a combination of these. In addition, some employment terms are imposed into contracts by statute.

While employers are obliged only to provide a written statement of the main employment particulars (see below), it is recommended that employees are given a full written contract, as it provides certainty and may help to avoid later disputes. However, even a written contract may not necessarily reflect all of the terms that apply in an employment relationship, and terms are often implied into a contract. These may be necessary to make the contract workable or may reflect custom and practice.

A contract can be for an indefinite duration, terminable on an agreed period of notice, or for a fixed term. Protection is afforded to a fixed-term worker so that he/she cannot be treated less favourably than an equivalent permanent worker, unless the treatment is objectively justified. In certain circumstances, fixed-term contracts automatically become permanent contracts.

Written particulars of employment

The Employment Rights Act 1996 obliges employers to provide employees with a written statement of employment particulars. The written statement is not necessarily a contract, but can provide evidence of the terms and conditions of employment. It must be provided to the employee within two months of the employment commencing and must contain certain basic information, including:

- the names of the employer and employee;
- the rate of remuneration and the intervals at which it is to be paid;
- the hours of work; and
- holiday entitlement.

An employee who has not been provided with the required particulars may make a complaint to the Employment Tribunal, which may award him/her between two and four weeks' pay. For these purposes, a week's pay is currently capped at £450, and this generally increases annually on 1 February each year.

Policies and procedures

Often written contracts are supplemented by the use of policies and procedures that describe the employer's more general employment practices, such as email and internet use.

MINIMUM STATUTORY PROVISIONS

In the UK, employees (and sometimes workers) are provided with minimum terms, which are aimed at providing decent minimum standards and promoting fairness at work. Many of the minimum standards were introduced in order to implement European directives, and consequently similar provisions apply throughout Europe. Minimum terms related to the following cannot be overridden:

- the national minimum wage;
- statutory sick pay;
- working hours;
- disciplinary procedures;
- notice periods;
- employers' liability insurance; and
- health and safety.

National minimum wage

The National Minimum Wage Act applies to almost all workers and sets minimum hourly rates of pay. The national minimum wage is reviewed annually. The rates vary for different groups of workers and as of 1 October 2013, were set as follows:

- £6.31 an hour for workers aged 21 and over;
- £5.03 an hour for 18-20 year olds;
- £3.72 an hour for all workers aged 16-17; and
- £2.68 for apprentices.

Statutory sick pay

Eligible employees are entitled to receive statutory sick pay (SSP) for up to 28 weeks in one period, or more than one linked period, of sickness (periods with eight weeks or less between them are linked). A helpful SSP calculator can be found on the HM Revenue and Customs website.[1]

The rate of SSP is reviewed annually and is currently £86.70 per week. In certain circumstances, an employer may be able to recover some or all of any SSP they have paid to their employees.

As a matter of policy, employers may choose to pay employees full pay (inclusive of SSP) for a limited period; this is referred to as "contractual sick pay".

Working hours

The Working Time Regulations implement a European directive aimed at protecting the health and safety of workers by ensuring that working time does not adversely affect a worker's health. In summary, the regulations provide details of:

- the 48 hour week;
- rest breaks; and
- annual leave.

The 48-hour week

An employer cannot require an employee to work more than an average of 48 hours a week, although there are a number of exceptions to this rule for senior employees and certain other categories of employment. Unlike many other European countries, Britain has negotiated an opt-out whereby this limit does not apply if an employee agrees in writing with his/her employer that it is not to be applied. It should be noted that the employer cannot compel the employee to opt-out and that the employee can reverse this opt-out by giving appropriate notice.

Rest breaks

Workers have the right to an uninterrupted rest period of at least 11 hours between working days, and to a 24-hour period clear of work each week. Additional rest breaks must be provided to workers whose pattern of work puts their health and

1 http://www.hmrc.gov.uk/calcs/ssp.htm

safety at risk. The regulations also provide the right to a rest break of at least 20 minutes after six hours of consecutive work. Special provisions apply to night workers.

Annual leave

Workers currently have the right to a minimum of 5.6 weeks' paid annual leave. This right applies from the first day of employment and accrues at the rate of one-twelfth of the annual entitlement per month worked. A "week" reflects the employee's working week. So, where an employee works a five-day week, he/she will be entitled to 28 days' annual leave, and if an employee works three days a week, he/she will be entitled to 16.8 days' annual leave. In practice, many employers offer employees the statutory minimum inclusive of bank holidays and will provide employees in senior roles with additional annual leave.

Grievance and disciplinary procedures

When resolving workplace disputes there is a requirement for both parties to comply with a code of practice developed by the Advisory, Conciliation and Arbitration Service (ACAS). The ACAS Code provides basic practical guidance to employers, employees and their representatives and sets out principles for handling disciplinary and grievance situations in the workplace. If an employee or employer is unreasonable in its failure to follow the new code of practice, employment tribunals will be able to order an increase or decrease in awards of up to 25 per cent.

Notice periods

The minimum legal notice periods to be given by an employer are:

- one week's notice if the employee has been continuously employed by the employer for at least one month but for less than two years; or
- two weeks' notice if the employee has been continuously employed by the employer for two years, plus an additional week's notice for each further complete year of continuous employment, up to a maximum of 12 weeks.

An employee's contract of employment may, however, provide for a longer notice period. An employment contract may be terminated without advance notice where the employee has committed an act of gross misconduct.

In the absence of any contrary contractual provisions, an employee who has been employed for one month or more must give their employer at least one week's notice to terminate their employment.

Employers' liability insurance

Every employer in the UK must have employers' liability insurance, which covers employers against damages and legal costs following injury or disease to its employees during their employment.

Health and safety

In the UK, employers have legal obligations to ensure a safe workplace. The health and safety obligations are extensive and if breached may give rise to criminal liabilities. Further details can be obtained from the Health and Safety Executive's website.[2]

WORK/LIFE BALANCE

Over the years, legislation has been brought in to enable employees to achieve a better work/life balance. It has been particularly targeted at parents to enable them to spend adequate time bringing up their children by allowing them to work around their commitments.

Maternity leave

All pregnant employees are entitled to 52 weeks' maternity leave. All employment benefits, including non-contractual benefits connected with an employee's employment that are not "remuneration", continue to be provided for the full period of maternity leave. For eligible parents, maternity leave can be transferred to the father where at least 20 weeks from the child's birth has passed and the mother has returned to work; this is referred to as "Additional Paternity Leave".

Employees on maternity leave who are eligible are also entitled to receive up to 39 weeks' statutory maternity pay (SMP) at the rate set by statute. The first six weeks of SMP are earnings-related, and an employee is entitled to 90 per cent of her average weekly earnings with no upper limit. The remaining 33 weeks are paid at a lower rate, which is currently £136.78 (or 90 per cent of earnings if this is less).

Employees who are not eligible for SMP are entitled to a Maternity Allowance for up to 39 weeks. This is currently £136.78 per week (or 90 per cent of earnings if this is less) and is claimed from the Department for Work and Pensions. Similar provisions to those set out above apply on the adoption of a child.

Paternity leave

Eligible employees whose partners are expected to give birth will be entitled to time off at or around the time of the birth. They are entitled to take either one or

2 http://www.hse.gov.uk

two consecutive weeks' leave as paid paternity leave. Statutory paternity pay is either 90 per cent of an employee's weekly earnings or the prescribed amount (currently £136.78), whichever is the lesser. Fathers may also be eligible for transferable maternity leave (see "Maternity leave" above).

Parental leave
Parents who have at least one year's continuous employment may take up to 18 weeks' unpaid parental leave for each child up to that child's fifth birthday (or fifth year of adoption). Parents of disabled children are entitled to the leave until the child's 18th birthday.

Time off to care for dependants
In the UK, all employees have the right to take a reasonable amount of time off, without pay, to care for dependants. The right to time off is intended to enable employees to deal with an emergency in the short-term and/or, where necessary, to make longer-term care arrangements.

Right to request flexible working
Employees who have at least 26 weeks' continuous employment may be able to make a request for flexible working, which will allow them to work modified hours of employment, if they either:

- have responsibility for the care of a child under the age of 17;
- have responsibility for the care of a disabled child under the age of 18; or
- care for an adult.

It is expected that later in 2013 the right to request flexible working will be provided to all employees who have 26 weeks' continuous employment.

Part-time working
Protection is also afforded to those who work on a part-time basis. Regulations have introduced provisions that prevent part-time workers from being treated less favourably than equivalent full-time employees, unless this is justifiable. Part-time employees should also have access to the same rights and benefits as full-time employees, albeit on a *pro-rata* basis.

EQUALITY PROVISIONS
In the UK the Equality Act 2010 outlaws discrimination on the grounds of sex,

race, disability, sexual orientation, religion or belief and age. Generally, the law recognizes the following types of discrimination:

- Direct discrimination: this is where someone is treated differently because of their sex, race, etc. It is not necessary to show an unlawful motive; it is the reason for the treatment that matters.
- Indirect discrimination: this is a less obvious form of discrimination. It occurs where certain requirements, conditions or practices imposed by an employer, although applied equally to all employees, have a disproportionately adverse impact on one group or other.
- Harassment: this is where one person subjects another to unwanted conduct related to their sex, race, etc, which has the purpose or effect of violating the other's dignity, or creating an intimidating, hostile, degrading, humiliating or offensive environment for them.
- Victimization: this is where a person is treated less favourably because they have started proceedings, given evidence or complained about the behaviour of someone who has been harassing them or discriminating against them.

Special provisions apply to disability discrimination and age discrimination. Under the disability discrimination provisions, an employee with a particular condition may receive additional protection where this amounts to a "disability" as defined under the legislation.

MISCELLANEOUS MATTERS

Whistleblowing

Protection is given to employees who disclose or "blow the whistle on" wrongdoings at work. Employees are protected if they blow the whistle and, if they are dismissed or receive detrimental treatment as a result of their action, they can present a claim in an employment tribunal. Compensation for whistleblowing is uncapped. Whistleblowers are protected where they disclose in good faith something that relates to:

- the commissioning of a criminal activity;
- failure to comply with a legal obligation;
- a miscarriage of justice;
- a health and safety issue; and/or
- damage to the environment.

Any disclosure must be made in the public interest.

Data protection
The UK has data protection or "privacy" laws. Data transfer to companies outside the EU is permitted only when the receiving country has data protection laws that are considered "adequate" by the European Commission. UK data protection laws may give individual employees access to information held on them by their employer, provided that certain conditions are satisfied.

Reporting and consultation requirements
The Information and Consultation of Employees Regulations 2004, (ICE) give employees the right to be informed and consulted about the business they work for, including information on the employer's activities and any possible threats to their employment. ICE applies to all undertakings with at least 50 employees. The aim of ICE is to encourage people to develop their own voluntary arrangements tailored to their particular circumstances.

Termination of employment
In the UK, employees have the statutory right not to be unfairly dismissed. If the employee's employment commenced on or after 6 April 2012, generally, after they have accrued two years' service they can only be dismissed for a "fair" reason. The reason for dismissal will only be "fair" if it falls under one of the following prescribed reasons, namely:

1. capability;
2. conduct;
3. avoidance of a legal enactment;
4. redundancy; or
5. some other substantial reason that justifies dismissal.

Even though a fair reason may be established, the employer should follow a fair procedure when dismissing an employee, and the parties are required to comply with the ACAS Code.

Where a dismissal is found to be unfair, an employee can recover compensation which is capped at the lower of £74,200 (reviewed annually) or one year's salary of the employee. There are, however, a number of circumstances, including in the event of whistleblowing or discrimination, in which an employment tribunal can ignore the cap on compensation and award unlimited compensation. If the reason for dismissal is redundancy, an employee is generally entitled to a statutory redundancy payment, up to a current maximum of £13,500.

Employers should note that there are special rules concerning redundancy. An employer who proposes to make 20 or more employees redundant must consult with the relevant trade union or employee representatives beforehand. Failure to do so may result in compensation of up to 90 days' pay for each affected employee.

Breach of contract

In addition to statutory rights that apply on dismissal, if an employer does not comply with a term of the employment contract, this may be a breach of contract. An employee can bring a claim for damages or "wrongful dismissal" if they do not receive their notice entitlement under their contract of employment. A fundamental breach of contract will also usually entitle an employee to resign and claim unfair "constructive dismissal". Similar principles apply where an employee breaches their employment contract.

When awarding compensation for breach of contract, UK courts will seek to place the innocent party in the position they would have been in had the contract been properly performed.

MERGERS AND ACQUISITIONS

Where a business or part of an entity is transferred to another by way of a business transfer, the employees in the transferring part are given significant legal safeguards under the Transfer of Undertakings (Protection of Employment) Regulations, 2006. These safeguards apply only when there is a transfer of assets and not where the employing entity is the same, as might be the case where the transfer is of shares in the company. These special provisions also apply in certain outsourcing situations. The special protections include:

- appointment of employee representatives who must be informed (and possibly also consulted) in advance of the transfer;
- inheritance of past (undischarged) liabilities of the employer by the buyer;
- changes to an employee's terms and conditions of employment being rendered unlawful; and
- dismissals in connection with the transfer being rendered unlawful, unless they are for certain specified reasons.

CONCLUSION

It might seem at first sight that employers in the UK are subject to a considerable amount of legislative requirements. It should, however, be borne in mind that many of the provisions, particularly in the area of equal opportunities, were introduced as a result of European directives and thus apply to all EU member states. Further, in many areas the UK has managed to water down the impact of the legislation by opting out of certain provisions. In addition, the UK Government is also consulting on a number of amendments to labour law which, in some instances, are aimed at increasing the UK's competitiveness in the global market in which we operate.

4.6 PENSIONS, INSURED BENEFITS AND EMPLOYEE INCENTIVE PLANS

Liz Buchan and Rhodri Thomas,
Watson, Farley & Williams LLP

INTRODUCTION

In the UK it is usual for an employer to provide its employees with a mix of benefits including one or more of: pension arrangements, insured benefits and/or stock/share options, in addition to basic salary. This chapter summarises these types of benefits.

PENSIONS

Occupational pension plans v personal plans

Currently pension plans can either be occupational or personal. Broadly, occupational plans are annuities provided by employers for their staff in order to provide an income in retirement. Occupational pension plans vary in size from large arrangements that have many thousands of members and assets worth many millions of pounds down to individual arrangements set up for single executives.

Occupational pension plans operate on a triangular basis. They are established by the employer and administered by a board of trustees who act in the interests of the third party - the beneficiaries. The employer and the trustees will agree the terms of the constitutional documents. In addition to these documents, the plan has to be run in accordance with UK legislation and HM Revenue & Customs ("HMRC") rules.

Personal pensions are different in that the primary legal relationship is between the employee and the personal pension plan provider, such as a life insurance company, a bank or another authorised institution.

Defined benefit v defined contribution

What differentiates between types of occupational plan is how they are funded. Some are funded on a defined benefit basis and others on a defined contribution basis. There is a significant difference between the two.

Defined Benefit

Here the pension which is provided for the employee is calculated according to a variety of factors which might include length of service, amount of salary at the retirement date and the "accrual rate" (often specified as a fraction, e.g. one sixtieth for each year of service). To the extent that there is a difference between the amount of contributions made by the employer and the employee, the employer will be responsible for making up this shortfall.

Defined Contribution

These plans take contributions from the employee and from the employer and invest them in such a way as to optimise returns with a view to providing an income for the employee after retirement. The investment risk falls on the employee, not the employer and this is the funding method chosen by most companies starting out new occupational pension plans.

Combined

On rare occasions a mix of the two or a "hybrid" plan is chosen. This may be a defined contribution plan with a defined benefit underpin (or vice versa) or a plan which permits a change from one to the other at a given age or service period. The uncertainty of cost and complexity of running such plans makes them rare choices.

Problems with defined benefit plans

Many companies have closed their defined benefit pension plans to new entrants to try and cap the under funding problems that such plans have caused.

Personal Pension Plans

The main other type of plan used by employees to provide for their retirement is known as a personal pension plan. A personal pension plan is the only type of HMRC approved pension arrangement that can currently be initiated by an employee who is not eligible to join an occupational pension plan.

A personal pension plan is a very simple form of pension contract. It is a defined contribution contract issued by a provider to an individual employee. The provider takes contributions from the employee, and invests them, with the contributions receiving certain tax privileges. Employees can take their benefits from age 55 and the value of the fund that an employee accrues over their period of membership (including investment income) will be used to provide an income after retirement. Employers can also make contributions to the arrangement.

Group Personal Pension Plans

Many employers offer a group personal pension plan. This is, essentially, a branding exercise and the "group personal pension" is merely a collection of personal pension policies arranged by the employer through its financial advisor. This does not change the fact that, for legal purposes, this is an arrangement between the employee and the provider.

Stakeholder Pension Plans

Between October 2001 and October 2012 all UK employers who employed five or more employees and who did not offer employees membership of an occupational pension plan or make contributions of at least 3% of basic salary to a personal pension plan had to comply with the stakeholder access requirements. There is now no requirement for new employers to comply with the stakeholder access requirements, but for employees who were already in stakeholder plans as at October 2012 certain transitional arrangements may apply.

Auto Enrolment

New laws came into force in October 2012 which require employers to automatically enrol eligible employees into a pension scheme. The new duties apply to all employers with employees working in the United Kingdom and are being implemented over five years from 1 October 2012, with larger employers being affected first. From the date an employer becomes subject to the new duties it must automatically enrol its eligible employees in a qualifying pension scheme, unless the employee is already an active member of the employer's qualifying scheme. This can be either an occupational or personal pension scheme (if certain quality requirements are met) or the employer can enrol its employees in NEST, which is the name of the central government-established scheme.

Qualifying employees must be over age 22, below state pension age and must earn at least £9,440 a year (in 2013/14). Employers can also choose to impose a three-month waiting period before a qualifying employee is enrolled. If an employer auto-enrols its eligible employees in a qualifying scheme, it must pay contributions of 3% of "band earnings" each year and the employee will be required to contribute 5% of band earnings; though the requirement to contribute will be phased in over five years. For 2013/14, the qualifying earnings band runs from £5,668 to £41,450.

Employees who have been automatically enrolled will have a right to opt out within prescribed time limits. However, if they do opt out, they will be automatically re-enrolled every three years. Employers will not be allowed to induce their employees to opt out of scheme membership or make job offers conditional on opting out. The Pensions Regulator will police employer compliance and has issued detailed guidance. Employers that breach the new duties will receive compliance notices and could face penalties of £10,000 a day. Criminal penalties could apply in the case of "wilful" failure to comply.

INSURANCES

Introduction

In addition to pension benefits, it is also very common for employers to provide employees with insured benefits, such as life insurance, private medical insurance and permanent health insurance. These benefits are summarised below.

Life Insurance

This benefit pays out a lump sum in the event of the death of the insured employee. Typical arrangements will provide for a lump sum payment based upon a multiple of the insured employee's annual salary, sometimes up to a maximum salary level. Where an employer provides this benefit through a group life insurance plan (see below), the level of cover that can be provided is capped at four times an employee's annual salary.

Where life insurance is provided as an employee benefit, this will usually be done by the employer establishing a group life assurance plan for which the employer pays the plan premium. Individual employees can then be entered into the plan. The provision of life insurance by an employer (where the group policy meets certain HMRC requirements) does not constitute a taxable benefit in the hands of an employee who is entered into the policy.

Private Medical Insurance

This benefit provides cover to meet the costs of treatment of short-term curable illness or injury of an employee, and consequently ensures that the employee has access to such treatment with as little delay as possible. Certain conditions may, depending on the scope of the policy, be excluded from the cover provided (for example, any conditions pre-existing on commencement of the policy will often be excluded).

Similarly to life insurance plans, group private medical insurance may be arranged by an employer, and individual employees may then be entered into the plan. This will usually decrease the 'per capita' cost of cover, as the employer is able to obtain lower premiums for the group policy than would be available to an individual. However, the value of the premiums paid by the employer in respect of an employee is a taxable benefit for the employee, and the employee will therefore be required to pay income tax on this amount (at the employee's prevailing marginal rate) to HMRC.

Permanent Health Insurance (PHI)

Where an employer provides this benefit to an employee, in the event that the employee becomes unable to work due to illness or accident, the insurer will pay a percentage (usually between 50 and 75%) of the employee's salary for the duration of the employee's incapacity. PHI policies will usually provide either that an employee must be unable to perform his or her own occupation, or that the employee must be unable to perform work of any kind, in order to receive benefits, although other forms of policy are available.

Payments will begin after a deferment period during which time the employee must be incapacitated (within the meaning prescribed in the policy). Deferment periods of six months are common, although the period may be longer or shorter. Shorter deferment periods will increase the premium payable on the policy. Often the employee will be eligible to receive company sick pay from the employer for some or all of the deferment period, following which the employee may become eligible to receive benefits under the policy.

Where an employer provides PHI as a benefit to employees, it will normally do this by establishing a group plan, into which individual employees may be entered. Where an employer sets up a plan in this way, the provision of PHI cover to an employee is not a taxable benefit in the hands of the employee. However, should an employee become eligible to receive benefits under the PHI policy, those benefits will be taxable as income (this is in contrast to where an individual arranges PHI independently, where any benefits received will not be subject to tax).

EMPLOYEE INCENTIVE PLANS

Introduction

There are various types of share and share option plans that an employer can establish as a tax efficient way of rewarding and incentivising its employees. The choice of plan or plans will depend on the needs and objectives of the employer. An employer will need to decide whether it wishes to put in place an option plan, (in which case Company Share Option Plans (CSOP), Savings-Related Share Option Plans (SAYE), and Enterprise Management Incentive Plans (EMI) may be of interest), a share plan, (in which case Share Incentive Plans (SIP) or Long-Term Incentive Plans (L-TIP) may be of interest) or a cash based plan which replicates an option or share plan (in which case a "Phantom" Plan may be of interest).

Various amendments to the legislation governing share and share option plans (and the tax treatment thereof) are due to be adopted by the UK in the latter part of 2013, but these amendments are generally relevant to matters beyond the scope of the following summaries, and have not, at the time of writing, come into force.

Further details in relation to share and share option plans can be found on HM Revenue & Customs' website: www.hmrc.gov.uk/shareschemes

Employee Shareholders

Additionally, while not strictly 'employee incentive plans', 2013 is expected to see the introduction of "employee shareholder" employment status in the UK, where an employee will give up certain employment rights/protections (including the right not to be unfairly dismissed in certain circumstances) in exchange for shares in their employer. The shares granted to an employee shareholder will need to have a minimum value (at the time of grant) of £2,000 and tax-favoured treatment is expected to apply to all grants of shares to employee shareholders up to a value of £50,000.

"Approved" and "Unapproved" Plans

Share and option plans are often categorised as "approved" or "unapproved" which indicates whether or not they are approved by HMRC. Again, employers will need to decide whether an approved or unapproved scheme, or even using an approved scheme together with an unapproved one, will best suit their objectives. It is also open to employers simply to grant standalone unapproved share options, outside of any formal scheme.

Broadly, an employee who is granted an unapproved option will not normally be charged income tax on the grant of the option itself, nor when the option becomes exercisable. Income tax will, however, be charged following exercise of an unapproved option on the excess (if any) of the market value, at the time of acquisition, of the shares acquired over the amount paid by the employee to acquire the shares. Capital Gains Tax ("CGT") may also be payable on any increase in value between the date of exercise and the date of disposal, although reliefs may be available to minimise any charge. There may also be PAYE and National Insurance implications for the employer on grant or, more likely, exercise of the option.

By contrast, options granted under the terms of an option plan "approved" by HMRC may, subject to conditions, be exercised without giving rise to a charge to income tax. The employee may still be liable to CGT when he ultimately sells the shares acquired on exercise, but certain approved plans do offer CGT benefits.

Company Share Option Plans (CSOP)
Summary
In a CSOP an employee is granted an option allowing him, during a set period of time, to buy up to a specified number of shares at a price fixed at the date of grant. The employer (or company in which the shares are to be acquired) must either be listed on a recognised stock exchange, or free from the control of another company. The price of the shares must not be less than the market value of the shares at the time of grant. To qualify for favourable tax treatment, CSOP options must generally be exercised by the employee not less than three years and not more than 10 years after the time of grant.

Under a CSOP the employer is, broadly, free to set its own rules as to the circumstances in which the options may be granted or exercised, provided that any performance-related conditions are objective and not subject to the exercise of a discretion by any one person, and that the plan's rules do not contain elements which are neither essential nor reasonably necessary to its operation.

Participation and Limits
The employer can decide on a discretionary basis which of its employees or full time directors can take part in its CSOP. There is, however, a limit of £30,000 on the maximum value of shares over which approved options granted under a CSOP may be held by an individual at any one time.

Further information on CSOPs can be found on the HMRC website.

Savings Related Share Options Plans ("SAYE Plans")
Summary
SAYE plans are capable of approval as approved plans, and as with CSOPs there

are eligibility requirements that an employer must satisfy to be able to use a SAYE plan. Employees are given a share option to buy a certain number of shares at a fixed price at a particular time. The shares can only be purchased using amounts saved under a special Save As You Earn (SAYE) savings contract. Employees are required to make savings contributions out of net income over a number of years.

At the end of the fixed period the SAYE contract pays back the contributions, interest thereon, and a bonus, out of which the shares can be purchased, by exercise of the share option. If employees do not exercise their options, they will still receive the proceeds of their SAYE contract, including the bonus.

Participation and Limits

SAYE plans are all-employee plans under which all qualifying employees and directors must be eligible to participate on similar terms. The employer may specify a qualification period of up to five years' employment. Participants may choose to exercise their options at the end of fixed three or five year terms and monthly savings must be between £5 and £250.

Further information on SAYE Plans can be found on the HMRC website.

Enterprise Management Incentive Plans (EMI plan)

Summary

EMI plans can be established by qualifying independent trading companies that have gross assets not exceeding £30 million. Certain trades (such as property development) are excluded. While EMI plans offer attractive tax benefits, there is no approval mechanism, although an employer can seek HMRC confirmation that it is eligible to grant EMI options.

Participation and Limits

There are no restrictions on the number of employees who may participate in an EMI plan. Options over shares worth up to £250,000 at the time of grant can be issued to each employee. However, there is an overall limit on the value of unexercised options at any time of £3 million.

There are no rules about when the options may be exercised (although options must be exercised within 10 years of grant to obtain tax and National Insurance relief) or about the price at which options may be granted. Tax relief is limited if the options are granted with an exercise price of less than market value at the time of grant.

A qualifying employer under an EMI plan must have fewer than 250 employees, must not be under the control of any other company and must be carrying on a qualifying trade. It must also have a permanent establishment within the UK.

Individuals, whether they are new recruits or existing employees, must work for the employer for at least 25 hours a week, or if less than 25 hours, for at least 75% of their working time, to qualify for EMI. The purpose of the grant of the option must also be to recruit or retain an employee, and not for the purpose of tax avoidance.

Further guidance on EMI plans can be found on the HMRC website.

Share Incentive Plans (SIP)

A SIP is an approved plan, which operates by providing employees of a company with shares in the company, through a trust. All shares acquired under a SIP must initially be held in a UK resident trust, whose trustees hold shares in the employer on behalf of the employees who join the plan.

In order to obtain the full tax benefits, employees must normally leave their shares in the plan's trust for at least five years. Cash payments are made to the plan's trustees, who buy shares in the employer which are then appropriated to each employee in the plan.

There are four ways by which an employee can obtain shares:

- Free Shares: An employer can award an employee up to £3,000 worth of free shares per annum (with a choice of performance related awards).
- Partnership Shares: An employee can buy shares out of pre-tax remuneration. The maximum percentage of salary which can be used to buy the shares is 10%, with an overall limit of £1,500 per annum.
- Matching Shares: An employer can match the partnership shares bought by an employee by awarding up to two free shares for every partnership share issued.
- Dividend Shares: An employee can use any dividends from their plan shares each year to reinvest in further plan shares.

Further details in relation to SIPs can be found on the HMRC website.

Long-Term Incentive Plan ("L-TIP")

Summary

This is a flexible, unapproved plan whereby employees receive a deferred right to shares, or to exercise an option to acquire shares at nil cost. Rights are generally made conditional upon the attainment of pre-set performance targets. The plan is intended to afford incentives for future performance over a period of (usually) three years. Many plans also provide that at the end of the period over which performance is measured, the employees' rights to sell the shares are deferred for a further period of another one, two or three years (i.e. up to six years in total). The plans are often aimed at company executives, to encourage them to become long-term shareholders in the employer.

When shares are ultimately transferred to (or sold on behalf of) the employee under an L-TIP, they receive the full value of those shares, not merely, as in the case of a traditional share option, the growth in the value over the option period. This is because, should the targets be met, shares are usually transferred to the recipient at no cost.

Participation and Limits

Any employee may participate in the plan at the discretion of the directors/shareholders. Since L-TIPs are not capable of approval, there are no limits on the amounts up to which individuals may participate in the plan.

Tax Treatment for the Employee

The tax treatment for the employee will be as described above in relation to "unapproved" plans, the employee generally being liable to income tax when shares are received. There may be PAYE and National Insurance considerations for the employer, which generally do not apply to approved plans.

"Phantom" Share Options ("Phantoms")

Summary

Phantoms are a type of deferred cash bonus arrangement, mirroring the cash benefits that would result from the grant and exercise of a share option, and the immediate sale of the shares acquired. As it is merely a method of calculating a cash bonus it is not subject to HMRC approval.

The amount paid as a bonus is calculated by reference to the increase in the market value of a fixed number of shares over the "option period". The employee is granted a right to call upon the employer to pay him a cash sum calculated as the amount of the difference between the "exercise price" (usually the market value at the time of grant) and the market value of those shares at the time of exercise.

Participation and Limits

Any employee or director, at the discretion of the directors/shareholders, is able to participate in the plan. As phantoms are not capable of approval there are no restrictions on the number of shares referable to, or on individual participation.

Tax Treatment for the Employee

The cash bonus paid forms part of the employee's emoluments and is subject to income tax and National Insurance Contributions.

Listed Companies

Listed companies are subject to various additional rules, guidelines and codes of best practice relating to the adoption and amendment of employee share and share option plans. In particular, certain provisions of the UK's Listing Rules and Corporate Governance Code will apply, and listed companies are expected to conform to the ABI Principles of Remuneration, issued by the Association of British Insurers and the Institutional Voting Information Service. The principles are designed to provide a framework to enable companies to operate the full range of employee share plans within prudent limits, which avoid undue dilution of the interests of existing shareholders.

Part Five

Industry Sectors of Opportunity

5.1 THE AUTOMOTIVE INDUSTRY

Mark Norcliffe, The Sourcing Solutions Ltd

Amid the gloom that has surrounded the automotive industry in Europe since the economic downturn of 2008-2009, the United Kingdom has emerged as a beacon of light, and growth. Whilst sales in other markets have continued to fall and chronic over-capacity has stalked continental assembly plants, the UK is recording solid growth, high productivity and record levels of automotive exports.

In 2012, light vehicle sales in Western Europe totalled 12.3 million units, approximately 30% lower than the aggregate figure for 2008. Some markets have suffered even steeper declines – Spanish car sales have halved since 2007 – and there are few signs of recovery. In the first half of 2013, the French and Italian markets fell by 11%, and even the powerful German automotive sector suffered a double-digit drop. In contrast, UK sales rose by 10% over the same six months. Whilst some European automakers have been reporting plant utilisation levels as low as 25%, vehicle manufacturers such as Nissan, BMW, and Jaguar Land Rover have been hiring workers and adding new models at their UK facilities, as productivity levels continue to rise.

For global automotive companies facing a range of production, marketing and technological challenges, the UK is currently an attractive investment haven.

AT THE CROSSROADS

At the end of the 20th century – a period once dubbed "the age of the motor car"

- the global automotive industry appeared to have entered a period of stability and continuity. The mature markets of the USA, Europe and Japan accounted for the lion's share of both sales and production. Vehicle development was evolutionary rather than revolutionary, and the internal combustion engine was the almost universally accepted form of propulsion.

After a period of rationalisation, a dozen multinational car manufacturers – each building more than one million units per annum – dominated global sales. A second group of regional manufacturers principally served their own domestic markets. A similar process of consolidation had also taken place in the components sector, with major tier 1 suppliers acquiring smaller companies, as they positioned themselves to produce whole vehicle systems for the car makers in whatever region of the world their customer chose to assemble vehicles.

However, barely a decade into the new millenium, fresh challenges have arisen to disrupt the established order. As vehicle sales in mature territories have slumped, the developing markets of China, India and Brazil have continued to grow. China has leapt past the USA to become the world's largest vehicle market, with annual sales now surpassing 20 million units. This change must be recognized as permanent, rather than a temporary phenomenon. India and Brazil have both continued to grow steadily during the economic downturn, and now boast domestic markets comfortably above 3 million per annum. The epicentre of the world auto industry is clearly shifting to the BRIC grouping of emerging economies, and vehicle styling, production and pricing must increasingly be tailored to the tastes of their growing consumer classes. At the same time, these newcomers are spawning indigenous automakers with the wealth, the ambition and – increasingly – the technologies to compete with their international rivals on the global stage.

These challenges to their established business strategies and production over-capacity in their home markets have rocked the global industry giants to the extent that General Motors briefly entered bankruptcy. Ford elected to sell off non-core brands, and Toyota has faced previously unheard of quality problems. European VM's, who have traditionally relied upon strong sales in their domestic markets served by local production plants, have struggled to adjust to the new order. Many of the component conglomerates, assembled only a few years ago, have unravelled. Increasingly, the new owners of unwanted or unprofitable automotive assets, divested by the traditional vehicle and component makers, have come from the emerging economies of India and China.

At the same time, auto companies are under intense pressure to develop a new generation of low carbon vehicles, which will simultaneously reduce dependency on fossil fuels and cut emissions. The best technologies, market potential and likely costs for such new-energy vehicles are still far from clear, but the development costs are already high.

In 2013, the future direction and development of the global auto industry appears much more fragmented and uncertain that it did a decade earlier.

This shifting landscape has major implications for countries and/or regions seeking to bolster their economies by attracting inward automotive investment. Potential new investors are appearing, but the scope and style of their projects, and the products, skills and infrastructure that they require are all changing. Meanwhile, existing investors are seeking to re-structure their existing operations to match the trends within the industry.

A SNAPSHOT OF THE UK MOTOR INDUSTRY TODAY

Today, the automotive industry in the UK is diverse, vibrant and world class. The combination of native engineering and production skills, capital and best practice injected by foreign investors, and the "open door policy" pursued by successive governments has created a resilient, modern industry that contributes substantially to the nation's economic performance.

Currently, seven global car manufacturers and eight commercial vehicle builders have production facilities in the UK. They are complemented by more than 30 niche vehicle makers to create the most diverse automotive mix in Europe. To support this range of production, 19 of the world's top 20 component suppliers also have a presence in the UK, and some 2,300 companies are actively engaged in the local supply chain.

Productivity levels in the sector have improved by 78% over the last decade, and continue to rise. The Nissan plant in Sunderland is regularly rated as one of the most flexible and efficient in Europe.

Total industry turnover is estimated to be in excess of £55 billion, including an annual R&D spend of approximately £1.3 billion. The sector provides employment – directly or indirectly – for around 700,000 and contributes some £12 billion in added value to the national economy. It also makes a substantial (11%) contribution to UK export earnings, and 80% of the vehicles manufactured in the UK are sold abroad. The strong, and increasing, demand for UK-produced premium brands in the emerging BRIC economies is a particularly significant trend, underpinning an 8% growth in vehicle exports for 2012.

In that year, UK passenger car production rose 9% to 1.465 million units. Commercial vehicles added another 112,000 to the total figure, whilst engine production fell just short of the record 2.5 million mark achieved in 2011.

AREAS OF SPECIAL EXPERTISE

One key reason for the continued success of the UK automotive industry is its global reputation for excellence in some of the most dynamic, competitive and technically innovative sectors.

Premium Cars

The UK is the world's second largest producer of premium cars, for which the enduring reputation of British skills, craftsmanship and heritage are strong selling points. The BMW-owned Mini is perhaps the most striking example of this trend. Annual production at the Cowley, Oxford plant now tops 200,000 – more than double the volume originally predicted. Both VW and BMW have found it advantageous to keep the assembly of their respective Bentley and Rolls Royce luxury brands within the UK, and to expand their product portfolios to appeal to new customers in global markets. VW's announcement of a £800 million investment to produce a Bentley-branded sport utility vehicle in Crewe is the latest manifestation of this strategy.

Tata Group has similarly invested heavily in expanding their Jaguar and Land Rover brands, with new models that include the long-awaited Jaguar F-type and Land Rover Evoque. With overseas demand booming – particularly from the Chinese market – these iconic British names now make a significant contribution to the Indian group's total automotive profits.

McLaren and Aston Martin – two leading examples of the many smaller, low-volume manufacturers, whose specialist "niche" vehicles both benefit from local engineering skills and appeal to British motoring enthusiast – are committed to building their new high-performance models at UK facilities.

Engine Development and Production

The UK is also a recognised centre for the development and production of modern, efficient engines. British companies that have been behind some of the world's most famous propulsion units – names like Lotus, Ricardo and Cosworth – continue to offer their design and engineering expertise to international customers for both conventional internal combustion engines and alternative energy electrical and hybrid systems. To utilise the advantages offered by the combination of these development skills and a sophisticated component supply base, global manufacturers – such as BMW, Ford, Honda, Nissan and Toyota - have chosen the UK as a key location for their global engine manufacturing.

The latest investor to join this grouping is Tata Motors, who are constructing an all-new engine plant at Wolverhampton, in the West Midlands. Meanwhile, in the construction equipment sector, JCB are producing the Economax T4 diesel, specially developed for off-highway vehicles, and now fitted in both their own and competitors' machinery.

Between 2011 and 2012, almost five million modern, efficient and environmentally-friendly engines were built on UK production sites.

Motorsport

In the high-octane world of motorsport, the UK is a clear global leader, and hosts more specialist sports car manufacturers than any other country. At the pinnacle of the sport, it provides the home base for eight of the twelve Formula One teams, who need a unique blend of engineering skills and rapid development capability. The FI teams, in turn, depend upon 300 specialist companies to meet their exacting design, testing and re-building requirements. In rallying, NASCAR and other racing disciplines, top competitors also rely on British experts to build, tune and maintain their cars.

Overall, the sector is estimated to provide employment for 38,500 workers. Frequently, the new technologies that they first develop for use in motorsport subsequently migrate into mainstream vehicle engineering – KERS (Kinetic Energy Recovery Systems) is one recent example.

Construction Equipment

With products that move rather more slowly, but that are no less technologically advanced, the construction equipment industry is another UK success story. In this sector, the UK ranks fourth in the global league table, and employs around 50,000 people. Exports, which go to over 200 countries, account for three-quarters of total production.

Britain's own global giant – JCB – manufacturers 300 different types of machinery at their various UK sites, whilst major international investors include Caterpillar and Terex from the USA and Komatsu from Japan. For Caterpillar, the UK represents their largest concentration of investment outside North America.

Academic and Industry Collaborative Research

A significant number of British universities have an international reputation for conducting advanced automotive research, usually in collaboration with industrial partners. At a time when automotive companies are faced with the additional challenge of exploring and developing new technologies (e g battery composition) alongside their "traditional" products, it is especially valuable to have access to such academic research resources.

AUTOMOTIVE INVESTMENT IN THE UK

The Rising Tide of New Investment

The recent volume, and variety, of investments flowing into the UK automotive sector has been truly remarkable, and demonstrates the confidence of both existing and new investors in the resilience of the industry.

Amongst the vehicle manufacturers, Nissan has led the way with a £1 billion programme that will bring to their Sunderland plant future production of the new Invitation model, a revised version of the best-selling Qashqai, the all-electric Leaf, and their Infiniti luxury brand. Their Japanese compatriots, Honda and Toyota, have also announced spending in excess of £300 million to introduce new vehicles to their respective Swindon and Burnaston plants. BMW is investing a further £500 million in the record-breaking Mini plant in Oxford, whilst Tata Motors is expending a similar amount on building a new engine plant at Wolverhampton, as well as committing a substantial sum to up-grading their West Midlands assembly facilities. In response to a co-ordinated campaign by government, management and unions and highly flexible working practices, GM/Vauxhall have designated Ellesmere Port as a key production location for the popular Astra models. They will also build the Vivaro LCV at Luton. In the commercial vehicle sector, Optare – now part of India's Ashok Leyland grouping - has opened a new bus assembly works at Elmet.

There have also been fresh investments in the luxury and high-performance car sector – an area of traditional British expertise. Aston Martin will locate the production of their new Cygnet model at Gaydon, whilst the exclusive McLaren MP4-12C sports car and the Jaguar C-X75 hybrid supercar will be built at Woking and Solihull respectively. The production volumes and model ranges for luxury brands Bentley and Rolls Royce are being further expanded by their respective German owners.

In the component sector, global names like Brose, Calsonic, GKN, Nifco, NSK, Unipres and Stadco have announced investments totalling more than £100 million, as they boost their capacity in the UK to meet increased customer demand.

Historical Precedents

The UK has, of course, a long tradition of attracting automotive investment, stretching back over 100 years to the early production sites of Ford and General Motors. In the 1980's, there was a significant influx of Japanese capital and know-how, when Nissan, Toyota and Honda all selected the UK as their initial manufacturing base within the European Community. These companies built new, modern plants in regions with a strong tradition of engineering skills, but high levels of unemployment. In each case, the vehicle manufacturers brought with them a core of key component suppliers, who also established local production facilities.

Latterly, a new investment surge has seen foreign vehicle manufacturers taking control of British luxury marques, whose global reputations offer strong sales opportunities in emerging markets. From Germany, VW and BMW have invested heavily in growing the Bentley and the Rolls Royce/Mini brands respectively. India's Tata Motors and China's SAIC plan similar growth for the Jaguar Land Rover and MG names that are now under their stewardship.

A Change of Direction

Whilst early automotive investment was largely directed towards vehicle production and assembly, more recent developments have focused increasingly on the acquisition, expansion and utilisation of research and development capabilities. Here, too, the UK has an impressive track record. Around 90% of the £1.3 billion spent annually in the UK on automotive R&D comes from overseas investors.

The Ford R&D facility at Dunton, Essex, which has become the company's global base for small and medium-sized car projects, is currently leading a multi-million pound engine development programme. Nissan's European R&D Centre at Cranfield has successfully re-engineered the Primera, Micra, Terrano and Qashqai models for the European market, whilst the company's London design centre ensures that future products are aligned to contemporary consumer tastes.

British engineering expertise is also eagerly sought by the new breed of VM's from emerging economies. Tata Motors are undertaking a 40% expansion of their Warwick-based European Technical Centre, whilst their fellow Indian automaker, Ashok Leyland, are opening research facilities in nearby Nuneaton. From China, Shanghai Automobile Industry Corp (SAIC), who took over the remnants of the failed MG Rover Group, has established its European Engineering Technical Centre on the old Longbrige site, and ChangAn Automobile Group has chosen Nottingham as the site for its European R&D office. As a result, the UK is now home to the European operations for two of the top automakers from both China and India, and British engineering DNA will be in many of the new models appearing in these rapidly growing markets.

MAPPING THE ROAD AHEAD

For more than 20 years, the UK has offered automotive investors an attractive combination of a stable, low-inflation economy, an open business environment, a resilient domestic market (not dominated by one domestic producer), good labour relations and flexible working practices from a skilled, professional workforce, and a network of research and development facilities, embracing world-class test sites, independent design engineering companies and academic institutions.

That cocktail, combined with the capital and best practice of overseas investors, has revitalised the automotive sector in the UK and made it a major contributor to the rebalancing of the national economy. This development is complemented by the fresh political emphasis on renewing and re-growing manufacturing industries.

Against that background, both government and industry recognise the importance of working together, within a clear and coherent strategy, to retain and further enhance the UK's advantages as a location for future investment.

The Automotive Council and the new Automotive Strategy

To achieve this objective, government and industry have come together to create the high-level Automotive Council, where senior executives and officials can identify and implement the measures necessary to maintain the UK's status as a preferred destination for automotive investment. The Council has done considerable work to create a road-map for development of the auto industry over the next 20 – 30 years, and to benchmark the UK's skills against future requirements. In July 2013, it launched a new Automotive Strategy that sets out an agreed future agenda under the key headings of:

- Technology
- Supply Chain
- Skills
- Business environment

It also established a dedicated Automotive Investment Organisation, tasked with ensuring that the UK can attract and proactively support future investment from global partners.

Technology

At a time when automotive products are undergoing both evolutionary and revolutionary change, the requirement is that the UK is at the leading edge of the most promising technology innovations. The Technology Strategy Board (TSB) channels funding and research into suitable projects, whilst Knowledge Transfer Networks (KTN's), such as Cenex and InnovITS, are tasked with encouraging information exchange and the sharing of best practice.

Examples of the projects undertaken include the creation of a new £1 billion Centre for Advanced Propulsion (jointly funded by government and the 27 founding companies) and the construction – on the MIRA site near Nuneaton – of a world-leading facility specifically designed for the testing and development of Intelligent Transport Systems in a controlled, but realistic, operating environment.

An additional encouragement to research and development work has been an amendment in taxation legislation to introduce the 10% R&D Expenditure Credit (RDEC). This essentially means that financial support for approved R&D activities now takes the form of a grant rather than a tax relief. As such, the benefit is attributable directly to the research budget holder, and effectively offers an 8% cash tax benefit.

The Supply Chain

Automotive Council research has determined that approximately 80% of a vehicle's components can be sourced from UK suppliers. It has also identified more than £3 billion worth of opportunities available to domestic suppliers and international companies wishing to invest in the UK.

A number of industry-led programmes, under the auspices of the Advanced Manufacturing Supply Chain Initiative, are underway to strengthen the component base in the UK, and to encourage vehicle manufacturers to increase their local sourcing. These include the Construction Supply Chain Competitiveness project, led by JCB and Perkins, which focuses on the construction equipment sector, and the Niche Luxury Vehicle Cluster Supplier scheme, involving Aston Martin, Bentley, Rolls Royce and McLaren, that seeks to develop local groupings of high-end luxury item suppliers.

In another, broader initiative, industry and government representatives are working with the banking sector to create a framework for co-operation that will offer innovative ways of providing finance to component makers for new tooling programmes.

Skills and Training

The Council has also addressed the need to refresh the UK's engineering and production workforce with a regular supply of suitably qualified entrants. As a result, the take-up of apprenticeships in the automotive and wider engineering sectors has increased by 85% in two years. To support this initiative, the government has instigated the Higher Apprenticeship Fund, with up to £6 million pounds available to companies offering suitable schemes to young employees.

For those already working in the industry, continuous on-the-job training and improvement courses are available through the National Skills Academy for Manufacturing and Industry Forum.

New Energy Vehicles

Perhaps the biggest technology leap presently facing the automotive industry is the migration from the internal combustion engine, which has – almost exclusively – powered vehicles for the last 100 years, to alternative low-carbon forms of propulsion. Both the timescale for the take-up of new-energy vehicles (NEV's) and the optimum alternative energy option (e.g. hybrid, pure electric, fuel cell) are currently uncertain, but funding is already available to encourage the early development and deployment of NEV's in the UK.

2013 will see the start of production in Sunderland of the Nissan Leaf – the world's first volume all-electric car. Meanwhile Toyota will launch the hybrid version of their Auris model, which utilises an engine wholly produced at their Deeside factory – the first time the company has built hybrid power units outside Japan. There are also strong hopes that GM's Ampera, which is powered by a combination of an electric motor supported by a conventional range-extender unit, will be produced at Ellesmere Port.

Buyer incentives of up to £5,000 are available to British purchasers of new-energy cars and light commercial vehicles, who can also benefit from tax and congestion charge exemption. The government has also allocated an additional £500 million to the Office for Low Emission Vehicles (OLEV) to support the development and roll-out of NEV's, and the associated charging infrastructure, until 2020.

DRIVING INTO THE FUTURE

The first quarter of the 21st century promises to be a challenging time for the automotive industry, with new markets, new players and new technologies coming to the fore. There will be many twists and turns, and a few dead-ends, on the road ahead.

To navigate this route successfully, automotive companies will need to be nimble and flexible, and able to operate in an environment that offers them both economic stability and a wide range of skills and technologies. The UK, with a well-established reputation as a world-class development and production base and a clear, coherent strategy for the future, endorsed by both government and industry, is well placed to meet those needs.

FURTHER INFORMATION AND KEY WEBSITES

Further information on automotive investment in the UK, and the support available, can be obtained from a variety of sources. These include:

Department for Business, Innovation and Skills	*www.bis.gov.uk*
UK Trade and Investment	*www.ukti.gov.uk*
The Society of Motor Manufacturers and Traders	*www.smmt.co.uk*
The Motorsport Industry Association	*www.the-mia.com*
The Construction Equipment Association	*www.coneq.org.uk*
Automotive Council	*www.automotivecouncil.co.uk*
Technology Strategy Board	*www.innovateuk.org*
Cenex	*www.cenex.co.uk*
InnovITS	*www.innovits.com*
Sector Skills Council	*www.semta.org.uk*
National Skills Academy for Manufacturing	*www.nsa-m.co.uk*
Industry Forum	*www.industryforum.co.uk*

5.2 INVESTING IN THE UK AUTOMOTIVE SECTOR

Will Harman and Tim Padgett,
Automotive Investment Organisation

INTRODUCTION

Three major forces are transforming the automotive industry: demand is shifting towards emerging economies; products are being more complex and customisable, and the pursuit of lower emissions and fuel costs demands new technologies and business models. This level of change is making investment decisions more challenging than ever. In the midst of uncertainty and sharply falling direct investment into Europe, the UK automotive sector has attracted over £6bn in overseas investment since 2011 (Source: SMMT).

Investors recognise that the UK is a global centre of excellence for the automotive business, offering investors:

- A great return on their investments, driven by growing global demand for UK automotive products, and £3bn in unfulfilled demand for UK-made components (Source: Automotive Council).
- A great place to grow through R&D, supported by cutting-edge universities and a world-leading motorsport sector.

- A great place to do business, with government and industry collaboration making the UK a very attractive location for automotive companies.

Many significant automotive companies have already invested in the UK, such as Jaguar Land Rover.

Case Study – ***Jaguar Land Rover***
"Jaguar Land Rover has invested significantly in the product creation process, in our advanced manufacturing sites and created more than 3,000 jobs during the fiscal year. This commitment is set to continue with a sustained programme of investment which will see us spend in the region of £2.75 billion on new product, people and infrastructure in the year to March 2014."
Dr Ralf Speth, Chief Executive Officer
Jaguar Land Rover

THE UK AS A GLOBAL CENTRE OF EXCELLENCE FOR AUTOMOTIVE MANUFACTURE

11 of the world's largest manufacturers assemble vehicles and engines in the UK. This includes 8 premium brands; the UK is second only to Germany in global market share (source: SMMT website). In addition, there are over 30 other specialist car manufacturers based in the UK, such as McLaren, Caterham and Morgan, and the UK is also the home of Triumph Motorcycles.

There are major UK operations for commercial and specialist vehicle manufacturers such as Dennis Eagle, Leyland Trucks and Wrightbus; as well as major off-road manufacturers including Caterpillar, Perkins, Terex, Komatsu and JCB.

The scale of the UK automotive industry is significant and growing:

- Total automotive revenues of £59.3bn in 2012, up 2.8% on 2011.
- Vehicle production is forecast to rise beyond 2m by 2017.
- 81% of UK-made vehicles and 62% of engines were exported in 2012, to over 100 countries. Around a third of UK-made vehicles are exported to emerging markets (SMMT).

A great business case for investors
The financial case for investing in the UK derives from strong market demand, the diversification of UK manufacturers and the growth of UK based OEMs. Growing global demand for UK-made vehicles and engines is the platform for a great return on investment. Contrasting with trends across most of Europe, UK automotive

production continues to increase. 2012 production of 1.58m vehicles represented an increase of 7.7% on 2011 and engine production was stable at 2.5m. Meanwhile production fell in Europe's largest 3 car-producing markets (down 8.1% in Germany, 16.6% in Spain, and 12.3% in France). (Source: SMMT)

Case study - ***Nissan***
We have been showing that you can operate a world-beating plant in the UK for almost 30 years and the construction of the battery plant is a vote of confidence in the country's ability to support high-technology manufacturing".
Andy Palmer, Executive Vice President
Nissan

The UK industry is highly diversified, providing an excellent platform for sustained growth. The UK exported 81% the vehicles it produced in 2012, and 49% of these were exported outside Europe. The fast-growing markets of China, Russia and the US make up 28% of UK vehicle exports. Source: SMMT and www.oica.net/category/sales-statistics/

For investors in the supply chain, the growth of OEMs has created an unprecedented opportunity

Total spending on components by UK vehicle and engine manufacturers is estimated at £31bn. The Automotive Council has identified an additional £3bn in annual components business that customers would like to source in the UK. Growth in vehicle and engine volumes will drive further demand for UK-sourced components (Source: Automotive Council, KPMG). In addition, eighteen of the world's Top 20 automotive suppliers have a presence in the UK.

THE UK AS A GREAT PLACE TO GROW THROUGH RESEARCH AND DEVELOPMENT

The UK has world class universities and centres of excellence for R&D, attracting total automotive R&D spending of £1.7bn in 2012. The motorsport industry is a perfect example of British R&D in action

UK motorsport leads the world and is increasingly relevant to mainstream automotive companies pursuing lower weight and innovative powertrains.

- In 2013 there will be 19 F1 races across five continents, and 8 out of 11 F1 teams will be based in the UK.
- 4,500 motorsport engineering companies investing around 30% of revenues in R&D.

*Case studies – **Motorsports industry in the UK***

Silverstone-based Flybrid Automotive developed its Kinetic Energy Recovery System (KERS) for the 2009 F1 racing season. Flybrid is now working on its first production application of the system with Wrightbus, Voith Turbo, Productiv and Arriva and has a target of launching on road vehicles in 2014, in a project supported by the government's Technology Strategy Board (TSB). (Source: Flybrid).

The UK-based motor-racing components maker Xtrac is a specialist in transmissions. Originally working only in motorsport, it's "Race to Road" programme is supporting advanced propulsion systems, energy recovery, and increased power density. Xtrac's products range from electric and military gearboxes to the gearbox for the new Pagani Huayara supercar. Source: Xtrac; Autocar.

Since its formation in 1958 and its origins in motorsport and high performance engines, Cosworth has become a world-leading provider of high performance technologies in a diverse range of industries including Automotive, Aerospace, and Defence. The company's head office in Northampton is home to leading edge engineering and manufacturing, and comprehensive test facilities.

The UK is pursuing co-ordinated, high-value programmes in low-carbon technologies:

The government's Office for Low Emission Vehicles (OLEV) aims to make the UK the premier market for Ultra-Low Emission Vehicles (ULEVs), by supporting R&D and infrastructure development, and providing consumer incentives. It has £400m in funding to 2015, supported by a further government commitment and an additional £500m to support ULEV development to 2020. (Source: BIS).

The government and automotive industry are jointly investing £1 billion over the next ten years in an Advanced Propulsion Centre (APC) to research, develop and commercialise the technologies for the vehicles of the future. Backed by 27 companies in the sector, including supply chain companies, the commitment is expected to secure at least 30,000 jobs currently linked to producing engines and create many more in the supply chain. (Source: BIS press release).

The High Value Manufacturing Catapult and the Transport Systems Catapult are supported by over £250m in government investment and physical centres. They are designed to accelerate the transfer and commercialisation of new and emerging technologies into world beating products and services, with a particular focus on low carbon mobility and innovative transport systems. They will be supplemented by private sector funds and collaborative R&D projects.

AND FINALLY, THE UK IS A GREAT PLACE TO DO BUSINESS

The UK is the leading European destination for inward investment, attracting one third of the European total in 2012/13. The UK automotive sector attracted more than £6bn in foreign investment during 2011 and 2012. (Source: SMMT).

There is long-term support for the automotive sector at local and national levels and in terms of both funding and technical support. This forms part of the UK Automotive Industrial Strategy, which sets out the actions that government and industry will take collaboratively to secure the next stage of automotive sector growth (http://bit.ly/1377Buv).

The Automotive Council is the platform for partnership between industry and government. The Automotive Council's members include all of the major OEMs operating in the UK, more than a dozen suppliers, key government departments and other stakeholders.

Automotive is a key strategic sector for the UK Government and as such there is a wealth of government support available at both a national and regional level:

- The Government has committed over £316 million to automotive sector projects through the Regional Growth Fund (RGF), almost £80 million of public and private investment through the Advanced Manufacturing Supply Chain Initiative (AMSCI) and over £180 million to support collaborative R&D through the Technology Strategy Board.
- Patent Box provides an effective corporation tax rate of 10% on profits from patents registered in the UK or European patent offices. In April 2013 the government introduced an "above the line" R&D tax credit, with a minimum rate of 9.1% before tax, making investments more affordable. (Source: SMMT).

Case studies

Cab Automotive – Regional Growth Fund: In July this year Cab Automotive was awarded £1.6 million of RGF funding and is investing £8 million in premises and new machinery. The funding will enable the specialist company to continue to supply its customers such as Aston Martin, Jaguar Land Rover and Toyota with high quality seats and interior trim. This has already safeguarded 198 jobs and allowed the firm to take on 20 new skilled staff.

"The RGF grant has given the Company the confidence to invest in new plant and equipment which has already proven dividends with new orders of over £10 million. This is exactly what the fund is for and as an SME this gives us the springboard for sustainable growth and job creation."
Richard McCulloch, Finance Director,
Cab Automotive

Zytek – Regional Growth Fund: Zytek Automotive is a vehicle engineering enterprise based in Staffordshire. It specializes in the design, development and supply of components for hybrid and electric vehicles for automotive manufacturers. The company received £1.3 million from the Regional Growth Fund for an innovative research and development project, which led to the introduction of some new and exciting products into a competitive market and the creation of 40 new jobs.

"The RGF funding has made a real difference to us at Zytek and alongside our own planned investment has enabled us to develop a number of new and exciting products for this emerging and highly competitive market. Training is very important to us and RGF has meant that we have been able to move closer towards closing the skills gap."
Kerry Diamond, Chief Financial Officer,
Zytek Automotive

NGF Europe – AMSCI funding: NGF EUROPE worked with the Northwest Automotive Alliance (NAA) and the Liverpool City Region Local Enterprise Partnership to secure a £500,00 AMSCI (Advanced Manufacturing Supply Chain Initiative) grant, enabling a £4m investment in the first fully integrated high tensile strength glass cord manufacturing factory in Europe, creating 24 jobs.

"The support from the NAA's Business Excellence Programme resulted in a successful bid for AMSCI funding, and the outcome will be the creation of the world's leading glass cord manufacturing facility here in the North West. The support from the NAA allowed us to put in a high quality bid which meant that we stood a greater chance of success."
Alistair Poole, Managing Director,
NGF EUROPE Limited

Labour costs, industrial relations and tax are competitive assets for the UK.

- The UK has one of the lowest industrial labour costs (23.4 euros) of any Western European nation. This is significantly lower than in Germany (35.4 euros) and France (36.7 euros), and is comparable to that in Italy (27.5 euros). Source: Eurostat - Total labour costs for industry (except construction) in 2012.
- The UK offers stable wage rates, with levels of wage inflation amongst the lowest in Western Europe. Investors in the UK achieve more reliable returns, and companies buying from the UK benefit from consistent prices. Average annual wage inflation during the period 2001-2011 (accounting for Euro/Sterling exchange) was 2% in the UK, 6% in France, 8% in the Czech Republic, and 10% in Romania. Source: KPMG Capturing Opportunity Report

- The UK has the lowest rate of corporation tax amongst the major European economies. KPMG's 2012 Competitive Alternatives report shows that the effective tax rate for a typical automotive component supplier in the UK was 18.4% versus France (24.4%), Germany (29.8%), Italy (34.9%) and the Netherlands (20.5%). Further tax advantages are available through targeted initiatives to encourage R&D and innovation.

Case study – ***Nissan***
Nissan's Sunderland plant, producing the Qashqai, Juke, Note and Leaf models, is one of the world's most efficient car plants.

- Around 80% of the 500,000 vehicles produced at the plant are exported, to over 97 world markets.
- Representing over £3.5 billion of investment, Nissan's presence in Sunderland has led companies such as Tacle, Calsonic Kansei, Hashimoto and Unipres to set up manufacturing bases in the region and now directly employs over 6,000 staff, with a further 24,000 posts supported in the North East and wider UK supply chain.

(Source: Nissan)

ABOUT THE AUTOMOTIVE INVESTMENT ORGANISATION

The creation of the Automotive Investment Organisation (AIO) is part of an innovative approach which will help further accelerate foreign direct investment in the UK automotive sector. Led by Joe Greenwell, formerly Chairman of Ford of Britain and Chairman and CEO of Jaguar Land Rover, the AIO brings senior automotive industry expertise into government.

We work by helping potential and current investors to understand the opportunities that exist within the UK automotive sector and determine the government support that may be needed. We also create compelling investment propositions and provide practical support. To fulfil this task we work closely with stakeholders across government and the UK automotive industry, often via the Automotive Council.

For more information on how the AIO can help you to achieve your investment ambitions, contact us today by telephone or email as detailed below:

T: +44 (0)20 7333 5442
E: enquiries@ukti-invest.com

5.3 INVESTING IN UK LIFE SCIENCES

Mark Treherne, Chief Executive, UKTI Life Science Investment Organisation (LSIO)

INTRODUCTION

In December 2011, the Prime Minister made a firm commitment to build on our scientific and commercial heritage and exploit innovation in the life sciences sector. The Government needed to understand why we should continue to invest in the sector and why industry should continue to invest in the UK. This questioning triggered a deep analysis of our existing capabilities and strengths. The challenges facing industry and health systems around the world are considerable: the rising costs and complexity of research and development and the need for products and services that provide clear benefits for patients and meet the needs of an ageing population. By working with organisations across the sector, we built an understanding of the changes we needed to make to prepare for the future. Published on the same day, the *Strategy for UK Life Sciences and Innovation, Health, and Wealth* demonstrated our commitment to the sector and outlined new initiatives for the future.

Since then, the changes and new investments we have made are already opening up our scientific, clinical and healthcare infrastructure to new partnerships, while at the same time establishing a more efficient and integrated life science ecosystem to attract and stimulate industrial growth. This UK Life Sciences sector is a combination of Government, our National Health Service, the UK research base, research charities and industry. It presents a new deal for businesses, our life sciences economy, and for patients, whereby all stakeholders share the inherent risks in research and development but also together reap the rewards. The UK is now the international partner of choice to tackle the global healthcare challenges and realise value for businesses and for patients.

THE LSIO COMMITMENT TO BUSINESS

The life science industry faces increasing challenges, from the rising costs and increasing complexity of research and development to marketplaces that are evolving in response to ageing populations, the prevalence of chronic diseases, and escalating healthcare costs. The UK's commitment to addressing these challenges was documented in the *Strategy for UK Life Sciences*, launched in December 2011.

The progress made to date focuses on improving the efficiency of the translation of scientific discoveries into innovative technologies, products, and services, making that process smarter, better and faster, and leading to quicker returns for patients, businesses, and investors. To get an update on progress to date, read *The Strategy for UK Life Sciences: One Year On*.

To help achieve these commitments and to signal the importance of the life science sector to the UK economy, UK Trade & Investment (UKTI) has established a dedicated unit to support overseas investment into the UK from the earliest R&D collaborations through to clinical trials, commercial operations and partnerships. The team in the UKTI Life Science Investment Organisation (LSIO) is here to support you to navigate the UK investment environment and to help global businesses invest and expand in the UK. We launched our new LSIO Prospectus in December 2012, which reiterates:

- the commitment the UK is making to improve the UK's life science ecosystem, benefiting both businesses and patients, and
- the commitment the UK is making to industry to be the preferred partner for international business in discovering, developing, and commercialising innovative life science products and services.

The LSIO recognises the need to support every component of the pathway. From bench to bedside, we are making it easier to discover, develop and deliver healthcare innovation in the UK. Business benefit from the support and investment we provide to protect the UK's vibrant research base and create the right environment for experimental medicine, clinical translation and commerciali-sation. Business also benefit from the opportunity to use the UK as a launch pad to other international markets, whether in Europe or beyond. The UK's excellent reputation in research, clinical development, health regulation, and health economics combined with UKTI's own global connectivity mean that the UK can help your business maximise the export potential of your health technologies or services. This process is illustrated in Figure 5.3.1 below:

Figure 5.3.1

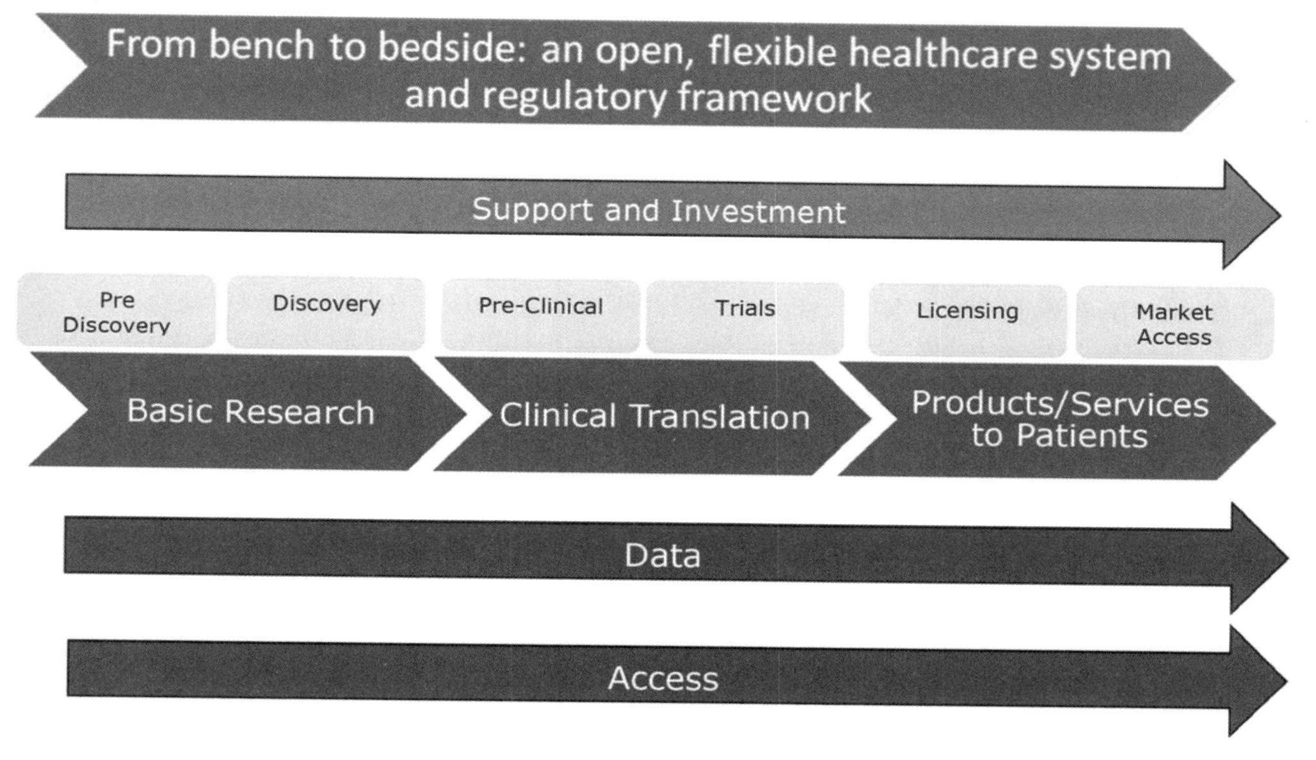

IMPROVING THE BUSINESS ENVIRONMENT FOR LIFE SCIENCES

With the increasing cost, risk and complexity of research and development, it has become continuously more challenging for life science companies to commercialise medical innovations. To address this challenge, the UK Government is introducing a suite of fiscal measures including targeted investment, funding initiatives and tax incentives to stimulate innovation and growth for start-ups and SMEs through to large global enterprises. By locating in the UK, a **non-European** business also becomes eligible for funding initiatives from the European Commission.

In April 2013 the UK Government introduced a Patent Box, which allows companies to elect to apply 10% rate of corporation tax to all profits attributable to qualifying patents, whether paid separately as royalties or embedded in the sales price of products.

R&D tax credits are the single biggest UK Government support for business investment in R&D. The scheme for Small and Medium Sized Enterprises (SMEs) is amongst the most generous in the world. The SME scheme provides relief worth approximately 25p on every £1 of qualifying expenditure. Companies claiming under the SME scheme can also claim relief for R&D subcontracted to other enterprises. Large companies applying to the scheme receive relief worth approximately 7p on every £1 of qualifying expenditure. From April 2013, large companies are able to claim an 'Above the Line' credit for their qualifying R&D expenditure. This is designed to increase the visibility and certainty of UK R&D relief and provide greater financial and cash flow support to companies with no corporation tax liability.

The Government's Regional Growth Fund (RGF) is a £3.2 billion fund operating across England. It supports projects and programmes that lever private sector investment to create economic growth and sustainable employment, ensuring that your company can thrive in a business-friendly English region.

The £300million UK Research Partnership Investment Fund (UK RPIF), managed by the Higher Education Funding Council for England (HEFCE), will lever more than double this in private investment into higher education research facilities and stimulate strategic research partnerships between university, businesses and charities. Projects relevant to life sciences were announced in 2012, securing £146.5million from the Fund.

The Biomedical Catalyst is a £180million programme of public funding designed to deliver growth to the UK life sciences sector. Delivered jointly by the Medical Research Council and the Technology Strategy Board, the Biomedical Catalyst provides responsive and effective support for the best life science opportunities arising in the UK and seeks to support those opportunities which demonstrate the highest scientific and commercial potential, irrespective of medical area.

Invention for Innovation (i4i) is a research award from the National Institute for Health Research (NIHR) which aims to support and advance the development of innovative medical technologies and their translation into the clinical environment for the benefit of patients in the NHS in England and Wales. It is a patient focused source of early or late-stage product development funding for R&D collaborations between UK healthcare academics, clinicians and industry.

There has been renewed interest in UK venture capital through 2012, with the announcement of a series of new investment funds focused on the life science and healthcare sector. The creation of these funds has created a new vehicle for start-ups to access early-stage investment.

Scottish Enterprise provides grants for investment projects via the Regional Selective Assistance (RSA) funds. In addition, grants to support commercially viable translational research projects (up to and including early phase clinical trials) are available to both research organisations and companies.

The Life Sciences Investment Fund is a £100million fund created for the life science sector in Wales. The new fund will contribute to an already well-established Welsh life science sector that employs over 15,000 people in more than 300 businesses, contributing around £1.3billion to the economy annually.

Invest Northern Ireland offer some of the most attractive incentive packages in Europe. They provide financial support to help set up your business in Northern Ireland, along with comprehensive advice to facilitate the investment process. Invest Northern Ireland supports commercial clinical trials that benefit from the Health & Social Care R&D clinical research infrastructure.

SUPPORTING THE UK'S VIBRANT RESEARCH BASE

The UK has a heritage of life science discovery that has transformed scientific knowledge and continues to unlock clinical and commercial opportunities. From the building blocks of the new genomic age, to the secrets of cells, to the physics that makes magnetic resonance imaging (MRI) possible, UK science is world-class, offering industry an opportunity to partner with globally recognised pioneers and innovators. The Medical Research Council (MRC), which celebrates its centenary year in 2013, is just one example of this heritage. The MRC's research institutes include the Laboratory of Molecular Biology where Watson and Crick uncovered the structure of DNA, which moved into its new building this year. Due to open in 2015 the Francis Crick Institute is a partnership between the MRC, Cancer Research UK, the Wellcome Trust, University College London, King's College London and Imperial College London. It will be one of significant developments in UK biomedical science for a generation. By fostering collaboration with other centres of excellence, the Crick will harness the full capacity of this country's brightest and best researchers for the benefit of patients and the economy.

The UK Government has protected the UK's science budget and is committed to supporting core science funding.

In the UK, partners work together to support a research and innovation culture that spans sectors and geographies, and supports the creation of a fully integrated life science and healthcare ecosystem that places the patient at the heart of the system as in Figure 5.3.2.

Figure 5.3.2 The UK Research and Innovation Culture

The UK has a uniquely powerful combination of:

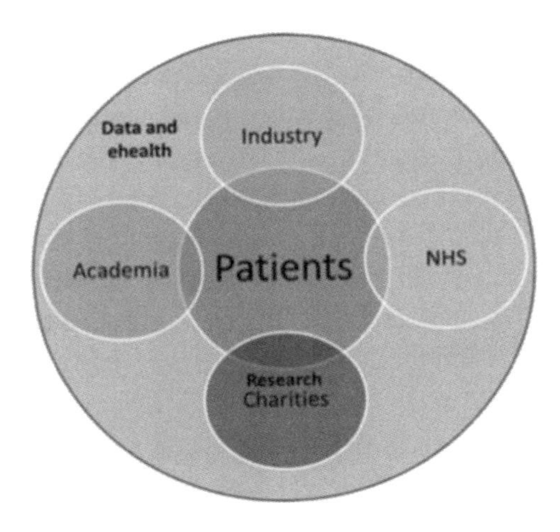

- World-leading universities, science facilities, and principal investigators
- Established industrial R&D, manufacturing and supply chain
- Translational research infrastructure and clinical network supported by key opinion leaders within the National Health Service
- Globally renowned research charities
- A national infrastructure for health research
- Access to unrivalled, clinically coded, granular health data that tracks patients throughout the whole care pathway.

IMPROVING THE QUALITY AND EFFICIENCY OF CLINICAL TRANSLATION

The UK is committed to making clinical study start-up more efficient, introducing the Health Research Authority to streamline approvals for clinical research and new performance metrics for patient recruitment. In future, the National Institute for Health Research (NIHR) funding for providers of NHS services undertaking clinical trials will be contingent on working to a benchmark of 70 days or less from receipt of a valid research application to recruitment of the first participant.

The UK is also committed to enabling every willing patient to be a research patient and embedding this commitment in the NHS Constitution. Through organisations like the UK Clinical Research Collaboration and the revamped UK Clinical Trials Gateway, the UK is encouraging more patients to participate in clinical research. This makes the UK an attractive location to initiate pivotal studies and a gateway to enter other European markets.

The UK spends circa £0.5billion annually on the National Institute for Health Research (NIHR), supporting experimental medicine research and clinical trials in the NHS.

The NIHR Office For Clinical Research Infrastructure (NOCRI) facilitates industry access to the UK's clinical research infrastructure, from early-stage collaborative research through to contract clinical trials. NOCRI can help your business access world-leading science and clinical expertise, world-class facilities, and well-characterised and diverse patient cohorts drawn from the 60 million people who use the National Health Service in the UK. NOCRI provides a managed process for collaborative research, has developed model partnership and contracting agreements for industry, and has set up and administers two NIHR Translational Research Partnerships in Joint and Respiratory Inflammatory Diseases and a new Translational Research Collaboration for Dementia Research.

PROVIDING ACCESS TO DRIVE HEALTHCARE INNOVATION

Demands on health and social care systems continue to rise as demographics change and the ever-increasing expectations from the public it serves. Add to this an increase in capability within the life sector, fuelled by advances in knowledge, science, technology and the development of new pharmaceutical treatments, diagnostics and devices. Innovation is the answer. By basing your business in the UK, you gain access to the largest national healthcare system in the world. Launched in December 2011, alongside the *Strategy for UK Life Sciences, Innovation Health and Wealth (IHW)* set out a delivery agenda to embed and spread innovation at pace and scale throughout the NHS. It included a number of ambitious actions that will deliver game-changing improvements in the quality and value of care delivered in the NHS. They are designed as an integrated set of measures that together will support the NHS in achieving a systematic change in the way it operates, delivering high quality care, value for money and driving economic growth.

The UK is a world leader in health technology assessment and home to the National Institute for Health and Clinical Excellence (NICE). With an increasing focus on clinical and cost-effectiveness globally, and the need to demonstrate value to the patient and to health systems, industry can leverage the UK's expertise to develop an evidence base to support market access, uptake and diffusion. Through NICE International, its non-profit fee-for-service consultancy arm, NICE works with governments and other organisations from around the world to promote efficiency and quality in healthcare systems.

Procurement plays a valuable role in driving growth and improving quality and value in the NHS. In May 2012, the Department of Health published 'Raising Our Game' which sets out the immediate steps that NHS organisations can take now to realise the efficiencies needed from procurement. This has been a good start, but we need to go further and be more ambitious, to take advantage of the enormous buying potential of the NHS to ensure value for money for taxpayers, more productive relationships with industry, and better patient access to the very best services, technologies, devices and medicines.

There has been an open engagement process with the NHS, industry and a range of stakeholders to move towards a modernised procurement function for the NHS that is as good as any internationally. This will result in:

- Procurement based on outcome rather than cost
- Having better access to data and to share this
- Putting clinicians at the heart of the procurement process
- Working together to harness the enormous buying power of the NHS.

UNLOCKING DATA TO DRIVE INNOVATION

UK science is informed by real world data and information, from bioresources to anonymised patient records, clinical practice, and outcomes data. Enabled by the National Health System and anonymised electronic patient records, business have access to unrivalled, clinically-coded health data, including linked datasets offering a unique opportunity to understand care pathways.

The NHS's rich output of data can help drive innovation of your business' technology and services by monitoring effectiveness, performance and value of the product through from primary, secondary and tertiary care in routine clinical practice. This enables your business to create clearer pricing and market access planning strategies and to undertake the required post launch benefit/risk requirements.

CREATING AN OPEN AND FLEXIBLE REGULATORY FRAMEWORK

The Prime Minister has stated that "The most crucial, the most fundamental thing we're doing is opening up the NHS to new ideas because time and again we've heard the same thing from industry. We've got the treatments that work, we've proved they're safe, they've been approved but we cannot get them into the NHS."

The UK Government is committed to ensuring there is a step-change in the research activities and adoption of new products into the NHS. The UK is also home to two internationally respected health regulators, MHRA at the UK level and the EMA at the European level. Their commitments are:

- the NHS is open to collaborate with your business on research
- new products are critically appraised to the highest standard.

The Government's ambition is that if successful, your technology is adopted into a healthcare system that is open to innovation, with access to real world data that can be tracked across care pathways to ensure robust appraisal and efficacy tracking of your business' product or service.

The NHS is a repository of innovative ideas based on unmet clinical need gained from the daily interactions NHS clinicians have with patients through all stages of the care pathway. The Government is harnessing this unique position by investing and incentivising NHS organisations to research and collaborate with industry in an aim to create innovative services and technologies to meet end patient benefit.

The UK is home to two globally-respected health regulators – the Medicines and Healthcare products Regulatory Agency (MHRA) and the European Medicines Agency (EMA).

The MHRA is an Executive Agency of the Department of Health and has UK-wide responsibility for the regulation of medicines and clinical trials and is the Competent Authority in regulating medical devices in the UK. The European Medicines Agency (EMA), headquartered in London, conducts scientific evaluation of medicines for use across the European Union, harmonising existing national medicines regulatory bodies across Europe. By undertaking health research in the UK and being assessed by rigorous and globally renowned health regulators your business can ensure better portability and prestige of your product(s) across the rest of the world.

HOW THE LSIO HELPS BUSINESS

The UKTI Life Science Investment Organisation (LSIO) is your partner acting as a simple interface to the UK Life Science sector. The LSIO is your guide to identifying research, development and delivery partners and will support you through every step of investing in and working in the UK. The LSIO team work closely with you to understand business needs and requirements, partnering companies with the right people in the UK.

Once a business has a presence in the UK, we consider it a UK company and open up UKTI's global trade services to help your business to launch in other international markets. The LSIO connects your business to subject matter and experts across the life science and healthcare sector in the UK.

www.ukti.gov.uk/lifesciences
@UKTI_LSIO

5.4 CHEMICAL AND RELATED INDUSTRIES

Chemistry Growth Strategy Group

INTRODUTION

This chapter is a summary of the report prepared by the Chemistry Growth Strategy Group (CGSG) and published in July 2013 detailing the strategy developed in cooperation with the UK Government for the chemical industries for the period through to 2030.

In 2012 the Gross Value Added contribution of the chemistry-using industries to the UK economy amounted to £195 billion. The strategy target is to increase the contribution by 50% to £300 billion by 2030. Chemistry is the bedrock of manufacturing and the success of the UK's key growth sectors, including aerospace, agriculture, automotive and life sciences, is dependent on chemistry - often delivered by SMEs through competitive supply chains.

Despite the downturn in the global economy, chemical producers and their users in the UK have remained very strong. However, much still remains to be done if UK chemistry is to deliver its full potential for economic growth and the formation of the Chemistry Growth Partnership will serve national interests to deliver a manufacturing renaissance.

ANATOMY OF THE CHEMICAL INDUSTRIES SECTOR

At the foundation of the UK's manufacturing industries, the chemical sector encompasses a diversity of products ranging from lightweight polymers through to medicines, clean drinking water and food. The success of all the UK's established growth sectors - including aerospace, agritech and life sciences - is chemistry dependent often delivered through competitive supply chains with SMEs playing an essential role as providers of design, manufacturing and service links.

The chemical sector itself has an annual sales turnover of £60 billion, sustains 500,000 jobs throughout the country and contributes a £5 billion annual trade surplus to the national balance of payments as the UK's biggest manufacturing contributor.

The chemical sciences are harnessed to generate four kinds of economic benefit:

- chemical manufacture
- process technology
- product development
- application and formulations skills

Together, they yield the following gross value added contributions from chemistry-using industries:

	£ billlion
Direct	
Chemical manufacturing	10
Pharmaceutical manufacturing	9
Indirect	
Consumer products	46
Automotive	11
Aerospace	7
Construction	23
Oil and gas extraction	24
Production of electricity	6
Other	59
Total	**195**

Source: ONS Annual Business Survey 15/11/2012

ACHIEVING THE GROWTH OBJECTIVES

In aiming for growth of 50% by 2030 to deliver a Gross Value Added contribution from the chemical-using industries of £300 billion, three critical ingredients have been identified for achieving this target, namely: secure and competitive energy and feedstock; accelerated innovation; and strengthened supply chains.

The CGSG has proposed that procurement of these three ingredients be entrusted to a joint industry/Government Chemistry Growth Partnership (CGP) to help the industry realize the potential growth opportunities envisioned in the strategy.

Securing competitive UK energy and feedstock supplies

Working with appropriate Government departments and other stakeholders the CGP will focus on policies to ensure that affordable, environmentally "clean" raw materials for chemical manufacturing are available. In particular, the CGP has tasked itself to provide proof of commercial viability for unconventional gas sources by 2014 to enable commercial flows by 2017 working with local communities on fracking issues and benefits.

In addition to the safe exploitation of unconventional gas, other CGP missions include:

1. The sustainable use of biofuels and optimal use of waste resources.
2. Exploring the potential to increase support for research into technically and economically viable options for carbon capture and storage, and usage on an industrial scale.
3. The continuing development of renewable resources through industrial industrial biotechnology and synthetic biology.

The potential benefits from work in each of these areas has been scoped but is, as yet, unquantifiable. For example, the potential for unconventional gas could be equivalent to twice that of conventional North Sea gas and, if realised, would reduce dependence on imported gas while strengthening the business case for investment in UK chemical capacity.

In the field of carbon capture there is potential to reuse and generate value from CO2 emissions by converting them into hydrocarbons and there is an urgent need for greater research on the benefits of commercialisation.

Biofuels and waste recycling also offer sources of feedstock and a route to lower carbon emissions from production. For example: mechanical recycling in plastics uses 25-60% less energy thasn that required to produce primary polymers as feedstocks.

Examples of technology achievement

Example 1

An outstanding example of successful work in building and operating industrial scale facilities for converting waste and non-food crop biomass into advanced biofuels and renewable power is provided by INEOS Bio using its own proprietary bioenergy technology. The first INEOS Bio facility in Florida USA has been operational since 2003 and an industrial scale plant using fully integrated gasification-fermentation-distillation processes broke ground in 2011 involving an investment of $130 million.

Example 2

Here in the UK, Oxford Catalysts, an SME spin-out from Oxford University, has exploited two platform catalyst technologies focused on the area of clean energy and fuels. Its US subsidiary Velocys acquired in 2008, developed an impressive portfolio of microchannel reactor technology which provided a perfect platform for the type of highly active catalyst enabled by Oxford Catalysts' own technology. In 2013 Oxford Catalysts raised more than £30 million through an oversubscribed placing on the London Stock Exchange bringing the total funding secured to over £55 million. Its Fischer-Tropsch reactors are now being are now being sold into the USA and Europe.

The catalysts have opened up the Gas-to-Liquids (GTL) market to the majority of energy and specialty chemical companies, permitting them to convert undervalued natural gas and waste biomass into valuable liquid transportation fuels and chemicals. Here at home, for example, where Solena Fuels are building municipal waste-to-fuels plant to supply British Airways with jet fuel at London City Airport by 2015, the Oxford Catalysts' Fischer-Tropsch technology has been specified for the project.

Accelerating innovation

The CGSG has endorsed the establishment of an open-access Innovation Centre for the formulation of chemical products. It is intended that the proposed Centre will complement the established centre for Sustainable Chemistry, Industrial Biotechnology and Materials located in the Centre for Process Innovation, which is a part of the High Value Manufacturing Catapult initiative, as well as the innovation programme developed by the Chemistry Innovation Knowledge Transfer Network.

Industry will be encouraged to leverage links with the Continuous Manufacturing and Crystalisation Centre (CMAC) in Scotland and optimise use of the available UK and European funding to drive innovation.

Three priority areas have emerged from the CGSG's work in identifying the areas with the greatest potential for growth and what is needed to accelerate innovations to exploit these growth opportunities:

- raw materials for the 21st century
- smart manufacturing processes
- design for functionality

The potential longer term benefits from exploiting these opportunities have been quantified:

Raw materials: Potential benefits of £8 billion from the use of biomass or waste as raw materials.

Smart manufacturing processes: Opportunities estimated at £10 billion from scalable, flexible and more resource-efficient processes in both chemicals and industrial biotechnology.

Design for functionality: A conservative estimate of £5 billion benefit from intervention on materials chemistry to create substitutes for materials currently imported. The formulated products market in the UK is currently worth about £180 billion. Chemical products designed for a "circular economy" offer additional potential of about £1 billion currently achievable through design for waste management and recycling and this opportunity could increase to £120 billion by 2020.

Rebuilding UK Chemistry Supply Chains

The CGP is working with Government and industry to refill the UK's hollowed-out chemistry supply chains, with particular focus on UK SMEs to serve down-stream industries. Reinforcing industrial clustering and infrastructure to effect economies of scale will be critical to success. Attracting foreign direct investment (FDI) into the UK will help to fill gaps in UK supply chains.

To achieve these objectives CGP will encourage chemical and chemistry-using companies to strengthen business ties with UK suppliers and customers while exploring new foreign direct investment opportunities. As a part of this activity

CGP will ensure that chemistry-intensive SMEs leverage business support available from UK initiatives such as the Advanced Manufacturing Supply Chain, the new national Manufacturing Advisory Service and the established Scottish Manufacturing Advisory Service.

The UK chemical and chemical-using industry has a long-established infrastructure in place which will provide a foundation for the rebuilding of supply chains - ethylene pipe lines, freight lines and ports in addition to sites such as Wilton, Runcorn and Humberside which provide a strategic advantage.

However, CGP recognizes that over the past decade key chemical building blocks , previously part of a more integrated UK chemical industry with many raw material products manufactured here, are currently imported as a result of commercial decisions. In some cases, the UK has relied dangerously on sole suppliers. More recently a trend has become apparent among large chemistry-using companies, most noticeably in pharmaceuticals, to rebalance the East-West proportions of their manufacturing. Both the increasing costs of doing business in Asia, as well as regulatory and quality issues have been influencing factors. The impact of converting imports to in-country sourced products would be significant. The aerospace industry alone bought in some £220 million of chemicals and plastic products in 2010 and including the embedded chemistry in other components would add considerably to the value. Other priority industries including automotive are showing similar signs of change.

There are also opportunities to attract FDI into the UK which will help fill gaps in UK supply chains and improve competitiveness in global markets, as in the case of Mexichem's Fenix Fluor project.

The focus on ensuring a thriving community of generally agile SMEs, well-connected to academic and other centres of excellence, is particularly important, not least because they are less likely than major corporations to move their operations, jobs and tax payments abroad in hard times. However, they are often in need of support from Local Enterprise Partnerships (LEPS) and local government to help build their business growth skills to survive during periods of downturn when they are less resilient than the majors.

THE UK CHEMICAL SECTOR IN A COMPETITIVE WORLD

The CGSG has identified five priorities on which chemistry-using industries need to focus in order to optimise growth:

- climate change solutions;
- government initiatives

- trade
- regulation
- finance
- skills

Climate change solutions

It is estimated that the global carbon framework and increased use of chemical climate change solutions across industrial sectors could cause average energy use by the EU chemical industry to increase by 22% through to 2030. However, given the right frameworks to harness energy efficiency and carbon reduction opportunities, there is also scope to reduce carbon emissions in the chemical sector by 30% in the same timeframe. Growth in chemicals from the energy sector alone could exceed 3% per year.

Kingspan Insulation, now a leading international provider of sustainable products for the construction industry is an outstanding example of ehat is achievable. Its projects range from evolutionary chemical and structural improvement across its products to more fundamental changes in materials and building envelope solutions. Kingspan Insulation declares 'its commitment to quality, performance and innovation which is, through the help of chemistry, delivering global solutions for the construction of lower energy and lower carbon buildings.'

For the chemical industry the task is to identify which technologies and innovations are likely to help reduce emissions and optimise heat use across the sector, and to reduce the chemical industry's own emissions while stimulating R&D programmes and facilitating technologies prior to commercialisation.

Leveraging Government initiatives

There are a number of Government initiatives already in place to support and encourage chemical and chemistry-using companies, particularly those in the SME sector. They include the Technology Strategy Board and Research Councils for R&D funding; and the Business Bank, Green Investment Bank and Enterprise Finance Guarantee Scheme for funding.

Having identified that a significant number of potential users are unaware of these facilities, the CGP will work with Government and industry stakeholders to improve SME's awareness and ability to make use of existing support and initiatives.

Trade

The potential for gaining business from international markets is self-evident; in 2011, for example, UK domestic demand for chemicals and pharmaceuticals was less than 2% of global demand. In the same year, the UK exported £53 billion sales value of chemical man-made polymer and pharmaceutical manufactures which sustained 150,000 direct jobs and more than 300,000 jobs in distribution and other commercial and industrial services.

The UK's two biggest markets for its chemistry-using industries are the EU, in which Germany is the predominant trading partner, and the USA where two-way trade in non-pharmaceutical products totals more than £20 billion. Every 1% increase in chemical and pharmaceutical exports, or a similar decrease through import substitution, equates to £500 million of UK-generated sales or the creation/safeguarding of 4,500 jobs within and around the UK chemicals supply chain.

With this incentive, the CGP will work with Government and industry stake-holder to target high-value sector and markets through export promotion campaigns and to push for the rapid conclusion of a free trade asgreement between the EU and USA.

Regulation

Foreign companies choose to buy chemicals from the UK because they can count on responsiveness, reliability, quality, service and local knowledge to complement the UK's strengths in innovation, R&D and formulation. A regulatory environment is needed to give more encouragement to international companies seeking to exploit these strengths by starting up in the UK. The CGP works with Government to help create a regulatory climate and culture that will strengthen international competitiveness and deliver growth.

Finance and funding

While most established chemical companies do not face significant barriers to finance for new projects, SMEs and start-up companies have difficulty in accessing finance on reasonable terms. Traditional banks remain averse to risk-based investment or fund requests of less than £5-7 million, and personal guarantees are still usually demanded from SME directors.

The Government is fully aware of the financing problem for SMEs that are the backbone of chemical and manufacturing industries and has introduced the Funding for Lending scheme to help business access bank finance by providing guarantees through the Enterprise Finance Guarantee Scheme, stimulated now by new non-bank financing through the Business-Finance Partnership and supplemented by the planned £10 billion Business Bank, the Business Growth Fund and the Green Investment Bank. The majority of the sector's financing needs are related to capital expenditure; therefore, the Government's £2.6 billion Regional Growth Fund is a positive step in this direction.

The CGP's mission is to SMEs and the financial community for a better understanding of each other's business requirements and to establish greater clarity on lending risk, investor benefits and product/business cycles.

Skills

Finally, a skilled, technical workforce is essential to a successful UK chemical industry; every 1% increase in the number of employees trained is asscoiated notionally with an increase productivity of 0.6%, worth £162 million to the sector's gross value added.

Although the chemical industry has a strong track record in recruiting graduates and apprentices, the workforce is ageing and looking out to 2030 businesses will require a new range of skills to address new technology and innovation and to drive growth through best manufacturing practice. The CGP will work with stakeholders, including the Chemistry Industries Association, the Royal Society of Chemistry (RSC) and Institution of Chemical Engineers (IChemE), to reinforce and strengthen improvements in higher level graduate, masters and post graduate training to meet professionally verified standards including the "Cogent gold standard" as a brand for excellence in chemistry skills.

Readers wishing to study the Chemistry Growth Strategy Group report in detail may access the full text on myviews@ukchemistry2030growth.co.uk.

5.5 HOTEL & LEISURE INDUSTRIES

Felicity Jones, Watson, Farley & Williams LLP

INTRODUCTION

Whilst the impact of the global recession continues to be felt and there is no escaping the significant gap that this has generated between the market in London and the rest of the United Kingdom, both in terms of occupancy and investor confidence, there are positive signs in both. This chapter focuses on the branded hotel and serviced apartment markets rather than leisure facilities, bars and restaurants (although some of the principles apply to all sectors of the market).

Just as any potential guest has a wide range of products from which to choose, the hospitality investor has to consider the type of hotel or serviced apartment and market that they wish to invest in (ranging from budget to five star), the location (city centre, provinces or London – which warrants a separate classification), the nature of the project (new development or established site – possibly trading below expectations) and the degree of involvement that they require (from Owner/Operator to a purely financial investor with a management contract with a major brand). All of these factors are fundamental in the assessment of any project, the attitude of potential funders and the degree of risk.

The experienced hotel investor will know the importance of taking advice at an early stage to understand the industry in terms of the location, feasibility and/or trading history issues that affect value and funding and the legal issues relating to the project. Whether new to the sector or not, it is vital to take advice at an early stage in relation to the valuation, financing and structuring of a transaction, the prospects (whether by a feasibility study or a review of existing trading) through to brand selection and asset management going forward. An experienced Owner may not need the full range of advice and it will benefit from knowing the industry generally but an understanding of the specific sector of the industry in the relevant location is crucial.

Whatever the industry sector in which you operate, the same basic legal principles will apply and elsewhere in this publication experts have addressed intellectual property, real estate and employment law. The hotel, serviced apartment and wider leisure sectors are likely to require advice on all of these aspects as well as planning, licencing and consents at the operational level.

Understanding specific industry concerns is important when looking at any potential investments and the expectations of the investor (and their funders) need to be discussed early in the process. The correct operating structure can assist an investor with relatively little experience and, managed properly, can assist an investor to maximise its return.

Assuming that the potential investor has decided upon the segment of the market in which it wishes to invest or where it sees the greatest opportunity, any investor in the hotel or serviced apartments markets needs to decide what degree of participation it wants in the management of its property and the degree to which its investment may benefit from introducing or removing a brand.

OPERATING STRUCTURES

Where an Owner (or its funder) requires a "flag" under which to operate or market its accommodation and services, and the benefit of the reservations, marketing and support that such a "flag" offers, one of the following structures will usually apply:

Leases

In recent years, a combination of factors has seen the profile and use of the hotel management contract in the United Kingdom grow at the expense of the lease structure. This trend has been due to accounting and stamp duty issues, the preferences of some brands and the investment community for the "Opco/Propco" division and the growth of investors and lenders with experienced asset managers who are comfortable with management contracts. While many experienced property investors prefer the comfort of a lease structure where the employees, maintenance obligations and business risk are primarily the tenant's responsibility, there is much debate as to whether the lease structure (or a hybrid version thereof) will become more common once again - but this is by no means certain.

Some budget brands have shown a willingness to continue to lease; in contrast to mid-market and upscale brands where few brand owners will lease. The "budget" leases typically focus on a limited service for longer terms of 15-35 years and, in some cases, the tenant offers minimum guarantees to appeal to the investors. Where the tenant is a budget brand with an investor following which is understood by the market, it is likely to be perceived to be a sound investment risk. However, the recent activities of one of the larger budget brand tenants has shown Owners that the leasehold approach by no means offers security (particularly where the product is tired and/or in the wrong location).

Management contracts

A management contract usually takes one of two forms: (i) where an Operator is also the brand owner, it will contract to "manage" or "direct and supervise" the operation of the property under one of its brands offering the benefits of the Brand System (e.g. in reservations and marketing) and the Operator appoints the management team on behalf of the Owner (with whom substantially all the business risk remains); or (ii) a third party independent management company may be appointed to operate under the hotel Owner's own brand or a franchise, i.e. the Owner enters into a franchise agreement to brand its hotel and also uses an independent experienced management company rather than operating the business itself. All management companies should understand the need to present flexible terms that do not adversely impact the bottom line in the early years of operation. The brand operator is more common for larger full service hotels.

Some advisers are of the view that Operators have become more realistic and more prepared to consider break options, incentive structures and soft loans to achieve a financial position that attracts debt funding. We believe that this is the exception rather than the rule where the Operators are the brand owners. Given the unusual nature of a management contract, in the next section we have outlined some typical terms. These terms primarily relate to where a Brand Owner is the Operator but some of the provisions will also be relevant where the hotel is operated by a third party under a franchise.

Franchise agreements

A franchise agreement is one under which the Brand Owner will license the Owner of the hotel to operate directly (or through a third party manager) under its brand. Franchises are rare in the serviced apartment sector but may well grow as the traditional Hotel brands expand their brand portfolios to include more long-stay products. The main difference is that the headline fees payable under a management contract should be significantly larger than those under a franchise agreement (broadly 8% of gross operating profit) but an Owner will still need to carefully review the additional costs and expenses that the Brand Owner may require and will need to assess the additional costs of an independent operator, where relevant, to make a direct comparison.

In spite of the economic climate, a number of property developers continue to use the franchise model to grow significant portfolios. As a result of the significant reduction in bank lending, those developers continue to look at different ownership structures and are taking more equity involvement but are tending to maintain the franchise model (with or without an independent operator).

Some brands are prepared to consider management agreements that convert to franchises based on pre-agreed conditions, but this is not usual in the UK.

COMPARATIVE BENEFITS AND MANAGEMENT CONTRACT ISSUES

The "flight to brand" continues but whether this is a flight to quality (or a more profitable option) will depend very much on the location, style of property and the proposed brand. The availability of a variety of online options and the development of alternative platforms has led some Owners to develop their own brands or use smaller brands, which are often more flexible (or more suitable to an independent Owner of a single or limited number of assets). Funders used to assessing operations are likely to be influenced by the perceived size and resources of particular brands although this may not necessarily benefit the Owner in the longer term. Those Owners who want a recognised brand but more control and lower fees should consider a franchise. A lease will only be considered by an Operator in limited circumstances. This leaves the management contract option. Before entering into a long term commitment the Owner needs to understand the nature of the management contract.

The following is intended to provide the traditional property owner who is more accustomed to acting as a landlord with a guide to some of the terms that it can expect to see in a management contract in order to appreciate how very different it is from a lease. There can be no doubt that under UK law it will be easier (for both Owner and Operator) to terminate an unsatisfactory relationship under a management contract than an underperforming turnover lease. It is therefore important for a potential Owner to understand the nature of the agreement, the liabilities it will be taking on and the limited liability of the Operator controlling its asset.

While some provisions will be key to the Operator, the Owner should seek to find a balance which gives it approval rights in relation to key liabilities. This chapter does not address whether a brand is actually essential to the success of the hotel or the contribution that the brand makes in terms of valuation; but certain rights and restrictions in the management contract will undoubtedly affect value and the Owner must take advice from its valuers. Recent years have seen the contract that assisted the Owner to obtain its funding result in a reduction in open market value on a sale.

The basic management contract provides that the Owner remains responsible for funding the operation of the hotel, the maintenance of the building and all other aspects of the operation. The Operator is paid a fee. The relationship will ideally be one of principal and agent but the Operator may insist that it is no more than a service provider and/or may seek to exclude itself from an agent's fiduciary duties. The Operator will endeavour to ensure that it has control over all matters necessary to ensure that the hotel is maintained and operated to the relevant brand standard (i.e. to protect and enhance the value of its brand). Whereas an Owner will produce a lease, the starting point with a management contract is invariably a standard form management contract produced by the Operator. While there is a general view in the industry that these agreements are becoming more Owner-friendly it is highly unlikely that the starting point will be favourable to the Owner and there is a tendency for the Operator, in seeking to protect its brand, to behave as if the hotel is its own asset (albeit funded entirely by the Owner).

Key points that the Owner will need to consider fall principally into the following categories:

Fees

The fee structure is generally divided into: (i) a base fee based on a percentage of turnover; (ii) an incentive fee, based on profit; and (iii) various other licence fees and charges for reservations, sales and marketing, accounting and other central services provided by the Operator throughout its portfolio. Broadly speaking the average base fee in Europe is 2-3% of revenue and the incentive fee is in the region of 10% of adjusted gross operating profit ("AGOP"), i.e. gross operating profit, adjusted by the deduction of the management fee and other specified items e.g. possibly non-property related insurances.

It should be noted that the level of fees and the adjustments are a matter of negotiation and the costs of property insurance, taxes and other costs generally payable by Owners are often not deducted in the calculation of AGOP. The Owner needs to be aware of the likely cost of ownership as well as debt service and where possible, seek a minimum Owners' return (either as a guarantee or as a priority payment). Sliding scale incentives are becoming more common on the basis that higher fees based on profits are a strong form of incentive.

Term and termination

The most common pattern in Europe still seems to be a term of approximately 20 years with up to two five year renewals (which should be subject to mutual agreement), however, some brands and serviced apartment operators are more flexible and will agree earlier termination based on liquidated damages. The renewal is a double-edged matter and if one side is not happy then it may wish to walk away. The Operator will often seek rights which make it unattractive to terminate on a change of Ownership (its aim being to achieve the security of a lease without taking the risk).

Operating standard

Whilst most contracts will provide that the hotel will be operated to the operating standard contained in the Operator's manuals, it should be made clear that it will also be operated to the objective standard of an experienced, prudent Operator with a view to profit. Clearly, the final negotiated position will be some variation of this which permits some fluidity to ensure that the brand can remain current.

Other payments

Licences and development service agreements include other fees and charges which need to be carefully reviewed (and included in the feasibility study). In addition to these and reservations fees, an Operator is likely to be looking for a contribution towards its head and/or regional office expenses for sales and marketing based on a percentage of rooms revenue. Whilst the Operator needs to be allowed flexibility to maintain the brand in its market it is important that the Owner has a clear idea of the central services (e.g. accounting, IT, purchasing, trade shows etc.) it will be required to pay for and the likely level of those fees (preferably with a cap).

Performance guarantees/non-disturbance

Whilst some Operators will give parent company guarantees or key money, the price of these may often be reflected in the remainder of the commercial terms. The Owner should consider whether it is more advantageous to share the risk by contractual methods such as performance clauses or guarantees and/or a subordination of incentive fee, rather than seek an equity investment from the Operator.

The Owner should also be wary of agreeing to allow an Operator to insist on a non-disturbance agreement between any funder and the Operator. If this is conceded, the form should be one approved by the lender which allows it to terminate for poor performance, or the costs of borrowing may increase and any disposal may be restricted.

Budgets/capital expenditure
The management contract will contain a process for the Operator to produce an operating and capital expenditure budget each year. The contract will usually provide that, if the Owner makes no objection within a specified time, then the budget is deemed to be accepted. The Operator will rarely allow an Owner discretion to refuse a budget and at the very least, the Owner should require any budget items in any dispute to be referred to an independent expert as opposed to including an arbitration provision which will inevitably prove more costly.

Many Operators seek to oblige the Owner to comply with its requests for capital expenditure for structural changes as well as standard repairs and works necessary to maintain the operating standards of the relevant brand. The Owner would be well advised to seek a position whereby the Operator can use funds in the case of an emergency or to comply with legislation but, unless agreed in the budget, consent must otherwise be obtained from the Owner.

CONCLUSION

In this chapter we have endeavoured to give a potential hotel investor some guidance as to the operational models it needs to be familiar with at an early stage if it has an interest in investing in the hotel/serviced apartment sectors in the United Kingdom, not least, because of the potential impact that the structure may have in relation to valuations, yield and financing.

5.6 A GUIDE TO INVESTMENT IN UK COMMERCIAL PROPERTY

Gary Ritter and Charlotte Williams, Watson, Farley & Williams LLP

The UK has historically had one of the most dynamic and transparent property markets in Europe, with a broad variety of property options, stable rents and flexible short term lease structures.

Commenting on the UK property investment market in April and May 2013, respectively, the London office of Cushman & Wakefield, one of the world's leading commercial property consultants, states that:

"The unfolding crisis in Cyprus produced a more cautious mood in March but sentiment towards prime property has been barely dented let alone derailed. Prime yields were largely stable, averaging 5.8%, and in fact a bi-product of events in Cyprus may be yet more demand for secure, liquid markets such as London and stable income assets such as prime property generally.

Prime yields were unchanged in April at an average of 5.81% across all sectors, a 419 basis point premium to 10-year government bonds. The trend going forward is also largely stable and with signs of downward pressure being noted, and not just in London, the yield outlook is in fact at its most benign since mid-2010."

This chapter will seek to provide a legal background for overseas entities or individuals considering investing in or renting UK commercial property, either to occupy them or for investment purposes. Importantly, there are no restrictions on foreign nationals or overseas companies buying or renting property in the UK, subject only to tax implications.

As well as acquiring the property directly, there are a number of structures through which to invest in property including:

- Property companies;
- Partnerships;
- Joint Venture Vehicles; or
- Real Estate Investment Trusts ("REITs"): A REIT is a quoted company that owns and manages income-producing property, either commercial or residential which complies with certain conditions and may achieve certain taxation benefits.

OWNERSHIP OF LAND

The form of ownership and legal rights over a property can be very significant to an owner and/or occupier. Statute has established two forms of legal estate in land, with a relatively recent addition, namely:

- A Freehold Estate - Where the property (both land and structures) is effectively owned by the freeholder in perpetuity. An investor may choose to own a freehold as this gives the most control, has a capital value and will enable the grant of leases, to secure an income stream. Of course, freehold ownership may still be subject to certain covenants, for example, restricting the use of the property and/or rights of others, such as rights of way for third parties across the property.
- A Leasehold Estate (i.e. renting the premises) – Where the leaseholder's ownership of the land is contractually limited in time to the length of the term of the lease. The lease will be granted out of a freehold or superior leasehold estate.
- Since 2004, a new form of freehold tenure known as "commonhold" now exists. Commonhold is similar to the "strata title" and "condominium" systems that exist in Australia and the United States. Essentially, this is where each owner of a unit in a development (e.g. a flat, office or shop) owns the freehold of their unit and is also a member of a commonhold association which owns and manages the common parts of the development.

The English system enables the "legal interest" in the property to be split from the "beneficial interest," should this be desired. The legal title holder will be the registered proprietor at the Land Registry or the legal owner on the title deeds, while the beneficial owner will be entitled to the pecuniary interest in the property and will receive the income. This would be of relevance in establishing structures for tax and accounting purposes.

As regards the beneficial interest, land can be held by more than one person in one of two ways; either as a joint tenancy or a tenancy in common. A joint tenancy is a form of ownership where, normally, should one owner die, the property will automatically vest in the surviving owner(s), regardless of the terms of the deceased's will. A tenancy in common however, is a form of ownership where on the death of one of the joint owners, the relevant share in the property will form part of the deceased's estate and will pass to their beneficiaries by their will or, where there is no will, in accordance with the law on intestacy.

LEASEHOLD

Key elements

A lease is a contract between a landlord and tenant which creates a leasehold estate.

It is characterised by the landlord granting the tenant exclusive possession of the property for a fixed time (i.e. for a specified term or a period which is capable of being brought to an end by notice).

If these criteria are not met, a personal licence may be created instead of a leasehold estate. This is significant in terms of whether third parties will be obliged to recognise the occupier's rights and also because statute contains substantial protection for tenants, but not licensees, for example, security of tenure for certain residential and business tenancies.

Main types of lease

- *The ground lease:* this is a (normally residential) long lease often granted for more than 99 years usually for a one-off sum, called a "premium", with a nominal rent payable (sometimes called a 'peppercorn') throughout the rest of the term. A ground lease may be perceived to be closer in nature to a freehold owing to its capital value. Residential apartments/flats are normally sold or held on a long lease.
- *The rack rent lease:* this is the most prevalent form of commercial occupational lease usually granted for around 5-10 years. The tenant will pay a full-market rent often quarterly with rent review provisions and usually with no premium.

- *Short term residential occupational leases:* these generally take the form of an "Assured Shorthold Tenancy" whereby at the end of the lease term the landlord is entitled to possession of the premises.

COMMERCIAL LEASES

Pre-lets

Companies can rent premises that are already available or may be entitled to enter into 'pre-let' agreements with developers to lease premises prior to the carrying out or completion of construction work (enabling the future tenant to specify the design, layout and fittings of the building).

Security of tenure

In most cases where a tenant occupies premises for business purposes, statute grants them the right to renew their lease on largely identical terms (subject to a review of rent and length of term) at the end of the term (the intention being to protect the tenant's goodwill at the premises established whilst in occupation).

Certain rights to compensation may also be available in the event that the landlord is able to rely on one or more of seven grounds to refuse to renew the lease (e.g. if it requires occupation of the premises for its own use or wishes to redevelop the property).

Nevertheless it is common for the parties to agree to exclude the tenant's right to security of tenure and right to compensation by "contracting out". A contracting out agreement will only be valid where the landlord serves a prescribed notice on the tenant (in a strict timeframe) and the tenant makes the appropriate declaration that they have received the notice.

If the lease is contracted out, then the tenant must vacate the premises when the lease expires with no right to renew and no right to compensation.

Restrictions on use

Leases usually restrict how the premises can be used. This is often linked to planning permission but sometimes e.g. with the leases of commercial units in shopping centres, the use stated may be very specific so as to ensure the landlord has a variety of businesses within the development.

Rent review

Where leases are granted for more than five years, it is standard to provide for a rent re-calculation (review) every fifth year. These reviews can be based on the open market rent which would be payable for a lease of the property on similar terms, may be linked to the Retail Prices Index or (less commonly) on fixed increases. Such provisions generally provide for 'upwards only' reviews.

Full repairing and insuring lease
The majority of leases of commercial premises in the UK are on a full repairing and insuring basis ("FRI lease") which means that the tenant is liable for the upkeep and decoration of the property and the costs of the landlord in insuring the building.

Service charge
Where a property is let to several different tenants the landlord will retain responsibility in relation to the structure and the common parts of the building. He will recover these costs from the tenant through charging a fee called a "service charge". The amount of service charge paid is generally proportionate to the size of the tenant's individual unit in relation to the rentable space in the whole building.

Break rights
Some leases include break rights giving the landlord and/or the tenant the option to end the lease before its expiry date. These provisions specify how much notice has to be given and may have financial implications.

Privity of contract
Where a lease is transferred to a new party, the original tenant will be subject to different liabilities dependent on the date of the lease.

For leases signed before 1 January 1996, the original tenant remains legally responsible for the rent and other commitments for the duration of the lease, regardless of whether they transfer the leasehold interest to a third party.

Subject to certain exceptions, in leases signed after this date, the tenant will not remain liable unless the landlord requests the tenant to sign a guarantee ("AGA"), where the tenant will remain liable under the covenants in the lease during the ownership of the new tenant to whom he has transferred the lease, but not the new tenant's successors.

PLANNING

Prior to making certain alterations, erecting new buildings or changing the use of an existing building, businesses must contact their local authority's planning department in order to obtain planning permission. UK planning applications are administered by the local authority covering the area in which the particular building or site is located (contact details are available on most council websites).

The UK system is largely discretionary and therefore flexible, unlike many other European Union planning systems. The usual timeframe for a planning application to be considered is between eight and 13 weeks from the formal application, depending on whether it is treated as a major application. The appeals system in the UK also follows a comprehensive process.[1]

REGISTERED LAND V UNREGISTERED LAND

Registered land

The majority of land in England and Wales is registered at the Land Registry. The register is a matter of public record and the title is guaranteed. It contains information concerning the type of estate (e.g. freehold or leasehold), the property description (through reference to a filed plan), current owner (known as the "registered proprietor") and details of all third party rights which have been registered against the estate or protected by notice (e.g. mortgages).

Not all information relating to the property will be displayed on the register. Certain third party rights ("overriding interests") will bind a purchaser of registered land regardless of whether they are recorded on the register, or whether a purchaser has any knowledge of them.

Unregistered land

Alternatively, where land has remained in the same hands for many years, there may not have been a trigger event requiring registration at the Land Registry and the land may still be unregistered. In the absence of a register entry, a landowner can only deduce title by proving an unbroken chain of ownership by reference to the title deeds and documents relating to the property. In practice, for a landowner to prove a good root of title, the chain of deeds must go back at least 15 years.

HOW IS LAND TRANSFERRED?

A typical sale and purchase transaction is a two-stage process involving an exchange of contracts between the buyer and the seller, followed by completion of the legal transfer. A seller's solicitor will issue a draft sale contract which will be negotiated and then exchanged with a deposit usually being paid. This is the point of no return, when both parties commit themselves to complete on a certain date. Up to this point, either party can withdraw without any liability to the other side.

Following exchange of contracts, the transfer of the property from the seller to the buyer is effected by completing the transfer deed and by complying with Land

1. http://www.planningportal.gov.uk/planning/appeals/guidance

Registry registration requirements. Completion is, in effect, moving day, when the money is paid to the seller's solicitors and the keys to the property are handed over to the buyer.

Principle of "Caveat Emptor"

In UK conveyancing, the principle of *caveat emptor* ("let the buyer beware") is key and places the responsibility for due diligence and searches relating to a property on the buyer. It is normally the task of a lawyer to consider and negotiate the legal documentation and discover as much information as possible about the property through a variety of searches and enquiries, including, but not limited to:

- Local search - list of enquiries about property sent to the local authority which includes questions about planning, highways, drainage etc.
- Environmental search – historical information about previous uses of the land.
- Preliminary enquiries – questions about the property which are sent to the seller's or landlord's solicitors requesting information about issues such as disputes with neighbours and use of property.

A physical survey of the property should be arranged by the buyer and carried out by a surveyor.

TAX IMPLICATIONS OF ACQUIRING AN INTEREST IN PROPERTY

Value Added Tax ("VAT")

Many commercial property transactions are subject to VAT. Whether it is subject to VAT will depend on a number of factors, mainly being whether it is regarded as a "new" property or the owner has opted to tax. In these cases, the current rate of VAT chargeable on commercial buildings is 20%.

Stamp Duty Land Tax ("SDLT")

This is a mandatory tax payable by the buyer on the purchase price, on completion or substantial performance of the contract (which generally means occupation or a payment of at least 90% of the price), whichever is earlier.

SDLT is currently chargeable at a rate of up to 15% of the purchase price or lease premium of residential property depending on the statutory value bands. In contrast, the maximum rate of SDLT currently applicable to UK commercial property is only 4%. Current rates are available on the website of HMRC.[2]

2 http://www.hmrc.gov.uk/sdlt/intro/rates-thresholds.htm

SDLT is also payable on the grant of a lease upon both the premium and rental payments. For more information on calculating SDLT please see the HMRC website.[3]

There are a number of transactions which may be exempt from SDLT, such as intra-group transfers within the same group of companies and the leaseback elements of a sale and leaseback of property.

Business rates

Business rates are a property tax that business occupiers pay towards the costs of local government services. They typically range from £20 to £130 per square metre (approximately £2 to £13 per square foot).

Details of business rates can be found at:

- England and Wales http://www.voa.gov.uk/corporate/index.html
- Northern Ireland – http://www.dfpni.gov.uk/lps/index/property-rating.htm
- Scotland - http://www.scotland.gov.uk/Topics/Government/localgovernment/17999/11199

This chapter gives a brief summary of the legal issues relating to investment in UK real estate. It is not intended to give any specific legal advice or take the place of advice from property experts.

3 http://www.hmrc.gov.uk/sdlt/calculate/calculators.htm

Part Six

Banking and Financial Services

6.1 COMMERCIAL BANKING AND FINANCE FOR COMPANIES

Jonathan Reuvid, Legend Business

COMMERCIAL BANKING ALTERNATIVES

Foreign companies or individuals entering the UK to do business will need, as a minimum, to open a UK banking current account in order to trade. If the bank in their home territory has a UK subsidiary, the simplest procedure is to open an account with the subsidiary on which it can draw cheques and carry out electronic banking transactions. Subsidiaries of foreign banks are classified as "Agency Banks".

Clearing banks and their processes

Alternatively, or in addition, companies or individuals can open an account in their own name with one of the 10 UK banks which are members of the Cheque and Credit Clearing Company Limited and enjoy the benefits of faster clearance of cheques and credits. The 10 UK "Clearing" banks, in alphabetical order, are:

- Abbey
- Alliance and Leicester
- Bank of Scotland (HBOS)
- Barclays
- Clydesdale

- The Co-operative Bank
- HSBC
- Lloyds TSB
- Nationwide
- Royal Bank of Scotland (RBS)

Four of these banks: Bank of Scotland, Clydesdale, Lloyds TSB (Scotland) and RBS are also members of The Committee of Scottish Bankers (CSCB) which is their representative body maintaining contact with the Bank of England.

The Bank of England, itself the core eleventh member of the Cheque and Credit Clearing Company Limited, supervises the overall interbank settlement process and associated interbank reconciliations.

There is a distinction between the cheque clearing process, as described below, and the credit clearing process which is effected without Inter Bank Data Exchange (IBDE) files.

In addition to the Cheque and Credit Clearing Company Limited and the Committee of Scottish Bankers, there is also a Belfast Bankers' Clearing Committee of which the current members are: Bank of Ireland, First Trust Bank, Northern Bank Ltd and Ulster Bank Ltd. Variations for the Scottish and Northern Irish Banks are the cause of extra days incurred through logistics and lack of IBDE files.

The cheque clearing process

In summary, the basic steps in the clearing process are as follows:

1. A cheque and credit slip are paid into a branch of the payee's Clearing Bank (Bank A). The cheque together with all the other cheques deposited at the branch is couriered to a regional centre which where the out-clearing is undertaken:

a. The amount of the cheque is read electronically using Image Character Recording (ICR) technology.

b. The sort code account number and cheque number are read electronically using Magnetic Ink Recognition (MICR) or ICR technology.

c. Cheques are sorted into batches corresponding to each clearing bank using the sort codes for identification.

d. From the electronically read information electronic files of cheque payment records are created for each Clearing Bank (IBDE).

e. Where applicable, the paper credit corresponding to each cheque is also converted into an electronic entry by similar (CR/OCR) technology and is put into an electronic file of credits for use in the internal accounting of the Clearing Bank at which the cheque was deposited.

f. The Clearing Bank on which a cheque was drawn (Bank B) will receive it together with others in the same batch of cheques presented by Clearing Bank A which is collected from the Exchange Centre at Milton Keynes.

g. In parallel with the physical exchange of cheques there is an electronic exchange of files of payments in the form of IBDE files which are transmitted over secure network connection from each clearing bank to another on a bilateral basis.

h. Both physical and electronic records are exchanged by 11:00 am on the morning of the next day (T+1).

2. The Clearing Bank A receiving the cheque feeds the electronic credit record into its accounting records (usually overnight). The bank will give its customer access to the funds for interest and/or withdrawal according to its own rules, credit policies and customer credit assessment. For customers of good standing the bank may give value and withdrawal from the first day, certainly in time for the morning of the day following (T+1). New customers considered high risk may gain same day access to the funds for interest purposes but are not allowed withdrawal until four days later (T+4).
3. Clearing Bank B performs the reverse process of identification and verification for cheques and IBDE received in batches for each other Clearing Bank. Electronic files of verified payments are passed into Clearing Bank B's accounting (usually overnight) on the night of T+1. The overnight accounting debits the account provisionally with what is called an AM entry, thereby earmarking the funds.
4. Decisions whether or not to pay the cheques that have been drawn on customers' accounts are taken during day T+2. Decisions not to pay are a mixture of computer based and human bases decisions which may be either account related (eg insufficient funds) or cheque related (ie technical or fraud reasons).

There are additional procedures for the return of unpaid ("bounced") cheques.

Clearing cheques drawn on Agency Banks

There are more than 400 banks in the UK that can pay or receive cheques who participate as Agency Banks. As well as the UK subsidiaries of foreign banks, this category includes small UK domestic banks and building societies.

Customers paying in their cheque and credit slip to their Agency Bank are subjected to an extended clearing process. The Agency Bank in effect acts as a post box. It collects the cheque and credit slip and sends them on to the Clearing Bank through which they do business. The method of transmission varies from Agency Bank to Agency Bank. Some highly centralised organisations will rush the day's cheques by courier or their own transport to the Clearing Bank on the night of the day they are received (Day T). Others with branch networks will post them by surface mail to their Clearing Bank which will receive them on day T+1. Others may use internal mail to send all the cheques and credit slips for the whole branch network to a single head office which will then courier them to the Clearing Bank, but still not in time to be processed as a part of day T intake.

The Clearing Bank then processes cheques in much the same way as for its own with the Agency Bank, maintaining an account with the Clearing Bank, referred to as a "settlement account". All cheque credits processed in out-clearing are credited to the settlement account as a part of its own accounting process on the night of T+2. The Agency Bank may then withdraw this money to pay its own customer accounts.

To assist the Agency Bank in identifying which account to credit, the Clearing Bank will typically provide an electronic file of credit records (derived from credit slip codelines) to be made to the Agency Bank's accounts – without which the Agency Bank may have neither an electronic nor paper record of the cheque payment. This electronic detail may be sent as a part of the out-clearing on T+1 or in the form of an electronic statement of the Agency Bank's account with the Clearing Bank after the accounting runs on the night of T+2.

The Agency Bank uses the electronic file of information as input to its own customer accounting processes, normally on the night of T+2 or T+3. As with Clearing Banks, Agency Banks have to decide when to give customers the benefit of their credits, both for interest and accrual purposes and for withdrawal.

The reverse process of in-clearing a cheque drawn against an Agency Bank which uses a Clearing Bank to perform its cheque clearing is subject to a similar timescale. At the end of the process, the Agency Bank against which a cheque is drawn can apply the cheque debit to its customer's account on the night of T+3 and make its pay/no pay decision on T+4.

These timescales represent the "worst" case of a cheque drawn on an Agency Bank and paid into an Agency Bank. Most Agency Bank transactions will involve one Agency Bank and two Clearing Banks. However, since steps in the process may involve post office delivery of mail next day which is not a guaranteed service. In extreme cases, where Agency Banks needs time to feel confident that a cheque deposited will not bounce, they may not give credit for value (withdrawal) until T+5 or T+6. Therefore, for customers with significant revenue flows, there are clear advantages in opening a current account with a Clearing Bank.

The Bank of England's Real-Time Gross Settlement (RTGS) system
As the name suggests, the RTGS system provides for real-time posting with finality and irrevocability of debit and credit entries to participants' accounts.
Institutions open accounts in RTGS so that they can participate:

(i) as a settlement bank in any of the interbank fund transfer systems for which the Bank acts as settlement agent and/or
(ii) as a member if the Bank's Reserve Scheme (part of the operational framework for delivering the Bank's monetary policy decisions since 2006).

In the Bank's role as settlement agent, the RTGS system is an integral part of two systemically important interbank funds transfer mechanisms: the CHAPS high-value payment system; and the mechanism supporting the CREST securities settlement system.

CHAPS is the same day electronic funds transfer service, provided by the CHAPS Clearing Company, owned by the commercial banks, that is used primarily for high-value/wholesale payments but also for other time-critical lower value payments. Individual CHAPS payment instructions are routed via the SWIFT network to the RTGS system and then settled across the paying and receiving CHAPS banks' settlement accounts.

Since April 2013, the Bank has provided a Liquidity Saving Mechanism (LSM) within RTGS which contains a "central schedule" that enables the CHAPS member banks to manage their cash flows centrally. Banks can decide whether their payments should settle via "urgent" or "non-urgent" streams. By October 2013 CHAPS had 19 direct members who settle their own, and several hundred indirect participants' CHAPS payments over their settlement accounts.

CREST is the UK's securities settlement system which has provided real-time cash against securities settlement - referred to as "Delivery versus Payment" or DVP - operated by Euroclear UK & Ireland (EUI) for its 35,000 members.

Securities transactions are settled under the CREST system in a series of high-frequency cycles throughout the day. Every CREST member must have a banking relationship with one or other of the 14 CREST settlement banks.

Other interbank payment systems

The Bank also provides a settlement service in RTGS for four additional payment systems:

- Faster Payments Service
- Bacs
- Cheque and Credit Clearing
- LINK

Direct members of these systems settle their obligations on a "deferred multi-lateral net basis" because the very high volume - and typically low value - of payments involved. The Bank receives a settlement message via the SWIFT network each day (three time for the Faster Payments Service) from each of the relevant payment systems, containing single net pay/receive figures fpr each of the systems' direct members.

FINANCE FOR COMPANIES

The UK offers the best range of options for obtaining finance in Europe that range from small, specialist seed funds to a full listing on the London Stock Exchange and including the largest venture capital market.

Debt finance

Inward investors have access to a wide choice of providers offering commercial loans, mortgages and credit facilities including the facilities available from the UK branches of their own banks.

In addition, the UK Government provides the “Enterprise Finance Guarantee” scheme which operates through commercial lenders providing a 75% Government guarantee on individual loans from £1,000 to £1 million to viable companies with an annual sales turnover 0f up to £41 million. The guarantee can be used to support new loans, refinance existing loans or convert all or part of an existing bank overdraft into a loan to meet working capital requirements.

The UK Government also provides access to working capital finance support for UK-based exporters, including both manufacturing and service sector companies, through its export credit agency, UK Export Finance.

Equity finance

The London Stock Exchange and other UK Exchanges

Key factors for companies choosing to list their shares in the UK are London's liquid international trading market, the high UK standards of regulation and corporate governance and access to emerging market investors.

There a four levels of market, depending on the size of company that is looking for a share listing and its specific requirements:

- The Main Market has around 1,350 UK and international companies with a total market capitalisation of more than £3.5 million.
- The Alternative Investment Market (AIM) is also a global market for young and growing companies which are not ready to bear the costs of a main market listing through an Independent Public Offering (IPO) and maintain the listing. The AIM is the most appropriate market for inward investors to consider and its operation is described in Chapter 6.2. It is viewed as a stepping stone to the Main Market.
- Plus Markets is an independent stock exchange that supports the financing of small and medium-sized companies. It offers significantly less liquidity than the two senior markets.
- ShareMark an online fundraising facility for small and medium-sized companies, operating through an electronic auction market which matches sellers and buyers.

Venture capitalists and business angels

Venture capital firms typically make investments of over £2 million in businesses with high-growth potential. The UK private equity and venture capital market attracted £6.6 billion in 2010, representing 30% of the European market (Source: The CityUK, 2012). The key organisation for this sector is the British Venture Capital Association (BCVA) with more than 400 member firms (www.bcva.co.uk).

Busines angels are high net worth individuals who either operate alone (investing between £10,000 and £250,000 typically per deal) or collectively in syndicates or networks where the total investment can be as high as £750,000 or even higher. They may be identified through the UK Business Angels Association website (www.angelinvestmentnetwork.co.uk). Typically, business angels will seek to benefit from tax relief under the Enterprise Investment Scheme (EIS).

Public sector equity funds
In England, the major available funds are:

- Enterprise Capital Funds investing a combination of public and private capital in small businesses at equity levels of up to £2 million;
- Business Angel Co. Investment Fund making initial equity investments from £100,000 £1 million in high-growth businesses.

In Wales, the principal source of public sector venture capital services is Finance Wales which provides equity investments from £5,000 to over £1 million.

In Northern Ireland, a range of funding packages are available including a specialist venture capital fund "Northern Ireland Spin Out Fund" for early stage companies.

In Scotland, private and public supported venture capital funds include:

- the Scottish Venture Fund: an initiative to invest between £500,000 and £2 million in company finance deals between £2 million and £10 million;
- the Scottish Co-investment Fund: a £72 million equity fund which can invest between £100,000 and £1 million in deals of up to £2 million; and
- the Scottish Seed Fund: supporting start-up and growing companies seeking loan or equity funding from £20,000 to £250,000.

Other sources of funds

Grants
There is a range of grants available in the UK provided by the EU and UK governmental organisations as outlined in Chapter 1.3.

Community Development Venture Funds (CDVFs)
Offering equity typically between £100,000 and £2 million to businesses located in deprived areas across the UK, CDVF information may be found on the websites of the Community Development Finance Association or Bridges Ventures.

Seed Funds
Usually operated by technology transfer organisations within universities, seed funds in the UK are strongly focused on supporting innovative technology projects. The National Endowment for Science, Technology and the Arts which

is mandated to invest up to £1 million in innovative start-up companies is a leading example.

Note: The second part of this chapter is based on data derived from a UK Trade & Investment fact sheet. The UKTI Investment Hub welcomes investment enquiries on +44 (0) 20 7333 5442 or by e-mail at enquiries@ukti-invest.com.

6.2 AIM – THE AIM MARKET OF THE LONDON STOCK EXCHANGE

Christina Howard and Gareth Burge, Watson, Farley & Williams LLP

INTRODUCTION

The global financial crisis has had a significant and well-publicised effect on the world's equity markets. The AIM Market (AIM) is no exception and the past few years have not been easy for London's junior market. However, there are signs of improvement, as companies and investors are returning to AIM.

AIM

The London Stock Exchange (LSE) launched AIM in 1995, as an alternative market for smaller growing companies, targeting businesses that either did not yet qualify for listing on London's main market or were otherwise not ready for this step. The LSE wished to provide a route to capital markets for companies that were at a relatively early stage in their development and smaller in size and resources than companies on the LSE's main market. Consequently, they required a more balanced and less burdensome regulatory environment in which to operate than was available on other markets. AIM was therefore structured with a measured level of regulation and with limited entry criteria.

The intention was to create an infrastructure that would enable companies to focus on growing their businesses rather than having to devote an inappropriate amount of management time and resources to regulatory compliance. This had to be balanced with the need to ensure the continued integrity of the market and the maintenance and enhancement of its reputation as a safe and effective place to do business. The result has been a highly successful capital raising market that now enjoys a global reputation.

THE GROWTH OF AIM

From its modest beginnings, AIM grew steadily and, by 2007, more than 1,500 companies had been admitted to AIM since its initial launch 12 years earlier. During the economic downturn, in line with other markets around the world, the number of admissions to AIM fell significantly, with 114 companies joining the market in 2008 and just 36 in 2009. There were 71 admissions to AIM in 2012 and so far there have been 21 admissions to AIM this year (as of April 2013). As of April 2013, 1,088 companies were listed on AIM, with a combined market capitalisation of £60.06 billion.

AIM has matured significantly in recent years. Companies from all sectors are now represented on the market and the number of international (i.e. non-UK) companies admitted to AIM has grown strongly. The increasing maturity of the market has also been demonstrated by the amount of funds raised by AIM companies. In 2004, the total amount raised by AIM companies by way of initial public offerings (IPO) or secondary fundraisings reached £4.6 billion – more than double the previous year's figure. In 2005, this figure was £8.9 billion and in 2006 a total of £15.7 billion was raised – again, almost double the figure for the previous year. This was even more remarkable in view of the slightly moderated admission and IPO numbers in 2006 compared to 2005 twice as much money was raised by a smaller number of companies. In 2006, AIM raised more money than NASDAQ for the first time.

2008 and 2009 were difficult years for AIM, as the effects of the global financial crisis became clear, with fundraising reducing in 2008 (to £4.3 billion) and in 2009 (to £5.6 billion). The ongoing effects of the global financial difficulties are continuing to have an effect on fundraising levels, with £3.15 billion raised in 2012 and £849 million raised so far this year (as of April 2013).

Figure 6.2.1 shows the growth in admission numbers and in the amount raised by AIM companies since the launch of the market in 1995, including the effect that the global financial crisis has had on AIM.

Figure 6.2.1 - Distribution of Companies by Equity Market Value

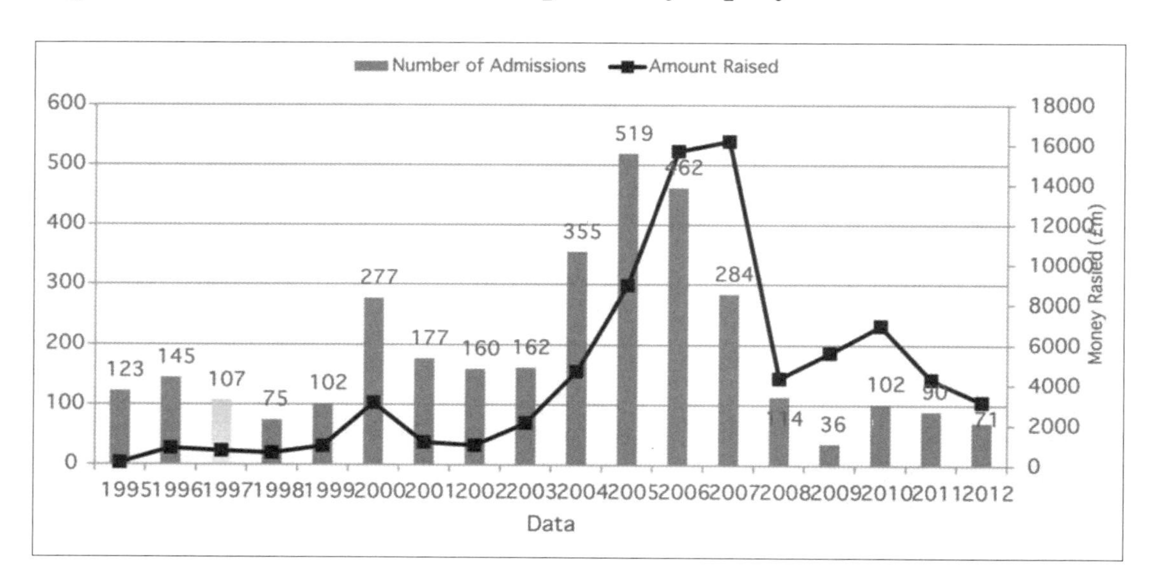

INTERNATIONAL COMPANIES

A significant development for AIM in recent years has been the growth in international admissions. As of April 2013, there were 222 international companies on AIM from some 30 or so jurisdictions, representing just over 20 per cent of the market. However, this does not take account of businesses that have incorporated a UK holding company into their group structure – a strategy adopted by many companies in view of certain benefits in doing so. Taking these companies into account, the proportion of international businesses on AIM is much higher – the number of non-UK companies listed on AIM, as per main country of operation[1], is over 500 (around 50% of the market). Much of this growth in international business has been driven by companies from Western Europe, Africa, the US, China and South East Asia.

In the US, for example, the regulatory environment, together with the difficulties faced by small or mid-cap companies to raise equity funds on domestic exchanges, has seen an increasing number of US businesses elect to pursue an AIM strategy.

As of April 2013, there were 50 companies with the US as their main country of operation listed on AIM, a substantial increase from around six years previously when just a handful were listed. The US Sarbanes-Oxley Act, 2002, has acted as a catalyst for this development, but it is rarely the principal or only reason for a business to choose AIM in preference to US markets; AIM is a market more suited

1 Main country of operation is deemed to be the geographical location from which an AIM company derives, or intends to derive, the largest proportion of its revenues or where the largest proportion of its assets are, or will be, located.

to a smaller growing business than other exchanges, including those in North America.

AIM is attuned to the needs of these companies. Besides its appropriate level of regulation and relative ease of entry, AIM has a highly developed infrastructure of advisory firms focused on the market, specialising in this area. These include nominated advisers ("nomads") that:

- provide the corporate advisory function needed for such companies;
- assess the suitability of companies wishing to join AIM under delegated authority from the LSE; and
- in many cases, also provide broking and fundraising services for their corporate clients.

MARKET CAPITALISATION

AIM is home to companies with a broad range of market capitalisations. Many AIM companies have a market capitalisation of £5 million or less; however, most AIM companies have a market capitalisation of between £5 million and £50 million. As of April 2013, 39 AIM companies had a market capitalisation of £250 million or more, with 16 of these having a market capitalisation of £500 million or more. The distribution of market capitalisation across the value range is illustrated in Figure 6.2.2.

Figure 6.2.2 - Distribution of Companies by Equity Market Value

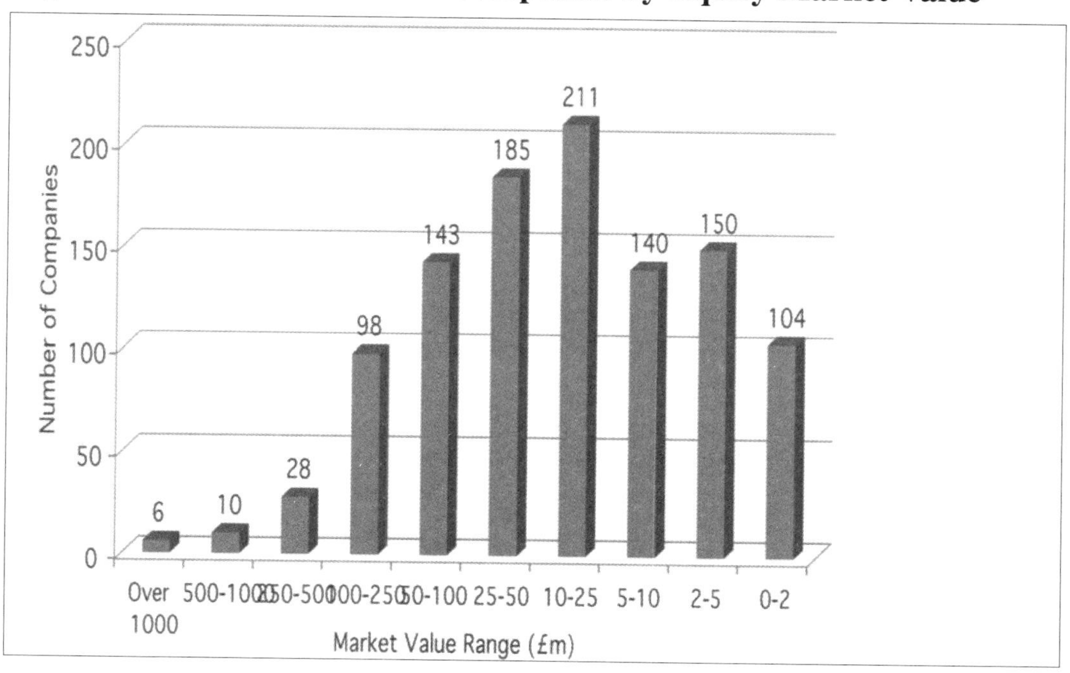

As of May 2013, the average market capitalisation of a company listed on AIM is £58.9 million.

REASONS TO SEEK A PUBLIC LISTING

There are a number of reasons for a company to seek a public listing. These include the following:

- accessing capital for growth;
- creating a market for its shares;
- obtaining an objective market valuation of its business;
- raising its profile;
- creating the ability to fund acquisitions with share capital; and
- providing incentives to employees through share ownership.

AIM provides all of the above benefits to a public company. In addition, AIM may be contrasted with other exchanges by virtue of the following:

- absence of onerous admission criteria;
- more straightforward admission process;
- simple secondary fundraising procedure;
- easier acquisition rules; and
- a more balanced regulatory environment.

AIM admission criteria

AIM imposes few eligibility criteria on companies wishing to join the market:

- There is no minimum requirement for a particular percentage of shares to be held in public hands.
- No trading record is required.
- Admission documents do not require pre-vetting by a regulatory authority.
- There is no minimum market capitalisation requirement.

Most other established exchanges require a particular length of audited trading history, a minimum market capitalisation and a certain percentage of shares to be held in public hands. In most cases, a prospectus or registration statement must be submitted to, and approved by, a regulatory authority in advance of listing, which can be onerous in terms of both timing and costs.

Although there are relatively few regulatory criteria for a company to qualify for admission to AIM, one of the essential foundations of AIM is the position occupied by the nomads, which act as the gatekeepers of the market.

ADVISERS

Nomads

Nomads are corporate finance advisers approved by the LSE. Their functions are to assist with the admission process and thereafter to advise on, and ensure compliance with, the ongoing requirements of AIM. The nomad's principal role in the admission process is to confirm that the company and its securities are suitable for admission.

Following admission, the nomad is responsible for advising the directors of the company as to their ongoing obligations, and for reviewing the company's actual trading performance and financial conditions against any profit forecast, estimate or projection included in admission documents or published elsewhere.

In view of their responsibilities to the LSE, nomads are required to carry out extensive due diligence on their clients in advance of admission. In February 2007, the LSE introduced a new rule book for nomads, The AIM Rules for Nominated Advisers, which codified the role and responsibilities of nomads based on existing best market practice. While most nomad firms conduct their businesses in accordance with best market practice in any event, the LSE was keen to ensure that all firms adopted the same standards in their review of prospective AIM companies.

The system of delegated authority from the LSE to the nomads forms one of the bedrocks of the balanced regulatory environment upon which AIM is based. It is a system that has been accepted by investors and has worked extremely well. Investor confidence in the system is reflected in the amount of funds invested in AIM securities, and the moderate additional rules that AIM has introduced are likely to enhance investor confidence further.

Brokers

Every AIM company is also required to appoint and retain a broker at all times. Brokers are approved by the LSE. The function of these firms is to provide market support for trading in the company's securities and to undertake fundraising activities for the company. The broker will also generally provide research and institutional sales support for the company, and provide information about the company to the market.

In many cases, the nomad and broker functions are combined within the same firm, although in separate divisions. There is no requirement for a single firm to adopt both roles, and some companies prefer for their nomad to be independent of their broker.

Other advisers

In addition to a nomad and a broker, a company wishing to be admitted to AIM will need to engage legal counsel, reporting accountants and, in most cases, a public relations firm.

The role of legal counsel will be to advise the company on the legal and regulatory requirements for admission to AIM and on applicable securities laws, and to play a principal role in the preparation and finalisation of the admission documents, working closely with the nomad in this regard. The lawyers will also advise on:

- any required corporate reorganisation;
- any required amendments to the company's constitutional documents;
- the terms of directors' service contracts; and
- the duties and responsibilities of the directors under applicable UK law.

They will also undertake a legal due diligence review covering matters such as the company's contractual arrangements, employment agreements, and legal and regulatory compliance and litigation, as well as any other matters required by the nomad in order to satisfy itself that the company is suitable for admission to AIM.

The nomad and broker will also engage their own legal counsel to provide independent advice on legal matters in relation to the negotiation of the placing (or underwriting) agreement.

The reporting accountants, who are distinct from the company's own auditors, will:

- undertake a review of the company's financial position and financial reporting procedures;
- generally produce a report containing the results of its financial due diligence review; and
- prepare with the directors a working capital report to demonstrate that the company will have sufficient working capital for at least 12 months following admission.

The role of the financial public relations firm will be to generate press and investor interest in the initial and any subsequent fundraisings, and to raise the profile of the company generally. The public relations firm will also work with the nomad, the company and its other advisers in agreeing the content of public statements.

ADMISSION PROCESS

Under the standard admission procedure, a company wishing to be admitted to AIM will be required to produce a formal admission document or prospectus that will include all relevant information on the company and its business. The content of the admission document is governed by The AIM Rules for Companies and is otherwise determined by reference to the UK's securities laws. Most AIM admission transactions are accompanied by a fundraising to institutional investors. If the fundraising constitutes a public offer of securities, is made to more than 150 persons in any member state of the European Union (EU) and is not otherwise exempted, a full prospectus under the EU Prospectus Directive (as amended) will be required. Such a document will require pre-vetting and approval of the UK Listing Authority (UKLA) prior to admission of the company to trading on AIM. For this reason, it is rare for a company being admitted to AIM to seek to raise funds through a public offer, and the vast majority of transactions are undertaken by way of an institutional placing exempt from the full prospectus and UKLA approval requirements.

The admission document will provide the basis upon which investors subscribe for shares. The broker will undertake a fundraising exercise, generally based on a marketing presentation and a near-final version of the admission documents. An AIM transaction is broadly similar to any other listing event, the principal difference being the absence of a regulatory approval process.

AIM has also introduced a streamlined secondary listing procedure, which is available to companies already listed on certain designated international stock markets. In such cases, companies can benefit from a streamlined regime under which the requirement to produce an admission document is replaced by an obligation to issue an expanded pre-admission announcement. The exchanges falling within the scope of the streamlined secondary listing procedure include the following:

- the Australian Securities Exchange;
- Deutsche Börse;
- NYSE Euronext;
- Johannesburg Stock Exchange;
- NASDAQ;
- the New York Stock Exchange;
- the UKLA's Official List;
- NASDAQ OMX Stockholm;
- Swiss Exchange; and
- the TMX Group.

Cost and timing

Although every AIM admission transaction is different, and while issues of both timing and cost will depend upon a number of factors, in most cases the admission process can be expected to take three to four months to complete. Some transactions are implemented in a shorter timescale, while others take longer, but this is a fairly reliable guide.

Similar variables apply in relation to the cost of an AIM admission. The largest single element of cost for an AIM admission with a fundraising is the commission payable to the broker or investment bank. This will generally be around five per cent of funds raised. Other costs include the cost of the nomad, legal counsel, the reporting accountants and, for certain sectors such as natural resources, competent persons who are required to produce reports. As a guide, companies would commonly expect the total cost of an IPO on AIM to be approximately seven to ten per cent of funds raised. This does, of course, depend upon the size of the fundraising.

POST-ADMISSION REQUIREMENTS

Once admitted to AIM, companies must comply with the AIM rules, as well as with applicable securities law. The AIM rules are written in plain English and are less prescriptively detailed than the rules on other major markets. AIM companies must provide certain information to the market on a regular basis and specifically upon the occurrence of certain events. To ensure that the market is kept fully informed, AIM companies are obliged to make similar ongoing disclosures to those required by companies on the other major exchanges, to ensure that the market is aware of the financial position of the company and its prospects.

Each AIM company is also required to publish accounts prepared in accordance with International Accounting Standards (IAS) as well as six-monthly interim results. Each AIM company is also required to notify the market of any changes in shareholdings of directors and to provide information to the market concerning substantial or related party transactions.

It should be noted that shareholder approval is generally not required for substantial transactions, which contrasts AIM with other markets. The only exception to this is in the case of a reverse takeover or a disposal resulting in a fundamental change of business, which requires the approval of shareholders in advance of the transaction.

Corporate governance

The UK has high standards of corporate governance applicable to public companies. The UK Corporate Governance Code is mandatory for companies with a premium listing on the Official List, regardless of whether they are incorporated in the UK or elsewhere. Although the UK Corporate Governance Code does not apply to companies trading on AIM, most AIM companies have sought to adhere to the provisions of the Code so far as is practicable, including ensuring that the roles of chairman and chief executive are exercised by separate individuals and that there is a balance between executive and non-executive directors on a board. The Quoted Companies Alliance (QCA) has issued the Corporate Governance Code for Small and Mid-Size Companies 2013, and although this guidance has no formal regulatory status, it does reflect a consensus position of the AIM advisory and investing community, as well as the key provisions of the UK Corporate Governance Code, with the caveat that the roles of chairman and chief executive may be exercised by the same person in exceptional circumstances. The National Association of Pension Funds has also published corporate governance and voting guidelines for AIM companies that are generally consistent with the principles published by the QCA, other than in relation to the sharing of the chairman and chief executive officer roles.

Tax benefits

For UK taxpayers, an investment in shares traded on AIM can provide certain tax benefits by way of tax reliefs that may be available to them. These will include:

- certain reliefs on gains realised on the disposal of shares held by individual investors or trustees; and
- the holding over of certain gains made on disposal.

Such tax benefits and reliefs are designed to encourage investment in AIM stocks, which have generally been companies in the early stages of their development.

CONCLUSION

The global financial crisis has affected all international stock markets. As governments continue their work to rejuvenate markets across the world, AIM, with its balanced level of regulation and history of past success should be well placed to maintain its position as a leading international IPO market.

6.3 ROLES OF THE NOMAD AND THE BROKER ON AIM

Tony Rawlinson,
Cairn Financial Advisers LLP

INTRODUCTION

A company seeking admission to AIM is required by the AIM Rules to have a Nominated Adviser (often referred to as a Nomad) and a broker. These advisers are so important to the life of a company on AIM that following Admission to AIM all AIM companies are also required to retain a Nomad and a broker at all times. Indeed, if a company finds itself without a Nomad, its shares will be suspended from trading on AIM, and if it is still without a Nomad after a month, its listing will be cancelled.

A Nomad is a corporate finance adviser which has been approved by the London Stock Exchange to act in the role of nominated adviser. It is responsible to the London Stock Exchange for ensuring that companies for which it acts adhere to the various rules and regulations applicable to AIM companies. The Nomad is privy to confidential, and often price sensitive, information on the company. Although its primary duty of care is to the London Stock Exchange, the Nomad's client is the company.

The function of the company's broker is to raise funds and manage the market in the company's shares. The broker may also make a market in the company's shares and produce research on the company, although these functions, whilst desirable, are not required by AIM. Brokers are dual facing with their corporate broking teams acting for AIM and other corporate clients and their private client or institutional sales teams acting for institutions or private individuals who invest in companies' shares and who are therefore not privy to confidential corporate information.

We examine the roles and responsibilities of both advisers in more detail below.

NOMAD

When the London Stock Exchange created AIM in 1995, it recognised the need to establish a flexible but effective way to regulate the market without overburdening the sort of younger, more entrepreneurial companies it wished to attract. The Exchange decided to do this by creating a new type of corporate finance adviser, the Nomad, which would have a responsibility to the Exchange for determining the suitability of a new applicant to AIM, and also an ongoing responsibility for monitoring the company and ensuring its compliance with the relevant regulations. Effectively the Exchange outsourced the regulation of companies quoted on AIM to the Nomads whilst the Nomads themselves are regulated by the Exchange.

The London Stock Exchange itself acknowledges on its website that the reputation and success of AIM since its launch is largely due to the dedication and professionalism of the network of Nomads. The introduction of the AIM Rules for Nominated Advisers in February 2007 codified the role and responsibilities of a Nomad, as well as the process and criteria that must be satisfied by a firm in order to become and remain registered as a Nomad, which include demonstrating a certain level of recent relevant experience, and employing a minimum number of qualified executives each of whom must have the requisite level of relevant experience.

As well as acting as a regulator, Nomads offer companies the sort of advice that one would expect from a corporate finance adviser, and from a company's point of view, the role of the Nomad is to guide the company through the process of admission to trading on AIM, and through its life thereafter as a publicly-quoted AIM company.

At the time of writing, there are just over 50 active firms registered as Nomads. Some will specialize in acting for larger companies some medium sized or smaller cap ones. Others may have specific sector or geographical focus. It is important for a company seeking a Nomad or broker to find the right fit and ensure they will get the level of commitment needed.

Obligations

The AIM Rules for Nominated Advisers set out the obligations of a Nomad in respect of companies for which it is the nominated adviser. The key responsibilities of a Nomad to the Exchange in respect of a company for which it acts are as follows:

General obligations

- To assess the appropriateness of a company on its application to AIM, and also when it takes on a company as its client. If a Nomad believes a company to which it is nominated adviser is no longer appropriate for AIM, it has a responsibility to contact the Exchange and discuss this;
- To comply with the AIM Rules for Companies, the AIM Rules for Nominated Advisers, and with any supplementary rules, procedures, notices, guidance, requirement, decision or direction issued by the Exchange; and
- To act at all times with due skill and care.

Nominated adviser responsibilities

- To advise and guide a company on its responsibilities and obligations both in respect of admission and on an ongoing basis. It must be available to give this advice and guidance to the companies for which it acts at all times and should allocate at least two appropriately qualified staff to be responsible for each such company.

Information obligations

- To provide the Exchange with any information that it reasonably requires, having first satisfied itself that the information provided is correct, complete and not misleading;
- To liaise with the Exchange when requested to do so either by the Exchange or by a company for which it acts;
- To seek the advice of the Exchange on any uncertainty on the application or interpretation of the AIM Rules, or on any concerns over the reputation or integrity of AIM;
- To advise the Exchange as soon as practicable if it believes that it or an AIM company has breached the AIM Rules; and
- To notify the Exchange in the approved manner on being appointed as Nomad to a company, or ceasing to act as Nomad to a company.

Independence and conflicts

- To demonstrate independence (both of the firm and its individual executives) from the companies for which it acts; and
- To avoid any actual or apparent conflict of interest.

Procedures, staff and records

- To follow the prescribed procedures, employ appropriately qualified staff and maintain sufficient records.

It is interesting to note that the stated responsibilities of a Nomad under the AIM Rules are all of a regulatory nature, and are owed to the Exchange rather than the company for which it acts. It may of course, subject to these responsibilities and obligations, also provide advice to these companies. It is the dual role of regulator and adviser that makes the relationship between a company and its Nomad such a unique one.

Responsibilities

A Schedule to the AIM Rules for Nominated Advisers contains a set of principles, with subsidiary actions, that a Nomad must follow in order to comply with its obligations. This codifies what had become best practice into required practice.

The principles are as follows:

- In assessing the appropriateness of an applicant and its securities for AIM, a nominated adviser should achieve a sound understanding of the applicant and its business;
- In assessing the appropriateness of an applicant and its securities for AIM, nominated adviser should (i) investigate and consider the suitability of each director and proposed director of the applicant; and (ii) consider the efficacy of the board as a whole for the company's needs, in each case having in mind that the company will be admitted to trading on a UK public market;
- The nominated adviser should oversee the due diligence process, satisfying itself that it is appropriate to the applicant and transaction and that any material issues arising from it are dealt with or otherwise do not affect the appropriateness of the applicant for AIM;
- The nominated adviser should oversee and be actively involved in the preparation of the admission document, satisfying itself (in order to be able

to give the nominated adviser's declaration) that it has been prepared in compliance with the AIM Rules for Companies with due verification having been undertaken;

- The nominated adviser should satisfy itself that the applicant has in place sufficient systems, procedures and controls in order to comply with the AIM Rules for Companies and should satisfy itself that the applicant understands its obligations under the AIM Rules for Companies;
- The nominated adviser should maintain regular contact with an AIM company for which it acts, in particular so that it can assess whether (i) the nominated adviser is being kept up-to-date with developments at the AIM company and (ii) the AIM company continues to understand its obligations under the AIM Rules for Companies;
- The nominated adviser should undertake a prior review of relevant notifications made by an AIM company with a view to ensuring compliance with the AIM Rules for Companies;
- The nominated adviser should monitor (or have in place procedures with third parties for monitoring) the trading activity in securities of an AIM company for which it acts, especially when there is unpublished price sensitive information in relation to the AIM company; and
- The nominated adviser should advise the AIM company on any changes to the board of directors the AIM company proposes to make, including (i) investigating and considering the suitability of proposed new directors and (ii) considering the effect any changes have in the efficacy of the board as a whole for the company's needs, in each case having in mind that the company is admitted to trading on a UK public market.

The relationship in practice

In practice an AIM company's relationship with its Nomad is one of the most important adviser relationships it will have. The Nomad is available to advise the company, but can also be held accountable by the Exchange if the company does not comply with the AIM Rules, for example if it does not announce an announceable event or is late in posting its accounts.

Accordingly, there must be regular communication between the company and the Nomad on all matters, including the trading performance of the business, its budgets and plans and any milestones that are reached or expected to be reached, any issues relating to directors and shareholders. The Nomad will need to be provided with full information on the progress of the business. This will typically include receiving copies of budgets, board pack and regular management accounts;

discussing any significant events in the business (both positive and negative); understanding any changes to shareholdings; and attendance at certain key board meetings.

BROKER

A broker is a securities house and must be a member of the London Stock Exchange. Its sole role under the AIM Rules is to use its best endeavours to find matching business if there is no registered market maker in a company's shares. However, in practice, the broker is a key adviser in the process of raising money in association with an admission to AIM or a secondary fund-raising, and in maintaining a sustainable market in a company's shares. The broker is normally responsible for running the fund-raising process, including advising on marketing materials, effecting introductions to potential investors, and coordinating the logistics of collecting funds and issuing shares.

Usually a company's broker also acts as a point of contact between the investment community and the company and, when requested, co-ordinates transactions in the company's shares with a view to maintaining an orderly market in those shares. It may also advise the Company on investment conditions and the pricing of its securities; and may produce research on the company for dissemination to the market.

Structure

Typically, a broker is divided into the company-facing corporate finance and corporate broking part of the firm and the market-facing part of the firm.

The corporate finance team advises client companies and is privy to confidential, often price sensitive, information on the company. It is focused on servicing the needs of the company, and its key function is to manage the broker's input into a flotation or other transaction.

The market-facing part of the firm includes sales people, who are engaged in selling the company's shares to institutional and other investor clients of the broking firm, and analysts, who are responsible for producing independent research on clients and other companies. This part of the firm is only entitled to receive information that is in the public domain, and once it receives information, it is deemed to be in the public domain.

Because these two parts of the broker have different objectives and are responsible to different clients (the company as opposed to the market), there are strict rules governing the interactions between them. These centre around protecting the confidentiality of information by the use of procedures that create and maintain a 'Chinese Wall'.

INTEGRATED HOUSE OR SEPARATE ADVISERS

Many city firms offer both Nomad and broker services, and it is quite common for a company to appoint such an integrated house to both roles. When this occurs, strict Chinese Walls separate the Nomad and broker functions, as in most cases information to which the Nomad is privy (in its role as quasi-regulator and corporate finance adviser to the company) must not be disclosed to the market-facing part of the broker.

Some companies prefer to keep the roles separate, choosing to appoint two distinct firms to fill these roles in order to safeguard the confidentiality of price-sensitive information and to ensure the independence of advice they are given. Keeping the roles separate has a number of advantages in that it can be time consuming and expensive to change Nomad whereas it is relatively easy to change broker which is more often than not the reason for wanting to change.

FURTHER INFORMATION

Further information on the roles and responsibilities of Nomads and brokers may be found on the London Stock Exchange website:www.londonstockexchange.com, in particular in the AIM Rules for Companies and the AIM Rules for Nominated Advisers. Alternatively, please contact Tony Rawlinson at Cairn Financial Advisers via their website: www.cairnfin.com

6.4 MERGERS AND ACQUISITIONS AND JOINT VENTURES

Tanvir Dhanoa, Watson, Farley & Williams LLP

INTRODUCTION

The phrase "mergers and acquisitions" (M&A) refers to the aspect of corporate strategy, finance and management dealing with the purchase, sale and merging of different companies and businesses. Unlike certain jurisdictions (notably the US), in the UK there is technically no concept of a true merger, in the sense of two or more separate entities combining to form one continuing entity (although the term M&A is used in the UK). The term "acquisition", also known as a takeover, is used to describe a wide variety of transactions involving the sale and purchase of either a business or a company. Through the acquisition of a UK target, an inward investor is able to gain immediate local presence, expertise and name recognition. The same principal issues are common to most acquisitions, whatever the size or nature of the parties or the entity being acquired.

The basic forms of business combination are:

- the purchase of shares of a target company;
- the purchase of the target's underlying business; and
- joint venture arrangements.

This chapter is divided into four sections: the first considers the private acquisition of companies and businesses; the second deals with the acquisition of public companies; the third covers joint ventures; and the final section provides an overview of merger control.

PRIVATE COMPANY AND BUSINESS ACQUISITIONS

There are generally two methods of acquiring a business: one is to buy the shares of the company that owns the business; the other is to buy the assets that make up the business. In either case, the buyer will achieve its commercial objective of acquiring the business that is being run by the target company, although the legal effects of the two types of acquisition are fundamentally different.

If shares in a company are purchased, all its assets, liabilities and obligations are acquired (even those that the buyer does not know about). The contract is made between the buyer and the owner of the shares (the seller). There is no change in the ownership of the business; it remains in the ownership of the company. Alternatively, the business may be purchased in its entirety as a going concern, together with all its assets and liabilities or, if appropriate, only those identified assets and liabilities that the buyer agrees to acquire.

A share sale is generally the quickest way to effect an acquisition because legally this only requires a share transfer. On a business sale, by contrast, transfer arrangements will need to be put in place for each asset being purchased. Tax issues will also play a central role in determining the best route to be followed.

Exclusivity

As an acquisition will involve a prospective buyer investing a substantial amount of time, effort and money, the buyer will often require the seller to agree not to negotiate with other parties for a given period while it conducts its due diligence exercise (investigation of the target business). An exclusivity (or "lockout") period for the buyer will often be agreed in a separate exclusivity agreement.

Confidentiality agreement

As most acquisitions will involve the buyer having access to significant information about the target business (and, to a certain extent, the seller and its group), some of which will be confidential, it is standard practice for a seller to ask any prospective buyer to enter into a confidentiality agreement requiring the buyer and its professional advisers to treat all disclosed information as confidential, and to agree that the disclosed information may only be used for the purposes of the acquisition or otherwise with the seller's consent.

Due diligence

For acquisitions subject to English law, the principle of caveat emptor, or 'buyer beware', will apply, which effectively means that there is only limited statutory and common law protection for a buyer under the law. It is, therefore, essential for a buyer to learn as much as possible about the target business and the issues that will be relevant to the acquisition as early as possible in the acquisition procedure through the process of due diligence.

Due diligence is intended to identify risks so that they can be allocated between the buyer and the seller. The review usually comprises legal, financial, tax and commercial due diligence, and will help to determine the contractual protections required from the seller, as well as the risks the buyer should avoid completely. The information-gathering process will aim to identify information that may impact upon the negotiation process and, in particular, on the price the buyer is prepared to pay. The buyer will seek to obtain contractual protection from the seller in relation to issues of concern to it and other risks in the form of warranties and indemnities in the acquisition agreement.

Warranties

In simple terms, warranties are contractual promises made by the seller to the buyer regarding the state of affairs of the target company/business.

Warranties serve two main purposes: one is to elicit information about the business from the seller by way of disclosure or qualification of the warranties—a process linked to the due diligence investigation discussed above; the second is to provide the buyer with a remedy (a claim for breach of warranty) if the statements made about the company/business later prove to be incorrect and the acquisition turns out to be other than as bargained for.

Indemnities

The buyer may seek further contractual protection in the form of indemnities included in the acquisition agreement (or sometimes in a separate deed). An indemnity is essentially a promise to reimburse the buyer in respect of a designated type of liability, should it arise in the future. The purpose of an indemnity is to provide a guaranteed remedy for the buyer, where a breach of warranty may not give rise to a claim in damages, or to provide a specific remedy that might not otherwise be available at law.

Stamp duty

Stamp duty is the tax payable when property or shares are transferred. Stamp duty land tax is payable when real property or land is bought, and either stamp duty or stamp duty reserve tax is payable when shares are transferred.

On an acquisition of shares, the buyer pays stamp duty at the rate of 0.5 per cent of the purchase price. On an acquisition of a business, the buyer pays stamp duty only on those assets that are taxable (essentially land and shares). On the purchase of commercial land, no stamp duty is payable if the value of the property does not exceed £150,000. Stamp duty on the purchase of real estate above this value is payable at varying rates up to four per cent.

Schemes of arrangement

A scheme of arrangement is a statutory procedure for business combinations effected under Part 26 of the Companies Act 2006, whereby a company may make a compromise or arrangement with its members or creditors. A company can effect virtually any kind of internal reorganisation, merger or de-merger restructuring under this section as long as the necessary approvals have been obtained, including the relevant shareholder approval and court approval.

Schemes of arrangement are becoming increasingly popular, and an inward investor should consider whether a conventional takeover offer or a scheme of arrangement would be the most appropriate method to acquire a target.

PUBLIC COMPANY ACQUISITIONS

The takeover market

The UK has a long history of takeover activity. Takeover activity has increased significantly since the Takeover Panel commenced work in 1968, and approximately three-quarters of all public takeover offers in the European Union (EU) occur in the UK. There are several reasons for this overall growth, including the fact that corporate balance sheets appear to be healthier and corporate earning expectations remain positive. In addition, the rising popularity of the AIM Market has continued and has generated significant takeover activity as companies on the market mature and consolidation of businesses becomes an attractive opportunity.

Regulation of takeovers

Transactions involving the acquisition of control of a public company (takeovers), and those involving the sale and purchase of public companies whose shares are listed on the London Stock Exchange, are subject to considerable additional regulation:

- The City Code on Takeovers and Mergers (the Takeover Code) is a set of rules developed by the Panel on Takeovers and Mergers (the Takeover Panel) and regulates takeovers in the UK. The Takeover Code applies to offers for public companies resident in the UK, the Channel Islands and the Isle of Man, irrespective of where their shares are listed or publicly marketed.
- The Listing, Prospectus and Disclosure Rules are made by the Financial Services Authority and regulate the process by which a company listed on the London Stock Exchange can make acquisitions or disposals.
- The Criminal Justice Act 1993 together with the Listing Rules, Disclosure Rules and Takeover Code, regulates insider dealings.
- The Companies Act 2006 contains the main legislation governing the formation and administration of companies.
- The Financial Services and Markets Act 2000 regulates the conduct of investment business and makes provision for the official listing of securities, public offers of securities and investment advertisement.
- Merger control provisions regulate the takeover of a UK company, which may require approval from the competition authorities of the EU or the UK.

Outline of a takeover

Takeovers are public transactions, and the Takeover Code prescribes a strict timetable to be adhered to. Unlike a private acquisition, it is not possible to simply announce the completion of a takeover. Under the Takeover Code, a takeover must be carried out publicly, and any takeover offer has to be held open for a fixed period of time. This in turn means that a potential rival bidder may make a competing offer to the target's shareholders.

In a "recommended bid", target shareholders are recommended to accept the offer by the target's directors. A "hostile bid", however, is an offer not supported by the target.

JOINT VENTURES

A joint venture describes a commercial arrangement between two or more economically independent entities for the purpose of pursuing an agreed commercial goal, in which the joint venturers share in agreed proportions the financing and control of the enterprise, as well as the profits and losses it makes.

Joint ventures may be structured through limited partnerships, limited liability partnerships or unincorporated associations. However, the most common joint venture vehicle is a limited company.

International joint ventures

Joint ventures are vital to the development of international business, and an alliance with a local partner can provide an inward investor with:

- an important means of business expansion;
- access to new markets;
- distribution networks;
- greater resources; and
- the sharing of risks with a partner.

International joint ventures (where an overseas party combines with a local party to undertake joint business in that local jurisdiction) will require consideration of a number of issues, including choosing the type of legal structure most appropriate to the joint venture vehicle, tax considerations, restrictions on foreign participation, licensing issues and the requirement for governmental consents.

Contributions and funding

Initial finance may be injected into a joint venture company in a number of ways. One of these would be a straightforward subscription by the partners for shares in the joint venture company in consideration for a contribution of cash or non-cash assets. Alternatively, capital may be injected by way of loan, either from the joint venture partners or from third-party lenders. The parties will also need to consider in advance how future finance is to be provided to the joint venture company.

Management

It is common for the partners to retain some level of control and influence in the joint venture's decision-making process, either through representation on the board of directors or through requiring certain key decisions to be referred to shareholders. The level of each party's control will depend on their respective shareholdings. The management structure should be reflected clearly in the joint venture agreement.

The joint venture agreement

The written agreement between partners should set out the precise terms and conditions agreed between them, and provide a framework for the ongoing alliance. It should specifically cover:

- the structure of the joint venture;

- the objectives of the joint venture;
- the financial contributions that each partner is to make;
- the management and control of the joint venture (e.g. the right to appoint directors and each partner's voting rights);
- how profits, losses and liabilities are to be shared;
- how any disputes between the partners will be resolved; and
- how the joint venture can be terminated.

MERGER CONTROL

Merger control provisions exist under both UK and European law. Inward investors merging with, acquiring or entering into a joint venture with a UK company should be aware that the transaction may require notification to the Office of Fair Trading (OFT) to assess its effect on competition in the relevant markets. As of April 2014, the OFT and the Competition Commission will be replaced by a new enforcement body, the Competition and Markets Authority as part of a package of reforms to the competition regime. Although notification is voluntary, the parties to mergers that meet or exceed the qualifying threshold criteria (see below) are well advised to notify their merger to eliminate the risk of investigation and possible sanctions.

A merger will be considered as "qualifying" for investigation in the UK where:

- two or more companies, at least one of which carries on business in the UK, cease to be distinct (brought under common ownership or control);
- the merging companies supply or consume goods or services that form part of the same market, and after the merger takes place, they will supply or acquire 25 per cent or more of those goods or services in the UK as a whole or in a substantial part of it; or
- the annual UK turnover of the company being taken over exceeds £70 million.

Larger mergers that have a "community dimension" will be reviewed by the European Commission under the European Community Merger Regulation (ECMR). For more details about merger control and an outline of the recent law reforms, please refer to the chapter on competition law.

Appendix I

Contributors' Contacts

Cairn Financial Advisers LLP
61 Cheapside
London EC2V 6AV
Tel: +44 (0) 20 7148 7900
Contact:
Tony Rawlinson
e-mail: tony.rawlinson@cairnfin.com

Carter Jonas LLP
6-8 Hills Road
Cambridge CB2 1NH
Tel: +44 (0) 1223 348 607
Contact:
Nick Hood
e-mail: Nick.Hood@carterjonas.co.uk

Chemical Industries Association (CIA)
King's Building
16 Smith Square
London SW1P 3JJ
Tel: +44 (20) 7834 3399

Contacts:
Neil Harvey
e-mail: HarveyN@cia.org.uk
Alan Eastwood
e-mail: EastwoodA@cia.org.uk

Legend Business
The Old Fire Station
140 Tabernacle Street
London EC2A 4SD
Tel: +44 (0) 20 7300 7370
Tom Chalmers
Direct line: +44 (0) 20 7300 7370
e-mail: tomchalmers@legend-paperbooks.co.uk
Jonathan Reuvid
Direct line: +44 (0) 1295 738 070
e-mail: jreuvidembooks@aol.com

Mazars LLP
Tower Bridge House
St Katharine's Way
London E1W 1DD
Contact: Toby Stanbrook
Tel: (0) 20 7063 4000
e-mail: toby.stanbrook@mazars.co.uk

PNO Consultants Limited
Dunham House
Brooke Court
Lower Meadow Road
Wilmslow
Cheshire SK9 3ND
Tel: +44 (0) 161 488 3488
Contact: Olaf Swanzy
e-mail: olaf.swanzy@pnoconsultants.com

The Sourcing Solutions Ltd
7200 The Quorum

Oxford Business Park North
Garsington Road
Oxford OX4 2JZ
Email: info@thesourcingsolutions.com
Tel: +44 (0) 1865 487 150
Contact: Mark Norcliffe
e-mail: m.norcliffe53@yahoo.com

UK Trade & Investment
Deputy Director, Investment
1, Victoria Street
London SW1H 0ET
Contact:
David McLean
Tel: +44 (0) 207 215 8775
e-mail: david.mclean@ukti.gsi.gov.uk

Investment Services Team
123 Buckingham Palace Road
London SW1W 9SR
Tel: +44 (0) 845 539 0419
Contact: Anna Francis
Direct Line: +44 (0) 207 333 5442
e-mail: Anna.Francis@ukti-invest.com

Life Sciences Investment Organisation
Tel: +44 (0) 7825 378 0101
Contact:
Mark Treherne
e-mail: Mark.Treherne@uktispecialist.com

Watson, Farley & Williams LLP
15 Appold Street
London EC2A 2HB
Tel: +44 (0) 20 7814 8000
Contact:
Asha Kumar
Direct line: +44 (0) 20 7814 8182
e-mail: AKumar@wfw.com